Evaluating the K Literacy Curriculum

As your school district undertakes the process of evaluating its K–12 reading program, literacy curriculum, or literacy instructional practices, this book will be your go-to resource. Pennell offers a step-by-step guide for educators, school leaders, or professional learning communities to evaluate high-quality instructional materials and standards-aligned literacy practices. It includes a wealth of tools such as timelines, full meeting agendas, stakeholder surveys, and evaluation rubrics.

Chapters cover key topics, including:

- Literacy leadership team meetings
- Reviewing foundational skills
- Comprehension and vocabulary
- Evaluating writing
- Selecting new materials
- Implementing new literacy materials
- Supporting educators through instructional coaching and professional learning

Pennell provides a straightforward framework for how educators can work together collaboratively to analyze, reflect, and ultimately evaluate their school district's literacy program. Each chapter is grounded in salient research on the *why* of literacy teaching and learning and helps you understand *how* instruction can be meaningfully aligned with current standards. The research and theory that support effective literacy instruction—including culturally responsive practices—are explained in an accessible and pragmatic manner.

The practical tools in this book are essential for administrators and educators tasked with evaluating literacy programs and practices, as well as graduate students who must learn how to audit a literacy curriculum. Whether you're a school administrator, teacher, or reading specialist, this book will ensure all your students can reach success in literacy.

Colleen Pennell is an assistant professor at Carroll University in Wisconsin. She was previously a K–12 reading specialist and elementary teacher in Wisconsin and the Southwest.

Evaluating the K–12 Literacy Curriculum

A Step by Step Guide for Auditing Programs, Materials, and Instructional Approaches

Colleen Pennell

Routledge
Taylor & Francis Group

NEW YORK AND LONDON

First published 2020
by Routledge
52 Vanderbilt Avenue, New York, NY 10017

and by Routledge
2 Park Square, Milton Park, Abingdon, Oxon, OX14 4RN

Routledge is an imprint of the Taylor & Francis Group, an informa business

Library of Congress Cataloging-in-Publication Data
Names: Pennell, Colleen, author.
Title: Evaluating K-12 literacy materials : a step by step guide to
   effective reading and writing programs and instruction / Colleen
   Pennell.
Description: New York, NY : Routledge, 2020. | Includes bibliographical
   references. |
Identifiers: LCCN 2019046438 | ISBN 9780367203627 (hardback) | ISBN
   9780367203634 (paperback) | ISBN 9780429261107 (ebook)
Subjects: LCSH: Language arts (Elementary)--Evaluation. | Language arts
   (Secondary)--Evaluation. | Literacy programs--Evaluation.
Classification: LCC LB1576 .P458 2020 | DDC 372.6--dc23
LC record available at https://lccn.loc.gov/2019046438

ISBN: 978-0-367-20362-7 (hbk)
ISBN: 978-0-367-20363-4 (pbk)
ISBN: 978-0-429-26110-7 (ebk)

Typeset in Palatino
by Cenveo® Publisher Services

Visit the eResources: www.routledge.com/9780367203634

Contents

Detailed Contents

Meet the Author

Colleen began her professional career in the Southwest, teaching elementary school in both New Mexico and Arizona. After several years, she moved to Wisconsin and served as a reading specialist, supporting both teachers and learners with diverse strengths and needs. Her work as a reading specialist also included evaluating the literacy curriculum, facilitating professional development, and implementing an equitable, multilevel system of support for readers and writers.

Colleen currently works as an assistant professor of literacy education at Carroll University in Wisconsin. In this capacity, she teaches preservice teachers as well as graduate students enrolled in the Reading Specialist program. Her work with future reading specialists has made her realize how critical it is for all literacy leaders to have a research-informed process for evaluating literacy materials and practices. Her passion for promoting high-quality instruction with aligned instructional materials was the impetus for this text.

Colleen holds a BS in elementary education, an MEd in curriculum and instruction, and a PhD in language and literacy.

eResources

Appendix C Composite Score Sheet can also be downloaded and printed for classroom use. You can access these downloads by visiting the book product page on our website: www.routledge.com/9780367203627. Then click on the tab that says "eResources," and select the files. They will begin downloading to your computer.

Introduction

Complex educational issues, like school-wide literacy achievement, cannot be addressed by quick fixes or silver bullets.

Rather, schoolwide literacy improvement requires a comprehensive approach that embraces all stakeholder voices and addresses the many dimensions involved in children's educational attainment. The purpose of this book is to help educational leaders address two areas that shape literacy outcomes: (1) literacy instructional practices and (2) literacy materials that support instructional practices. The goal of the text is to help educators and leaders understand *why* certain aspects of literacy must be taught, as well as *how* that instruction could occur. This book is not about adopting the next fashionable reading curriculum, but rather is about building administrator and teacher knowledge of literacy acquisition to inform a curriculum adoption.

Through a collaborative, bottom-up process that embraces the voices of all stakeholders, the outcome of this evaluation will help ensure that the instructional practices implemented across the school district, as well as the corresponding materials, provide all readers with access to a high-quality, culturally relevant literacy education.

Ensuring a quality literacy education for all children, is nuanced and complex—it cannot be distilled to a checklist of "look-for's." For instance, teachers need to understand the nitty gritty of word recognition. How does the brain learn to crack the code of written language? We know that children who develop phonemic awareness and alphabet knowledge by first grade are less apt to experience ongoing reading difficulty. What practices support this learning, and how can a strong foundational skills program support instruction?

We also know that content knowledge is critical for reading comprehension and yet since the recommendations of the National Reading Panel (2000), isolated strategy instruction has dominated many classroom contexts; some schools have even lessened their focus on science and social studies instruction. As educators and school leaders, how do we adequately ensure that our curriculum, as well as our instructional practices, support deep knowledge acquisition?

This book aims to help answer and understand those questions and more. It is written for individuals who are tasked with evaluating literacy program(s) and practices, as well as for reading specialists or graduate students in a reading specialist program who want to evaluate programs and practices as part of their coursework. Additionally, this book can be used to evaluate an entire K–12 literacy curriculum or one aspect of a literacy program (e.g., foundational skills).

Key to a successful review and materials adoption is voice: student, family, educator, and administrator. You will find that this text provides stakeholders an opportunity to share their input on the materials and practices that shape instruction. For example, Appendix B provides surveys for teachers, administrators, students, and families to anonymously complete. These surveys ask questions about instructional practices, as well perceptions of current curricula materials. The surveys, along with school-wide achievement data, will be used to inform the district leadership teams about the current needs of the district (Figure 1). The district leadership teams will compile these data and use them to adopt new materials or strengthen existing use of the current materials. The district leadership teams can also provide recommendations regarding instructional practices that need to be embedded, strengthened, or abandoned.

The chapters in the book are laid out as follows:

Chapter Title	Purpose	Main Topics Covered
Introduction	How to use this book	
Chapter 1: Organizing Teams and Gathering the Data	Written for the administrator in charge of leading the materials review and adoption process. Provides steps for beginning the evaluation.	• Organizing the district leadership team • Collecting data • Setting the agenda for the first meeting
Chapter 2: Literacy Leadership Team Meeting #1	Describes the agenda for the first leadership meeting and explains the review process.	• Establishing a positive literacy leadership team • Analyzing school-wide data and teacher surveys • Beginning the review
Chapter 3: Evaluating Foundational Skills	Small-group literacy leadership team reviews foundational skills program and practices.	• Concepts about print • Phonological awareness • Alphabetic knowledge • Word recognition/phonics • Fluency

Chapter Title	Purpose	Main Topics Covered
Chapter 4: Evaluating Comprehension Grades K–3	Small-group literacy leadership team reviews K–3 comprehension program and practices.	• Oral language • Bilingual learner comprehension • Read-alouds with discussion • Informational text/content-based approaches • Cognitive strategy instruction • Writing to learn
Chapter 5: Evaluating Comprehension Grades 4–12	Small-group literacy leadership team reviews 4–12 comprehension program and practices.	• Discussion-based approaches • Informational text/content-based instruction • Cognitive strategy instruction • Writing to learn • Disciplinary literacy • Online reading comprehension
Chapter 6: Evaluating Vocabulary Grades K–12	Small-group literacy leadership team reviews vocabulary program and practices.	• Purposeful, explicit culturally relevant instruction • Wide reading • Code switching • Bilingual learners • Morphological/structural analysis • Dual coding • Graphic organizers
Chapter 7: Evaluating Writing Grades K–12	Small-group literacy leadership team reviews writing program and practices.	• Writing framework • Narrative writing • Argument writing • Informational writing • Digital composition • Handwriting • Writing conventions
Chapter 8: Evaluating Classroom Libraries and Independent Reading	Small-group literacy leadership team reviews additional considerations outside of a literacy curriculum.	• Independent reading • Inclusive classroom libraries
Chapter 9: Literacy Leadership Meeting #2: Concluding the Evaluation and Making Recommendations	Finishes the initial evaluation of the current literacy program and instructional practices.	• Finish evaluation • Reporting findings • Investigating solutions
Chapter 10: Literacy Leadership Team Meeting #3: Evaluating the New Literacy Program or Materials	Evaluates new programs for potential adoption.	• Review new curricula • Make recommendation

(Continued)

Chapter Title	Purpose	Main Topics Covered
Chapter 11: Pilot-Testing Recommendations	Explains the process for pilot testing the new program.	• Piloting the new literacy curriculum
Chapter 12: Implementing a New Literacy Program: Professional Learning and Coaching	Describes the steps for curriculum mapping, rolling out the new curriculum and planning professional learning.	• Rolling out the new literacy curriculum

How to use this book: Since this text is written to support the administrator who must organize a school- or district-wide evaluation as well as the literacy leadership team (LLT) tasked with the evaluation, not every chapter must be read by all. If you are the administrator facilitating the evaluation (referred to as the LLT facilitator), you need to begin with Chapter 1. This chapter will guide you through selecting the LLT, collecting and organizing data, and preparing for the first meeting.

If you are on the LLT, you will want to begin with Chapter 2. This explains the process of the review and gives an overview of the agenda for the first meeting.

Chapters 3–9 are organized for small subgroups of the LLT to evaluate constructs of literacy. The overarching constructs being evaluated are:

- Foundational Skills
- Comprehension (K–3)
- Comprehension (4–12)
- Vocabulary
- Writing
- Classroom Libraries and Independent Reading

In the first literacy leadership meeting, individuals are placed in an expert group that is charged with evaluating one of these constructs. Before the review takes place, members of the expert group will want to read their designated chapter and get a feel for how the evaluation will proceed. Then, the expert group will work through each topic discussed in the chapter. Throughout the chapter, team members will be prompted to pause and evaluate these topics. For example, the expert group evaluating the construct of Foundational Skills will read about phonological awareness and then evaluate phonological awareness; they will read about phonics and then evaluate phonics, and so on. Note, that the book is written to allow districts to evaluate: (1) instructional practices, (2) the current reading program, and (3) the programs up for adoption. As such, a three-part rubric is provided to evaluate each of these areas:

 Phase One Rubric: Evaluates current instructional practices for each construct
 Phase Two Rubric: Evaluates the current reading materials provided to teachers
 Phase Three Rubric: Evaluates the quality of the program up for adoption.

NOTE: The LLT can decide if they want to complete all three phases of the evaluation or streamline the process and complete only one or two phases. For example, if you know you are going to adopt a new curriculum, you may only want to evaluate current instructional practices and the quality of programs up for adoption. Thus, you would only use phase one and two rubrics.

Why do we evaluate both materials and instructional practices? In some schools, materials for teaching reading are available but may not be utilized. Think of that dusty phonics program in the resource room that no one uses. Or in other cases, teachers are instructing phonics but relying on their own materials or websites like Teachers Pay Teachers. In these contexts, each teacher uses different and inconsistent materials that may or may not be aligned to your state's reading standards. Evaluating the materials that are currently available as well as current instructional practices helps a district administrator know the needs for materials, as well as ongoing professional learning and literacy coaching.

If you are only evaluating one aspect of your literacy curriculum, begin by reading Chapter 1 (collecting and organizing data) and then read the chapter aligned to the construct you are evaluating. Appendix C provides forms to evaluate the construct.

Once the LLT has evaluated the current reading curriculum and instructional practices, Chapter 10 provides steps for evaluating new literacy curriculum materials. When the LLT makes a recommendation for materials, Chapter 11 provides guidance on how to pilot-test program recommendations. Finally, once a new literacy program has been selected, Chapter 12 provides an outline for how to roll out the literacy curriculum. The appendices contain surveys, evaluation recording forms, supplemental lesson plans, and resources.

In closing, my hope is that you find this book useful, insightful, and a tool for change. There are no silver bullets in literacy education, and this book is no exception. However, if we commit to utilizing quality materials with aligned and meaningful instructional practices, we can support literacy acquisition for all learners.

1

Organizing Teams and Gathering the Data

Chapter Preview

This chapter is written for the facilitator of the reading evaluation process. It describes the pre-planning that needs to be done prior to the evaluation and first literacy leadership team meeting. The following elements are covered in this chapter:

- Selecting the literacy leadership team
- Organizing assessment data
- Preparing for the first meeting

Introduction

Evaluating your school district's literacy program and practices while further adopting new curricula can be a daunting process. There are numerous details to consider and plan for, including: Who will serve on the committee, and how will they be selected? When should meetings take place? What data are needed to begin this process? What should the agenda include for the first meeting? Rest assured that this chapter will provide you with detailed steps for embarking upon this journey. Keep in mind that as you begin, you may need to leverage your district's reading specialists or other school district personnel who can assist you in preparing for this year-long process.

Professional Learning Communities

This text is framed by a professional learning communities (PLC) process that is focused on building the collective capacity of educators within a school district. The educators on your literacy leadership team (LLT) will be charged with effectively evaluating your current and future reading program and practices. This PLC will work together over the course of the upcoming year. However, for reading achievement to improve in your school district, it is necessary for PLCs to also form within grade levels and scrutinize student reading behavior, assessments, and instructional practices (see DuFour & Marzano, 2011). Combined with the work of the LLT, your school-based PLCs will only positively enhance your district's literacy outcomes.

Yearlong Calendar and Tasks

The following calendar provides a timeline for the evaluation process and includes time commitments for the LLT as well as other support personnel. This timeline is flexible and can be adjusted to meet your specific school district needs. However, note that this timeline provides you with the most detailed evaluation process. Some leaders might be tempted to skip right to evaluating a new program. However, the curriculum review process will be much stronger if you build the capacity of your educators regarding existing materials and practices.

Thus, the timeline begins by **only** evaluating the current reading curriculum and instructional practices. New materials **are not** evaluated until the third meeting. Again, you may need to adjust this calendar as needed (Table 1.1).

Step 1: Select the Literacy Leadership Team

Early in September, you will want to begin the process of selecting the LLT. The composition of this team is critical to a successful evaluation outcome and should have diverse representation from each grade level, department, and specialty area (Chenoweth & Everhart, 2002). Ideally, members will have a variety of perspectives about literacy, have a strong knowledge base, be willing to learn from others, and be comfortable challenging ideas as needed. Most importantly, the LLT should be composed of individuals who are committed to literacy improvement.

In schools where leadership teams have been suggested to be the most successful, they have been composed of volunteers who chose to serve and not of individuals who were mandated to be there (Marzano, Waters, & McNulty, 2005). Thus, as you begin this selection process, you will want to seek out your volunteers and not insist that certain teachers participate. This process is too important to have any resentment or negativity attached to it.

Before soliciting for volunteers, you will want to decide how many full-day meetings will be required, how much summer work is expected, and if a stipend will be provided. The framework described in this text contains three full days of meetings (see Table 1.1).

Table 1.1 Suggested Year-Long Process for Full-Scale Evaluation

Suggested Year-Long Process for Full-Scale Evaluation		
Month	**Task**	**District Personnel Responsible**
August/September	Compile data for leadership team meeting #1 (pre-leadership meetings)	Curriculum director (typically)
September	Leadership meeting #1 Data dive, begin the evaluation	Literacy leadership team
October	Leadership meeting #2 Expert groups finish evaluating current literacy program and practices Recommend new curricula to evaluate	Literacy leadership team
November	Leadership meeting #3 Expert groups evaluate **new programs** and make official recommendations	Literacy leadership team
December–January	Materials for piloting are ordered	Literacy leadership team
February–May	Materials are pilot-tested in select classrooms Data on materials and programs being piloted are captured and monitored	Reading specialist leads classroom pilot Building administrators
June	Final recommendation is made New literacy materials are purchased Create curriculum map Create assessment plan	Curriculum director
July	Create year-long professional development plan Create coaching cycle/expectations	Reading specialists/ literacy coaches Curriculum director Building administrators Teacher leaders
August–June	Implement new program(s) Provide continuous K–12 professional development Provide ongoing literacy coaching	Reading specialists/ literacy coaches Curriculum director

Once you are ready, send an email to all the educators in your district. In the email, describe the literacy initiative and include the time commitment and any stiped that will be provided. An example email is provided here.

Dear Educators,

Our school district will be engaging in a review of our reading curriculum and instructional practices. The outcome of this review will provide suggestions for new and/or improved curriculum, as well as ideas for professional learning for educators. For this review to be successful, we need committed volunteers who are willing to serve on this committee. If you are interested in serving on this committee and possess the following characteristics, we strongly encourage you to apply:

- Passionate and knowledgeable about literacy teaching and learning
- Have a growth mind-set
- Have a positive working relationship with colleagues and grade-level team
- Have demonstrated leadership ability or potential
- Have effective interpersonal skills
- Can complete work in a timely fashion

To apply, please provide a brief write-up (no more than one page) describing your strengths and how you are a good fit for this committee. Address the previous points. Please include a statement of recommendation from your building principal. Optionally, include a resume.

If you are asked to serve on the committee, the time commitment is as follows:

Year 1: Three full-day leadership meetings (substitute teachers will be provided). During these meetings you will participate in a PLC grade or discipline alike workgroup for evaluating literacy programming and eventually piloting recommendations.

Stipend: Serving on the committee will provide a stipend of:

Please submit application materials to _____. Due date for application is _____.

We will notify you by _____.

Thank you for your ongoing commitment to our learners.

Sincerely,

Once you have received the applications, use the following questions to reflect on the strengths of applicants:

Applicant Name Grade Level Content Area (if applicable)	
	Comments
Does the applicant demonstrate passion about literacy teaching and learning?	
Does the applicant show an advanced knowledge base or needed perspective of literacy or content knowledge?	
Does the applicant describe a positive working relationship with colleagues?	
Does the applicant have a favorable recommendation from the building administrator?	
OVERALL RECOMMENDATION:	

Each school district is different. However, you should aim for a minimum of five members per expert group. If you are in a small district, you may only have two members. In a larger district you may have as many as ten. I would not have more than ten members per group, or the efficiency of the evaluation could erode.

Step 2: Organizing Assessment Data

After you have sent your email and while you are waiting for volunteer applications to pour in, begin organizing your literacy assessment data. You will need to compile data on assessments, curriculum, and literacy practices. Begin by sending out your literacy practice surveys.

Literacy Practices and Curriculum Surveys

These surveys are intended to understand the practices that dominate reading instruction and the resources teachers rely upon to teach. Appendix B contains several surveys based upon the main evaluation sections in this text. Table 1.2 explains who

Table 1.2 Literacy Practices Survey

Survey Type	Who Receives It	When to Administer
Early Literacy Practices and Curriculum	K–2 teachers Literacy coaches/reading specialists Special education teachers	May of year prior to the evaluation year OR late August/early September of evaluation year
Comprehension Practices and Curriculum K–3	K–3 teachers Literacy coaches/reading specialists Special education teachers	
Comprehension Practices and Curriculum 4–12	4–12 Teachers Literacy coaches/reading specialists Special education teachers	
Vocabulary Practices and Curriculum	All teachers Literacy coaches/reading specialists Special education teachers	
Writing Practices and Curriculum	All teachers Literacy coaches/reading specialists Special education teachers	
Independent Reading and Classroom Libraries	All teachers Literacy coaches/reading specialists Special education teachers	
Family Survey	Parents and caregivers with children in the school district	
Student Survey	All students in the school district	
Administrator Survey	All administrators in the school district	

will receive which survey. Ideally, you would want stakeholders to complete these surveys in May of the year prior to the evaluation. This will allow people time to reflect on an entire school year. However, if that is not possible, administer the surveys during the very beginning of the school year. This will give you enough time to organize the data prior to the first leadership meeting.

Reading Assessment Data

Next, you will want to gather all the reading assessment data, including the following:

- State-level data
  - State assessment results
- District/building data disaggregated (examples include):
  - Measures of Academic Progress (MAP) if used
  - (Dynamic Indicators of Basic Early Literacy Skills) DIBELS
  - ACT
  - Aspire
  - Advanced Placement (AP) exam data
  - Attendance rates

Once you have these data, consider meaningful ways to organize them into categories. For example, disaggregate by race, gender, economic status, and disability status. Use trend data to provide five-year trends for literacy achievement across grade level and subgroups. See Table 1.3.

Create summative trend data for reading scores based on discrete categories. An example is shown in Table 1.4.

A template for organizing your data is also provided in Appendix A.

Table 1.3 Ways to Organize Assessment Data

State Data	Grade-Level Trends	Subgroup Trends	Itemized Trends Grade Level	Itemized Trends Subgroups
District Data	Grade-Level Trends	Subgroup Trends	Itemized Trends District Data	Itemized Trends Subgroups

Table 1.4 Example of How to Categorize Trend Data. % Proficient or Above in Reading by Learning Disability Subgroup

Grade	2015	2016	2017	2018	2019
3	45	46	48	47	45
4	51	46	47	51	45
5	55	55	43	46	53
6	47	56	56	42	44

Step 3: Prepare for the Meeting

Once your data are organized, read through the guiding questions provided in Chapter 2 (p. 17). These questions will help frame the discussion with the LLT. Are there additional questions that you would like the LLT team to consider? If so, make sure to provide them during the data analysis in the first leadership meeting.

The following checklist can be used to prepare for the first LLT meeting.

TASK	Check When Complete
Organize teams: Once you have selected your LLT, you will want to place individuals into small teams that align to the sections of this book: Chapter 3: Foundational Skills Chapter 4: Comprehension K–3 Chapter 5: Comprehension 4–12 Chapter 6: Vocabulary* Chapter 7: Writing K–12 Chapter 8: Independent Reading and Classroom Libraries* *These are shorter chapters and can be combined so one team addresses both.	
Assign a chair for each team. The chair is responsible for maintaining minutes of the meeting, recording evaluation data, and reporting on data.	
Send an email to each LLT member for full details regarding the first meeting: • Define roles on the committee (make sure to describe the role of the chair) • Provide dates for future meetings • Request that they get a substitute teacher in advance for all meeting dates • Lunch: Will team members need to bring a lunch, will one be provided, or can they leave to grab a bite to eat?	
Order copies of this book for each group member. These can be distributed at the first meeting.	
Prepare assessment data: Prepare all assessment data in a format that can be easily read and analyzed by all team members.	
Prepare survey data: Prepare all survey data in a format that can be easily read and analyzed by all team members: • Teacher surveys • Student surveys • Family surveys • Administrator surveys (if including)	
Create an opening "Community Builder" for the first leadership team meeting. See Appendix A for list of ideas.	
Create an agenda with times. Include breaks and lunch.	
Gather additional materials: chart paper, markers, books	

2

Literacy Leadership Team Meeting #1

Chapter Preview

This provides an outline of the first literacy leadership team (LLT) meeting. The following elements are covered in this chapter:

- Introduction
- Community builder
- Group norms
- Data dive
- Discussion of data findings
- Begin evaluation

Introduction

Welcome to the first literacy leadership team meeting (LLT). As a member of the LLT, you are charged with analyzing assessment data and teacher surveys, exploring current and proposed instructional materials, and making recommendations for improvement. Throughout this work, the following questions should be kept at the forefront of your analysis. They will guide your thinking for the next days, weeks, and months:

1. What are our expectations for literacy achievement for *all* of our students?
2. What instructional practices and assessments are currently employed?
3. Do the instructional practices align with what research suggests?
4. What do the assessment and survey data tell us about how the reading skills, strategies, and content are being learned and taught?

5   What happens when our readers are not typically developing?
6   What happens when our readers are progressing beyond typical reading development?

What Is Skilled Reading?

As a member of this committee, it is essential to begin with a foundational understanding of the cognitive science of reading. One helpful way to view reading acquisition is through the lens of Hollis Scarborough's Reading Rope (2001) (Figure 2.1). In this metaphor, skilled reading consists of strands that weave together tightly to create a fluent reader who fully comprehends written text. If any of the strands are loose, reading skill will suffer. For example, the strands of word recognition are the foundational skills required for breaking the phonetic code of the English language. If a child struggles with phonological awareness and decoding, then the child will not be an automatic reader. If a student has strong word recognition skills but a weak vocabulary when reading a discipline-specific text, comprehension may suffer.

You can also use the Reading Rope (Scarborough, 2001) to think about writing instruction and acquisition. For example, instead of decoding print to speech, children use writing to encode speech to print. Yet both the skills of phonological awareness and sight word recognition inform the encoding process and determine how fluent an emergent writer is. Likewise, effective writers use their background knowledge to convey meaning, use rich vocabulary, and understand that written language

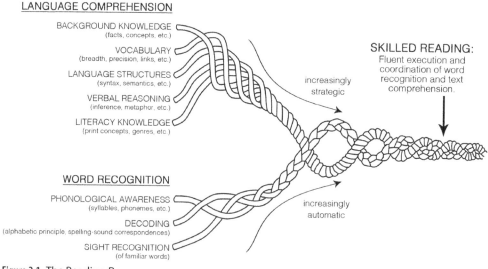

THE MANY STRANDS THAT ARE WOVEN INTO SKILLED READING

Figure 2.1 The Reading Rope.
Image credit: Scarborough, H. S. (2001). Connecting early language and literacy to later reading (dis)abilities: Evidence, theory, and practice. In S. Neuman & D. Dickinson (Eds.), *Handbook for research in early literacy* (pp. 97–110). New York: Guilford Press.

is structurally different from conversational language. Just like the strands of reading, these weave together to form skilled writing.

Although the Reading Rope (Scarborough, 2001) is an important framework to use to understand the cognitive science of reading, it does not address socioemotional or motivational factors that also shape reading outcomes. For example, self-efficacy of the learner (and the teacher!) and engagement in the task are key to learning. In this text, the Reading Rope is used to consider key aspects of curriculum and instruction that are needed to develop skilled reading. However, you will always want to keep motivation, engagement, and learner self-efficacy at the core of your instructional decision-making.

Why Not Just Buy a Program that Was Positively Reviewed Online?

Throughout this process, you are charged with exploring the materials *and instructional practices* that are used in your school or district to support skilled reading. But why not just explore curriculum? Isn't that the most important piece?

Although curriculum is central to supporting student learning, the quality of instruction matters more. Interestingly, educators often attribute student performance to **neither** instruction **nor** curriculum. Instead, teachers believe student characteristics (e.g., student motivation, home life, or attitude towards school) are why learning does or does not occur (Evans et al., 2019). Instruction, even though it is the most essential factor to learning, is often not reflected on as important. Thus, this book aims to shift that thinking by highlighting instructional practices that are pivotal to student learning.

The chapters in the text are aligned to the Common Core State Standards (CCSS). However, additional aspects not included in the CCSS, such as the classroom library, independent reading, handwriting, motivation, and nuanced elements of instruction, are also detailed and aligned to research. The "why" behind instruction is elemental to this book.

The goal of this text is improvement—improving curriculum and improving instruction to improve literacy outcomes. I challenge you to eliminate deficit talk from your discussions and think about what is working for your students and what can be done, instructionally, for your collective team of educators to improve. Moreover, believe in your own ability to adapt, change, and achieve. Research suggests that teachers who hold a positive self-efficacy (belief system) can positively affect the collective efficacy of the school (Goddard, Hoy & Hoy, 2004). Moreover, these beliefs can shape learning and achievement.

Keeping improvement at the forefront of the LLT will help you select or refine your reading curriculum and strengthen instructional practices. Before we begin, let's take a few moments to establish our own, healthy learning community.

Opening the Meeting Today: A Community Builder

As a member of this LLT, it helps to create a community that welcomes risk taking, idea sharing, and critical questioning. Each of you serves an essential role in supporting the literacy learning of all students. Thus, a strong professional learning community will foster meaningful results for this evaluation process.

[Facilitator leads community builder]

Establish Group Norms

Step 1: At tables, you will work together to co-construct group norms for how you will communicate with one another during meetings. Begin by forming a small group with your colleagues.

Step 2: Within your group, discuss ideas and generate a list of norms you believe are important for the success of the whole leadership team undertaking this process. Jot these down on chart paper.

Following are ideas to consider for establishing group norms:

- Beginning and ending meetings on time
- Avoiding sidebars
- Listening/not interrupting
- Soliciting each other's ideas
- Assuming positive intent
- Avoiding inappropriate humor about gender, ethnicity, or even our students
- Speaking respectfully—seek understanding

Step 3: Allow time for each group to share their ideas. Once that is complete, come back together as a large group, and collapse and synthesize the norms into one collective list that will guide current and future meetings. The facilitator of the LLT will write out the final group norms and share them.

Diving into the Data

During the next phase of the meeting, you will work in small groups to assess school-wide literacy data and survey results pertaining to literacy instructional practices.

Expert teams breakout. To begin exploring the assessment data, you will work with a small team based on your expertise. The team will be charged with reviewing one part of the literacy program based on the following components. This text is organized by these components as well.

Expert Team	Chair of the Team
Early Literacy Skills	
K–3 Comprehension	
4–12 Comprehension (can be divided into two groups)	
Vocabulary (can be combined with Classroom Considerations)	
Writing	
Classroom Considerations (can be combined with Vocabulary)	

Expert teams generate hypothesis about data. In your small group, you will be provided assessment data and results from the instructional practices survey that correspond to your assigned evaluation. Begin by reviewing the data individually. What do you notice? Come back together as a small expert team and use the following list of guiding questions to help make sense of what you are noticing. (*Note: You may want to begin with assessment data first and then move on to the literacy practices survey data second.*)

As you begin to respond to the questions, generate a hypothesis of what you are observing. These can be tentative and subject to change. The key is that you are noting patterns and consistencies in teaching and learning. A template for documenting your hypothesis can be found in Appendix A.

Guiding Questions for Reviewing Data

- What are the demographics in the district? In each school? What are the demographic data for each subgroup?
- What trends in the data do you notice?
- What do the data reveal about the district? Subgroups? Itemized data?
- Are students doing better in some areas of literacy than others?
- Does one weak area shape another? For example, do you notice that weak foundational scores in fifth grade are potentially influencing weak comprehension scores?
- What underlying factors might account for areas that are weak or strong?
- Do we know what our learners' out-of-school literacy practices are? Are we leveraging these in our instruction?
- What do the literacy practices survey data tell you about instruction?
- What are teachers doing in their classrooms to promote effective reading instruction?
- Are students' cultural and linguistic backgrounds recognized as relevant to high-quality curriculum and instruction?
- What are teachers doing when students struggle to acquire grade-level reading?
- In what areas of literacy do teachers describe a need for professional development?
- What are the perceptions of the current literacy curriculum?
- Is the present curriculum culturally relevant? Are the texts used for teaching and learning culturally diverse and representative of all of the students in our schools?
- Are biases and stereotypes reinforced through the present literacy curriculum and materials?
- Are there aspects of the literacy curriculum where teachers do not have adequate resources or guidance?
- Is there agreement between the achievement data and the literacy practices data? For example, are teachers stating they need more professional development on phonics, and assessment data show word recognition scores are low in second-grade students? Can you observe any potential correlates in these data?
- Who is not achieving with the current curriculum and instruction? Why?

Once you have analyzed and discussed, begin to condense and record your main findings. The committee chair can take chart paper and title it with the group name and the word "hypotheses" next to it (e.g., Foundational Skills Group Hypotheses). Next, engage in a discussion about the emerging hypotheses that were discussed. As a team, condense these into three to five main hypotheses (the chair can record these). Once you have agreed to three to five hypotheses, the chair of the expert team can post the team's chart paper somewhere visible in the room where others can view it.

Small-group data analysis and discussion should take between one and two hours.

Gallery walk. Now that you have discussed and analyzed the data, rotate through each of the group's documentation of their findings. As you read, write comments, questions, and suggestions or ideas on the chart paper.

Discussion of Data

Literacy leadership team whole-group discussion. After the gallery walk, engage in a larger discussion about what was observed about literacy practices and the curriculum within your district. You can use the following questions to guide this discussion:

- The data tell me that reading outcomes in our district are…
- What are you proud of in our schools with regard to literacy?
- Literacy programming in our district would be better if…

Lunch Break

Begin Evaluation

Expert groups begin evaluation. An audit of the current reading program/materials and instructional practices begins today and concludes at the next meeting. Directions are provided next.

Materials needed. Pens, literacy survey data, assessment data and hypotheses, individual score sheets (corresponding to the chapter) for each member of the expert group, and one composite score sheet for the chair. These can be found in Appendix C.

Expert group work. The LLT should break into their expert groups, and the chair of each group should distribute materials. Each member of the group should skim through their assigned chapter and read the introduction. After the introduction, each chapter is divided into sections pertaining to a literacy construct that the expert team will score. Directions are as follows:

1   Begin by reading through the background information about the construct you are reviewing. This is important, since a research base and examples of essential instructional practices aligned to the construct are provided. You will be assessing whether your school or district is aligned to evidence-based practices and what the needs are.

2   Once you are done reading, use the guiding questions to discuss the construct/section. An additional reference(s) has been provided if the expert group wants to learn more about the topic.

3   Next, you will see this sign ⚠ **STOP AND EVALUATE**, which indicates it is time to evaluate the topic you just read about.

4   Using the reading evaluation document, each member of the expert team will rate and evaluate the literacy components outlined in the chapter under review. There are three parts to the evaluation, but you will only begin with the first two areas: (1) Instruction and (2) Current Materials. Part 3, **Materials Under Review**, should be evaluated once a full audit of the present reading materials and instructional practices is complete.

Three-Part Evaluation Rubric	Explanation
(1) Instructional Practices	This is the first part of the evaluation rubric and explores instructional practices. When evaluating, use the survey data to consider the instructional approaches used by most teachers.
(2) Current Materials	This is the second evaluation rubric and explores materials currently available in the classroom. When evaluating, consider the reading program that is currently being used in the school and/or is available to teachers.
(3) Materials Under Review	This is the last part of the evaluation rubric and explores a new program or materials. This is for evaluating new materials for potential adoption. *Note: Typically, this is the last step of the process and occurs at a subsequent meeting once a full audit of the present program and instructional practices has been completed.*

5   The chair collects the scores, averages the ratings, and inputs them on the "Composite Score Sheet."
6   The chair of the group will also curate the qualitative comments and provide them below the average score of the group.
7   Once the expert group has evaluated each construct provided in the chapter, the chair gives all forms to the facilitator of the LLT.
8   The facilitator of the LLT should record these scores on a digital spreadsheet for future reference.

Note: Both the vocabulary chapter and the cross-cutting chapters are shorter and follow a streamlined version of these directions.

3

Evaluating Foundational Skills

Chapter Preview

The chapter begins with a research overview of how word recognition develops. Then the main foundational skills for K–5 readers are explained and evaluated. Research, instructional practices, and aligned assessments are provided for each of the following constructs:

- Concepts about print
- Alphabet knowledge
- Phonological and phonemic awareness
- Phonics and spelling
  - ○ FAQs on phonics and word recognition
- Fluency

Evaluation: A three-part rubric is used to evaluate all constructs:

Phase One Rubric: Evaluates alignment of current instructional practices	**Phase Two Rubric:** Rates the quality of the current reading program provided to teachers	**Phase Three Rubric:** Rates the quality of the program up for adoption

Anchor Standards: The following Common Core Anchor Standards are addressed in this chapter:

Reading: Foundational Skills

Print Concepts (K–1)
Phonological Awareness (K–1)
Phonics and Word Recognition (K–5)
Fluency (K–5)

Introduction

In this chapter, you will have the opportunity to discuss and evaluate the following constructs:

1 Concepts about print
2 Alphabetic knowledge
3 Phonological and phonemic awareness
4 Phonics/word recognition
5 Fluency

The journey to becoming a proficient reader is complex. We know from decades of research that learning to read is not a natural process and that for many children, it is one of the most cognitively demanding skills to acquire. As discussed in Chapter 2, the Reading Rope (Figure 3.1) (Scarborough, 2001) illustrates the complexity of the reading process by showing how several components must weave together to create automatic, fluent readers who comprehend what they read. The goal of this chapter is to deconstruct the various (and sometimes nuanced) foundational skills that are embedded within the word recognition strands of the Reading Rope.

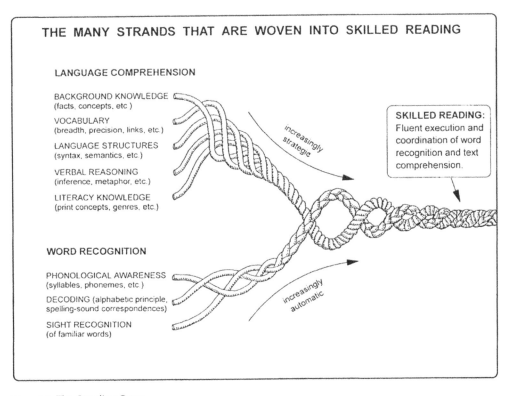

Figure 3.1 The Reading Rope.

Pendulum Swings in Reading Instruction

Historically, approaches for teaching word recognition have shifted back and forth with phonics instruction going in and out of favor (Snow & Juel, 2005). For example, in the late 1800s, phonics breathed throughout instructional resources as teachers relied upon McGuffey readers that taught students to learn and apply the alphabetic code. However, an 1886 study led researchers to infer that memorizing whole words would be more efficient than having children learn individual letters and sounds. Thus, phonics took to a back seat to a new type of instruction called whole word reading (also known as the "Look Say" method). In this approach, children were taught to read by memorizing whole words in books like Dick and Jane.

A "back to basics" movement in the 1970s popularized phonics once again with phonics workbooks proliferating the literacy landscape. However, by the 1980s "Whole Language" methods began to infiltrate classrooms and phonics workbooks were deemed unnecessary. Within the whole language approach, phonics was not explicitly taught but rather word recognition was believed to develop naturally, like language. In a whole language approach, researchers (Goodman, 1967) believed that skilled readers use multiple cues when reading (syntax, semantic, and visual/phonological) and that instruction should balance the teaching of these cues. The philosophy of whole language was that reading should be taught as a "whole" and not broken down into distinct parts like phonemic awareness or phonics.

Despite the popularity of whole language, by the mid-1990s, stakeholders again debated the role of phonics in early reading instruction. By this time, there was mounting evidence that phonics was essential to early word learning (Ehri, 1994; Share, 1995; Stanovich, 1986). Thus, legislatures and school boards were demanding more phonics instruction while maligning whole language practices (Spiegel, 1998).

Responding to the criticism, researchers (Pressley, 1998; Spiegel, 1998; Strickland, 1996) suggested that *balanced literacy* was a reasonable — and evidence-based — peacemaker for defusing the reading wars. In such an approach, educators would balance content and process, direct and indirect instruction, phonics and comprehension, and authentic texts with textbooks. In 2000, the National Reading Panel (NRP) worked to provide further clarification about the role of phonics and released an influential report that underscored the importance of decoding, citing both phonemic awareness and phonics as key pillars of reading instruction.

Nevertheless, twenty years after the NRP (2000) report, the debate over best practices for word learning persist (Hanford, 2018). These critics suggest that little has changed since the 1990s and balanced literacy is a euphuism for whole language where "multiple cues" are taught while systematic, explicit phonics instruction is neglected.

In the chapter that follows, I provide clarity on this issue by describing key research findings that pertain to word learning. I begin by explaining Linnea Ehri's (1994) phases of word learning. This is a useful theory for educators to understand and refer to when evaluating programs and practices. I then describe key foundational skills needed for word recognition and include the instructional approaches that align to teaching those skills. By having this research informed knowledge, you are better equipped to select high-quality instructional resources.

Phases of Word Learning: One Theoretical Model that Teachers Should Know

For educators to plan systematic instruction that meets readers' needs, it is essential to explore the nuanced aspects of how the brain acquires the ability to decode words and automatically recognize them by sight. Linnea Ehri (1994) identified four phases that readers progress through when learning automatic word recognition: *pre-alphabetic, partial alphabetic, full alphabetic, and consolidated alphabetic.* Ehri's phases of word learning are sequential, yet fluid in the sense that movement through them can overlap.

Pre-Alphabetic Phase

The first phase of reading occurs before children know the alphabet, typically in preschool and early kindergarten. During this time, children have not acquired the alphabetic principle and read by using logographic skills (looking at the shapes of letters) or guessing words through environmental context. Literacy is also developing through high-quality play, storybook read-alouds, and oral language experiences. To foster movement into the next phase of reading, instruction in letter identification and phonological awareness—namely phonemic awareness—is critical (see Table 3.1). Phonological awareness is the ability to detect and manipulate the units of spoken language. It encompasses the ability to auditorily detect whole words, rhymes, syllables, onset/rimes, and individual phonemes (phonemic awareness).

Partial Alphabetic Phase

In this phase, children can identify the sounds of several consonants and will couple this knowledge with context cues to guess at a word while reading. Our growing readers are working hard to secure the alphabetic principle and are evolving in their awareness of print concepts, including the concept of words. Knowledge of complex graphophonic patterns such as vowels, digraphs, and diphthongs has yet to be acquired. Explicit instruction on phoneme/grapheme relationships, including the flexible nature of vowels, is necessary for advancing into the next phase of word learning. Opportunities for writing and spelling are also essential as these strengthen phonemic awareness and alphabet knowledge.

Full-Alphabetic Phase

As readers move into this phase, they now possess the alphabetic principle, understand the flexible nature of vowels, and can segment and blend single-syllable words. These marvelous abilities allow readers to orthographically map many words, store them into long-term memory, and instantly recognize them by sight. However, at the onset of this phase, decoding is typically labored so explicit phonics instruction with repeated practice in connected text is needed. Readers in this phase can also begin to use analogy to identify an unfamiliar word by comparing part of a word (a rime) to an already known word.

Consolidated Alphabetic Phase

Learners in this phase are reading larger chunks of words, including roots, affixes, suffixes, syllables, and onset/rime. High-frequency spelling patterns (such as -ing, -ed, -er, etc.) begin to be retained and automatically mapped to correct spellings and

Table 3.1 Phases of Word Reading: Observations and Ramifications

Phase of Reading	Observed in Children	Instructional Implications
Pre-Alphabetic	Do not possess knowledge of letters and sounds Rely upon environmental cues to identify words Without environmental cues or pictures, children cannot read words in isolation	Provide explicit instruction in letter names, sounds, and formation Allow children to practice letter sound correspondence through letter awareness and invented spelling Teach phonological awareness such as word awareness Begin basic phoneme awareness of initial and final sounds in words Teach proper articulation of letter sounds
Partial Alphabetic	Apply phonetic cue reading by looking at the initial letter in a word or by using just the initial and final letter in a word Unable to fully decode a word due to insufficient alphabet knowledge and incomplete phonemic awareness	Continue alphabet knowledge instruction so children are proficient Continue instruction in phoneme/grapheme relationship with close attention to vowels Continue developing phoneme awareness through blending activities and identifying sounds within single-syllable words. Practice "reading" with predictable texts that reinforce finger pointing and concept of word
Full Alphabetic	Possess alphabetic principle and phonemic awareness Can decode unfamiliar words, but process can be slow Knowledge of recognizing words by sight increases substantially	Practice decoding in connected text by teaching the blending of all letters and sounds in single-cvc syllable words Varied practice reading texts for fluency development Teach reading with analogy (onset/rime)
Consolidated Alphabetic	Readers begin to internalize larger orthographic patterns, including syllables, affixes, and roots Instead of reading by decoding (letter by letter), readers use analogy to break words into meaningful parts	Increased focus on reading with analogy Provide strategies for breaking apart multisyllable words Continue fluency practice to develop increased automaticity and prosody

pronunciations. Instead of reading one letter at time, readers in this phase process larger units of words and strengthen their use of analogy.

Once readers graduate from consolidated reading, they are considered automatic word readers (Ehri, 1994). Throughout the rest of the chapter, I explain the key constructs that are needed to become fluent readers. I describe how these constructs are aligned to Ehri's model and provide suggestions for lesson design that educators can use to support word recognition within a comprehensive literacy framework (Table 3.1).

Concepts About Print

What Is It?

Concepts about print (CAP) refer to a child's understanding of how print works. It is typically taught in kindergarten and first grade. Children who possess concepts of print understand that written language carries meaning and that print has unique conventions.

Why Does It Matter?

Many children have well-developed concepts of print when entering preschool. Children who have been read to have greater print awareness than children who were not read to (Adams, 1990). The National Early Literacy Panel (2008) noted that CAP in kindergarten possesses a moderate-to-strong predictive value for later reading proficiency. Moreover, young children who are read aloud to and taught to focus on print during the read-aloud are found to outperform their peers in print awareness measures (Justice & Ezell, 2002).

How Is It Assessed?

Concepts about print are easily assessed in kindergarten through a checklist. In this assessment, the teacher works one on one with a child and measures the student's awareness of print concepts. This assessment provides a baseline for future instruction. Additionally, educators can assess children's writing to gather insight into their print awareness and use of conventions. A checklist for CAP might include:

Indicate if the child can:	Yes or No
Identify the title of the book "Show me the title of the book."	
Identity where to begin reading on page "Where would I begin reading?"	
Demonstrate left to right directionality "Show me how my finger should move as I read across the page."	
Demonstrate return sweep "What do I do when I get to the end of the sentence?"	
Identify a letter (concept of letter) "Can you show me a letter?"	
Identify a whole word (concept of word) "Can you show me a word?"	
Demonstrate voice/print match "Point to the words as a I read."	

Aligned Instructional Practices

- **Shared reading:** Using big books, the teacher reads aloud, points to words, and explicitly states how print functions. It is critical that during shared reading, the teacher is attending to the print as she reads. Children naturally focus attention on pictures, so teachers must direct them to the function that the print is serving. Preschool and kindergarten classroom teachers should rely on shared reading as a method of daily instruction, especially for children whose CAP scores are low (Justice & Ezell, 2002;

Justice, McGinty, Piasta, Kaderavek, & Fan, 2010). Specific print referencing strategies include:

- ○ Running a finger under the words
- ○ Noting specific features of print and letters (e.g., "This is a capital letter")
- ○ Asking children where to start reading the book
- ○ Counting words in a sentence
- ○ Pointing out print within pictures or speech bubbles

- **Shared writing:** Children benefit from shared writing—it supports concepts about print and positively affects young children's literacy development (Hall, Toland, Grisham-Brown, & Graham, 2014; Roth & Guinee, 2011). During shared writing, children compose a message, and the teacher models how print moves from left to right, has a return sweep, and uses specific punctuation to provide meaning. Shared writing can be composed in a whole setting but is especially powerful as small-group intervention. This instructional practice can improve print awareness, as well as phonological awareness, spelling, and reading (Craig, 2003).

- **Print-rich classrooms:** Classrooms should be filled with a diverse library of books and tools for writing. Labeling the classroom with words, although an implicit form of instruction, underscores the idea that print carries meaning. In kindergarten, creating literacy-rich dramatic play centers that include menus, grocery lists, mail, labeled groceries, etc., provides engagement with print but further allows the teacher to observe what children know about print and leverage that knowledge in instruction.

Guiding Questions for Discussion

- Is CAP assessed? How? What do the assessments tell about our program and practices?
- Are the effective practices routinely implemented to teach CAP?
- Are adequate instructional resources provided to teach CAP? If not, what resources are needed (be specific with quality and quantity)?
- Is professional development provided or needed on this topic (always consider teachers new to the profession)?
- Does the current or proposed curriculum include adequate lessons and resources to teach CAP?

Further reading

To extend your knowledge of the ideas presented in this section, read the following:

- Zucker, T.A., Ward, A.E., and Justice, L. M. (2011). Print referencing during read-alouds: A technique for increasing emergent readers' print knowledge. *The Reading Teacher*, 63(1), 62–72.

⚠ **STOP AND EVALUATE CONCEPTS ABOUT PRINT**

Table 3.2 Why Letter Names Are Confusing

The sound of the letter isn't in the letter name	The sound the letter represents is first and followed by a vowel sound. For example:	The sound the letter represents is second and begins with an inconsistent vowel sound	The letter name is entirely represented by the same sound	The identity changes when the letter is flipped around or upside down
h, w, y	*b, c, d, g, j, k, p, q, t, v, z*	*f, l, m, n, r, s, x.*	*a, j, e, i, o*	*b, d, p, q*

Source: Block and Duke, 2015

Alphabet Knowledge

What Is It?

Alphabet knowledge refers to a child's ability to identify the letter names, sounds, and symbols that are contained in the alphabet. There are 26 letters in the English alphabet, 44 English phonemes (sounds), and even more graphemes (letter and letter combinations) that represent those sounds. For example, the phoneme /j/ has numerous graphemes that correspond to it, including **j** as in jump; **g** as in gym, **dge** as is ridge, **dj** as in adjourn, and **di** as in soldier. Children first learn letter names, shapes, and finally sounds that correspond to the letter names.

Why Does It Matter?

Children's ability to identify the name, sound, and symbol of letters of the alphabet is a significant predictor of later reading ability (National Early Literacy Panel, 2008). Children who do not know the letters and sounds by the end of kindergarten are at a greater risk for reading difficulty by second grade (Gallagher, Frith, & Snowling, 2000). Knowing more advanced letter/sound representations (e.g., the letter combination of c and h makes the /ch/ sound) supports phonics understanding. Additionally, letter names are confusing to learn (Table 3.2), so clear and explicit instruction matters.

How Is It Assessed?

There are various aspects of assessing alphabetic knowledge:

- Letter naming: The child is provided letters of the alphabet (out of sequence) and asked to identify them.
- Letter sounds: The child is asked to say the sound the letter makes. Assess for both uppercase and lowercase sound recognition.
- Letter production: The child is asked to write the letter.

A strong reading curriculum will assess children's ability to identify both names and sounds of uppercase and lowercase letters.

Aligned Instructional Practices

- **Systematic and differentiated instruction:** Research suggests that explicit, differentiated, and systematic alphabet instruction in small groups based on children's needs is the most effective way to accelerate letter learning

(Stahl, 2014). This instruction should be brief (10 to 15 minutes per day) and introduce one letter per day (Jones, Clark, & Reutzel, 2012). Teachers should have a clear plan for systematically and explicitly teaching letters and sounds. Daily instruction should occur and begin around the first week of school. Here are considerations for teaching:

- ○ Lesson plan format: Jones, Clark, and Reutzel (2012) created an alphabet knowledge lesson plan that follows a clear, three-step process: (1) letter name and sound identification, (2) recognition of the letter within connected text, and (3) explicit teaching of letter formation in uppercase and lowercase form.
- ○ Differentiate instruction: Letter/sound identification should be instructed to small groups.
- ○ Letter sound correspondence: Once children can recognize the names and sounds of at least half of the letters and are able to segment and blend sounds together in a regular cvc word (see phonemic awareness section), they can move into traditional decoding instruction.

- **Correct pronunciation:** A critical step for developing alphabet knowledge is correctly modeling each letter sound and clipping pronunciations as needed. For example, the letter "b" is a clipped pronunciation and not a continuous "buh." Likewise, the letter "t" is clipped and not pronounced "tuh." In both letters, the schwa (an unstressed vowel pronounced like a short u sound) is not attached to the sound. This nuanced letter pronunciation is important when teaching phonemic blending. For example, when you are teaching phoneme blending of the word "bat," you would not want children to add in an extra schwa sound and pronounce it as buh+aa+tuh. Ensuring correct letter/sound pronunciations is an essential first step in eliminating confusion for developing readers.

- **Alphabet charts and key word considerations:** Alphabet charts are used as a scaffold to assist in letter identification and sound recognition. Although they are an implicit teaching tool, they are important. Typically, they include the letter and a picture of an object with a key word(s) representing the sound(s) of the letter. As educators, we need to ensure that our alphabet charts and corresponding key words do not confuse our readers (Duke & Mesmer, 2018–2019). For example, the keyword should have the dominant sound and not begin with a blend or r-controlled vowel: **A** is for *apple,* not **A** is for *airplane*. **E** is for *egg,* not **E** is for *elephant*. Using elephant to teach the letter /e/ is confusing because the "el" of elephant is the same pronunciation of the letter "l." Instead, use a key word like "egg," which is less apt to confuse. Using a cake to teach the letter /c/ is confusing because the letter "k" is in cake.

- **Letter name cues:** Letter names and sounds are more apt to be learned when the letter provides a cue to its sound. For example, the letters "b" and "l" give cues to their sounds /b/ and /l/ within their names. Other letters like "w," "y," and "h" do not.

- **Letter frequency:** Teach the most frequently used letters first (a, s, t, m). Avoid letter-of-the-week instruction. Focus on small groups based on readers' needs.

- **Phonemes and graphemes together:** Letter names should be instructed while concurrently emphasizing letter sounds (Piasta, Purpura, & Wagner, 2010). Thus, a combination of teaching both letters and sounds together promotes letter sound knowledge better than teaching letter sounds alone.

- **Explicit handwriting instruction:** See Chapter 7.
- **Name awareness:** Teachers can leverage children's names as a starting point to teach letter sounds. For example, Jamal begins with a /j/. Children are 11 times more likely to know the initial letter in their first name than a letter that is not in their name (Justice, Pence, Bowles, & Wiggins, 2006). We can use "Name Walls" with photographs of our readers that represent the letter/sound in their name.
- **Shared and interactive writing:** This activity supports letter learning and the alphabetic principle (Hindman & Wasik, 2012). During shared writing, the teacher holds the pen and writes a message or brief story; during interactive writing, children share the pen and compose a message with the teacher. In both approaches, letter formation and recognition of letter sounds are explicitly attended to.

Further reading

To extend educators' knowledge of the ideas presented in this section, the following article is suggested:

➢ Dougherty Stahl, K.A. (2014). New insights about letter learning. *The Reading Teacher 68*(4), 261–265. doi: 10.1002/trtr.1320

Guiding Questions for Discussion

- Is alphabetic knowledge assessed?
- Does my school or district provide a clear sequence of how letters and sounds should be taught?
- Is instruction differentiated based on the unique needs of readers?
- Is instruction clear and explicit?
- Is the use of invented spelling routinely provided to emergent readers?
- Is handwriting instruction provided?
- Are adequate resources and training provided to educators to teach alphabetic knowledge?

⚠ STOP AND EVALUATE ALPHABETIC KNOWLEDGE

Phonological and Phonemic Awareness

What Is It?

Phonological awareness is a broad term that refers to the ability to detect (hear) and manipulate the units of spoken language. Phonological awareness is an **auditory skill**. Thus, it does not include the ability to visually recognize letters or parts of words.

Varying in linguistic complexity, phonological awareness skills are on a continuum with segmenting words into syllables—the simplest skill to master—and phonemic awareness—the most complex (Schuele & Boudreau, 2008) (see Figure 3.2). *Phonemic awareness* is a distinct metalinguistic skill that is defined as the ability to segment and manipulate (e.g., blend, delete, substitute) each individual sound, or phoneme, within a word.

Phonological awareness encompasses the following distinct skills:

Concept of word: This refers to the ability to hear and detect individual words in a sentence. For example, if the teacher asked how many words are in the following sentence "I like my dog," a child who possesses concept of word could answer that there are four words in that sentence. Concept of words in print is a critical skill to possess for traditional reading. Children need to be able to point to each word as they read and demonstrate voice/print match.

Rhyming: This is the ability to detect and produce rhyming words. For example, the teacher might ask a child if two words rhyme: "Cat…Bat. Do they rhyme? Dog…Frog. Do they rhyme? Bird…Mouse. Do they rhyme?

Syllabication: This is the ability to segment and blend words into syllables.

Onset-rime: This is the ability to segment and blend the onset and rime of certain words. An onset is the first sound in a one-syllable word like cat. The onset is /c/. The rime is the vowel and letters that follow: /at/. Rimes are sometimes referred to as phonograms or word families. There are 37 common rimes in the English language. Note that the word "rime" differs in meaning from the word "rhyme."

Phonemic awareness: This is the ability to hear and manipulate each individual sound within a word. There are 44 sounds in the English language. For example, the word ship contains three sounds: /sh/, /i/, and /p/.

Why Does It Matter?

The term *phonology* refers to the sound system within language. Typically developing children enter kindergarten with a well-developed phonological system. However, they haven't been taught awareness of this phonological system and how to identity and manipulate the sounds of language. These *phonological awareness* skills are necessary for becoming a successful reader (Cardoso-Martins, Mesquita, & Ehri, 2011). The development of phonological awareness can be thought of in a hierarchy from basic to advanced. However, instruction can be fluid, meaning that children do not need to master one concept before moving on to the next.

Phonemic awareness is the most advanced phonological skill and an accurate predictor of successful reading acquisition (Adams, 1990). Phonemic awareness is a requisite for successful word recognition as it equips readers with a conscious awareness of the sounds of spoken language, which is needed when decoding and encoding words. Indeed, kindergarten children's level of *phonemic awareness* is a robust

Figure 3.2 Complexity of phonological awareness skills (Schuele & Boudreau, 2008).

predictor of future reading success (Anderson, Hiebert, Scott & Wilkerson, 1985; Catts, Fey, Zhang, & Tomblin, 2001; Snow, Burns, & Griffin, 1998).

Phonemic awareness instruction is most advantageous during the pre- and partial alphabet phases of word learning when small-group lessons focus upon one or two skills at a time (Armbruster, Lehr, Osborn, & Adler, 2009; National Reading Panel [NRP], 2000). For example, when we work with readers in the pre-alphabet phase, we might teach a lesson on how to isolate the initial phoneme of a word and identify a common phoneme across words (e.g., /m/ in mat, mud, mix) (Table 3.2). As our learners transition to the partial-alphabet phase of word reading, we can use Elkonin boxes (sound boxes) and letter cards to teach phoneme segmentation and blending. Blending is especially important for efficient decoding of words.

The NRP (2000) noted that approximately 5 to 18 hours of phonemic awareness instruction was sufficient for most readers, with segmentation and blending activities having the greatest effect on word reading. Nevertheless, phonemic awareness is a complex linguistic skill, and some readers may need engaging instruction that extends beyond 20 hours. Additionally, although the NRP (2000) found that infusing letter instruction into a phonemic awareness lesson was more advantageous than attending to sounds alone, researchers (Kilpatrick, 2016) advise educators to proceed cautiously and begin instruction at the sound level first (without letters). As children are strengthening their phonemic awareness skills, letters can eventually be infused as placeholders within phonemic awareness instruction. Although the addition of letters technically qualifies as phonics, phonemic awareness instruction with letters should be closely focused on segmentation and blending. Once readers can demonstrate how to segment and blend single-syllable words and can identify several letters and sounds in the alphabet, phonemic awareness instruction will smoothly transition to systematic phonics instruction. Here, children will learn increasingly complex phonics patterns and apply that knowledge within connected texts and writing activities.

How Is It Assessed?

Phonological awareness assessments such as the Phonological Awareness Literacy Screener (PALS), the Phonological Awareness Sensitivity Test (PAST), or the Comprehensive Test of Phonological Processing (C-TOPP) can be administered to students. Whatever screener is used, it should measure all aspects of phonological awareness and provide a clear path for instruction. Formative assessments should also be consistently used; teachers can use various checklists and document the development of children's phonological skills over time.

Table 3.3 provides a hierarchy of phonological skills, as well ideas for practice. Some children will naturally acquire phonological awareness without much direct teaching (Torgesen, Wagner, & Roshette, 1994); the assessments you use will determine this. However, other children will arrive at kindergarten needing more instruction, and some will need intensive teaching.

Aligned Instructional Practices

- **Daily small-group instruction**: Instruction should be differentiated in small groups based on needs. Research suggests students should receive 10 to 15 minutes per day of phonemic awareness instruction, yet no more than

Table 3.3 Hierarchy of Phonological Awareness with Instructional Practices

Phonological Awareness Concept	Typical Age of Achievement	Instructional Practices
Awareness of words	Age 5	Once children can count words in an oral sentence, begin instruction on voice/print match in text by using predictable texts with picture support (see phonics section for appropriate use of predictable texts)
Syllabication	Counting syllables: age 5	Assess, monitor, and teach in kindergarten
Rhyme	Recognition: age 5 Production: age 5.5	Assess, monitor, and teach in kindergarten
Initial phoneme awareness	Initial sound awareness: age 5.5	A bulk of phonological awareness instruction should focus at the phoneme level. Begin with easier tasks (identifying the first sound of a word); infuse letter symbols with instruction
Onset and rime manipulation and blending	Blending onset rime: age 5.5	Assess, monitor, and teach in the latter part of kindergarten
Phonemic segmentation and blending of CVC words	Blending two and three phonemes: age 6 Phoneme segmentation of simple CVC words: age 6 Phoneme substitution to build new words: age 6.5	Full segmentation tasks Instruction that combines alphabet awareness with phonemic awareness, such as invented spelling, positively shapes phonemic awareness ability. Instruction can extend through K-2.

Source: Adams et al., 1998; Blevins, 2017; Goswami, 2000

20 hours per school year (Edwards & Taub, 2016; Kilpatrick, 2016). Readers who struggle may need more intensive support with phonemic awareness, while other children may need much less. Your assessments will guide you to understand each child's unique needs.

- **Explicit instruction**: A sequence for explicit instruction (Kilpatrick, 2016) can proceed as (1) teacher explanation, (2) teacher demonstration, (3) student practice, and (4) teacher feedback.
- **Systematic instruction:** Teachers should have a clear sequence for the skills they are teaching and a way to assess proficiency.
- **Phonemic awareness focus:** The bulk of phonological awareness instruction should focus on phonemic awareness. This is essential instruction and should also be done systematically beginning with identifying initial sounds. The following activities support phonemic awareness:
  - ○ **Elkonin boxes**: Children can use sound/segmentation boxes to attend to phonemes at the beginning, middle, and/or end of words.

Instruction is also effective if it incorporates letters within instruction (NRP, 2000).

❍ **Phonemic awareness with rime units**: Kilpatrick (2016) suggests having children practice phoneme segmentation with rime units. For example, children can work with the rime /at/ and manipulate the vowel and consonant sounds through deletion and substitution tasks "Say /at/. Say /at/ again but don't say /a/." For a substitution task: "Say /at/. Say it again but instead of /t/ say /m/."

❍ **Blending activities**: Children should be taught how to blend syllables, onset/rime, and phonemes together. "When I say c-a-t, I can blend it together and say cat." Blending is an effective skill to use when eventually reading words. Thus, it is important that teachers do not just focus on phoneme segmentation but also on blending sounds together.

❍ **Five to eighteen hours of instruction**: The NRP recommends that for typically developing readers, no more than 18 hours of instruction is needed. The amount of instruction should be based on the needs of the students.

❍ **Invented spelling**: Writing with invented spelling is another tool that educators can rely upon to foster children's phonemic awareness. Research suggests that young children benefit greatly from applying invented spellings in their writing (Ehri & McCormick, 1998; Ouellette & Sénéchal, 2017; Snow, Burns & Griffin, 1998). This metalinguistic activity provides the opportunity for children to attend to individual sounds in words, apply letter knowledge, and develop vocabulary. Not only does this practice sharpen phonemic awareness, it develops the concept of words, which is an essential skill for children to possess when they begin reading in connected texts (see Bowling & Cabell, 2018). Moreover, teachers' analysis of children's approximations at spelling provide a window into their alphabetic and phonemic understanding. Children should apply their phonemic awareness by using invented spellings to write words, stories, poems, etc. As children progress in grade levels and become more aware of correct spelling patterns, they should be expected (and taught) to spell words correctly.

• **Phonological awareness focus:** Additional phonological awareness instruction can include:

❍ **Hearing words and sentences:** Children can learn to clap the words in sentences before they write them. This can be utilized in a shared writing format or as children are composing their own stories.

❍ **Rhyming activities:** There are many ways to teach rhyming. Children can produce rhymes, detect the "odd ball" in a rhyme sequence, play rhyming games, and read rhyming poetry and stories.

❍ **Syllable activities:** Children can learn to hear the syllables in words through clapping, tapping, and finally blending syllables together to create words.

❍ **Shared writing:** Children can engage in shared writing as they share the pen with the teacher and compose a short message (see "Concepts About Print" for a description). In shared writing, the following skills are reinforced: word awareness as children clap how many words are in a sentence and phoneme awareness as children hear and identify each sound in a single-syllable word. Shared writing promotes phonological awareness, phonemic awareness, and letter/sound identification.

Guiding Questions

- How is phonological awareness being assessed by teachers?
  - Is phonemic awareness instruction assessed?
  - How are the results used?
- Is the most amount of time spent on phonemic awareness instruction (as opposed to other aspects of phonological awareness)?
- Is instruction differentiated?
- Is the instruction explicit and direct?
- Is additonal support provided to children who are not progressing?
- Are materials and lessons provided to teachers, or is it haphazard?
- For readers with well-developed phonological awareness, are they being challenged?

Further reading

To extend your knowledge of the ideas presented in this section, read the following:

→ Hogan, T.P., Catts, H.W., & Little, T.D. (2005). The relationship between phonological awareness and reading: Implications for the assessment of phonological awareness. *Language, Speech, and Hearing Services in Schools*, 36(4), 285–293.

⚠ STOP AND EVALUATE PHONOLOGICAL AWARENESS

Phonics/Word Recognition

What Is It?

In this section, I use the term *word recognition* to describe instructional processes that can be used so children learn to automatically recognize words by sight.

Phonics is an approach for decoding written language by using letter sound knowledge to sound out and blend words for correct pronunciation. Phonic decoding allows a reader to pronounce an unfamiliar word in a text by sounding it out and blending it back together. To advance through the phases of word learning, students must be provided phonics instruction within a well-designed sequence, also known as *systematic phonics* (Ehri & McCormick, 1998; Ehri, Nunes, Stahl, & Willows, 2001; NRP, 2000).

Spelling refers to encoding written language. Both phonics knowledge and spelling have a similar trajectory of development, yet spelling tends to lag slightly behind phonics as children are learning to read (Ehri, 2000). Additionally, spelling requires you to expend more memory as you map a word to its written form. For example, reading the word "excellent" involves retrieving the correct pronunciation and meaning. Spelling "excellent," on the other hand, involves recalling each letter and letter combination in the exact sequence using the exact graphemic representations. Despite these differences, learning to read supports spelling knowledge, while spelling instruction supports decoding and reading ability. A well-designed phonics program will leverage both.

Unfortunately, spelling has often been ignored in educational policy (e.g., the NRP) and, consequently, instruction. However, your district's comprehensive reading program should include both phonics and spelling as integral components to reading acquisition. Since phonics and spelling are reciprocal in nature, they should be instructed in tandem (not in isolation) and build off children's emerging phonological skills. Thus, it is important to play close attention to your readers' developing skills. As they become more and more secure with phonological awareness, particularly the ability to segment and blend individual sounds, and they have mastered over half of the letters and sounds in the alphabet, they are ready for formal phonics and spelling instruction.

Why Does Phonics Instruction Matter?

Instructionally, phonics facilitates the brain's ability to glue alphabet patterns into long-term memory. Ehri and Flugman (2018) described the process by stating, "When specific words are decoded, their spellings are mapped onto pronunciations and retained in memory along with meanings" (p. 427). This process is referred to as *orthographic mapping*. Typically developing readers only need to decode and phonologically recode a word a few times for it to be embedded into long-term memory (Share, 1995). For example, when a reader sees the word "dish," he or she automatically knows how to pronounce it as practice decoding and blending the phonics patterns together in connected text successfully wired the orthographic image into the brain's circuitry. Unfortunately, readers who struggle will need multiple exposures for the same word—which is why explicit phonics instruction for all emergent readers is needed.

The research is clear that emergent readers must be provided sequential and explicit phonics instruction (NRP, 2000). Readers must be able to automatically recognize words by sight—phonics instruction aids in this ability. As children progress in their phonics knowledge, they can read fluently and effortlessly. This automaticity is necessary for the development of reading comprehension. Unfortunately, 65 to 75 percent of children who have reading disabilities in the early grades will continue to struggle with reading through adulthood (Scarborough, 1998). Thus, phonics is an essential skill for emerging readers to master. The following quote (Troia, 2004) summarizes this idea nicely:

Although the ultimate goal of reading is to derive meaning from text, it is well established that recognizing single words is the sine qua non of reading achievement…. In fact, the chief problem encountered by children identified with reading disabilities (RD) is slow and inaccurate word recognition…. Prevention and intervention efforts are crucial to avoiding the potentially chronic and debilitating effects of poor word recognition skills. (p. 98)

How Is Phonics Assessed?

Universal screeners: Many districts rely upon universal screeners such as Standardized Test for Assessment of Reading (STAR) or Measure of Academic Progress (MAPS) to assess early literacy skills. There are pros and cons to using these screeners, which is why teachers should rely upon multiple measures of data.

Classroom-based assessments: Educators can also administer their own classroom-based assessments that give information about their students' word recognition abilities. A valid and reliable phonics assessment is the Consortium on Reading

Excellence–Phonics Survey (CORE-PS). The CORE-PS includes a battery of assessments that begin with letter sound/identification and assess both pseudo-[1] and real-word identification. Another classroom assessment is the Basic Phonics Skills Test (BPST-III).

Informal reading inventory: Informal reading inventories should be used to assess how students are applying phonics, fluency, and comprehension skills in connected text. The Qualitative Reading Inventory-6 (Leslie & Caldwell, 2017) is a valid and reliable assessment that has been extensively field-tested.

Spelling assessment: For spelling instruction, a spelling inventory (Bear, Invernizzi Templeton, & Johnston, 2016 or Gentry, 2007) can provide teachers with information about a child's spelling development.

Formative assessments: This is the heart of your teaching. Educators should keep track of readers' progress during small-group instruction. Having a record keeping system helps you record children's use of phonics patterns or ability to analyze word structure can help you decide future instruction.

What Should Phonics and Spelling Instruction Look Like?

There are various approaches to teaching phonics, so it is important to understand how they are designed. *Analytic phonics* teaches children to use a familiar word to read an unknown word by processing its larger orthographic units, such as the onset and rime (Gaskins, et al., 1988). For example, the child might know the word "sick" and the word "her." When the child comes across the unknown word "kicker," he or she will analyze the word by searching for known parts, breaking it down, and pronouncing it correctly. *Synthetic phonics* begins with the parts of words and teaches children how to synthesize graphemes and phonemes together. Some synthetic phonics programs prioritize a *print-to-speech* approach that focuses on intensively teaching phonic patterns, connecting those patterns to the sounds they make, and decoding them in words. A *speech-to-print* approach prioritizes encoding (spelling) as readers connect sounds to the written word. Table 3.4 provides a description of each.

Both analytic and synthetic approaches are important to understand, as both have been shown to have positive effects on decoding (Henbest & Apel, 2017; NRP, 2000; Torgerson, Brooks, & Hall, 2006). For instance, Ehri and Flugman (2018) showed positive results on word reading by using synthetic approaches with first-grade learners. In a different study, researchers found that teaching rime units helped emergent readers develop efficient word recognition skills (Walton, Walton, & Walton, 2001). Understanding your readers' word recognition development can help you utilize both approaches as needed.

Additionally, it's imperative that educatorshave a well-defined scope and sequence that include daily, small-group lessons based on readers' needs. Instructionally, all phonics lessons—synthetic, analytic, or a hybrid of both—should be active, engaging, and relatively brief (15 to 30 minutes depending upon need) (Blevins, 2016; Duke & Mesmer, 2018).

Aligned Instructional Practices

- **Explicit:** Phonics must be directly taught and should not be through discovery or chance. Synthetic phonics is more explicit and teacher directed. Yet educators can and should provide clear and attentive instruction as readers engage in analytic phonics.

Table 3.4 Phonics Approaches

	Synthetic Phonics	Analytic Phonics	Encoding/Orthographic Approaches
Definition	Part-to-whole instruction. Students learn to convert letters into sounds and blend them together to make words. Focuses on six syllable types: closed, open, vowel consonant e, vowel team, consonant le, r-controlled.	Whole-to-part instruction. Students are taught to analyze a word and break it down and analyze its parts.	Instruction is organized by hearing the sound in a word and then learning how to orthographically represent (spell) the sound. Readers then learn to map phonemes and strings of phonemes to the written word.
Research Base	The NRP (2000) concluded no statistically significant difference in effectiveness between analytic and synthetic phonics. Encoding approaches use both analytic and synthetic methods.		
Teacher Expertise	Teacher's knowledge of word recognition is key. Teachers should have a strong understanding of the progression of phonics and be familiar with how to deliver different types of instruction. Teachers must be able to adapt their instruction for readers who need more or less of one approach. Districts should not expect teachers to rely upon a one-size-fits-all approach. Ongoing professional development is essential for K–2 teachers.		

- **Systematic:** The NRP (2000) noted that effective phonics instruction is systematic. Thus, teachers should have a system for teaching phonics patterns. Use only one consistent scope and sequence. Instruction should not be random or haphazard. While there is no single order of instruction that has been suggested to be the most effective, Table 3.5 represents an acceptable sequence.
- **Frequent small-group instruction:** Teachers should differentiate instruction in small groups based on need. The quantity of instruction depends on each reader's individual needs and their responsiveness to instruction. However, as a guide, emergent readers should be provided daily phonics instruction (15 to 20 minutes per day). Readers who struggle with phonics should be provided more intense instruction. Children who do not know their letters and sounds and cannot demonstrate essential phonemic awareness abilities (e.g., segmenting a consonant-vowel-consonant [CVC] word) will need intensive instruction at the phonemic and alphabetic level before instruction in larger orthographic units can begin.
- **Repeated practice and application:** Phonics lessons should incorporate students' ability to segment sounds in words, map those sounds to graphemes (spelling), blend the sounds to read words, and, finally, practice decoding and reading words in connected text. Emerging readers need generous practice reading phonics patterns within connected texts (often decodable texts—see later for additional information on text types). Blevins (2017) suggests a five-step process that integrates connected texts within instruction: (1) warm-up with repeated reading, (2) direct teaching of phonics pattern, (3) blending and word building, (4) practice in connected text, and (5) dictated writing. A reading program or phonics approach should include

Table 3.5 Sequence of Phonics Instruction

Approximate Grade	Phonics Skill
K–1	Initial consonants
K–1	Less common initial consonants
K–1	Consonant digraphs
K–1	Short vowels
1–2	Initial consonant blends
1–2	Final consonant blends
2	Less common digraphs
K–1	Long vowels with a final e
1–2	Vowel digraphs
1–2	R-controlled vowels
1–2	Diphthongs
2–3	Consonant/consonant digraphs
2–3	Irregular vowel sounds

activities like these. Following are a few examples that you might observe in a phonics lesson:

○ **Phonic blending** (Blevins, 2017) is an activity that builds on phonemic blending by adding letters to the task. Provide students with magnetic letters and explicitly demonstrate how to blend the sounds of the letters together by moving from one sound to the next: /mmmaaaat/ /mat/.

○ **Word building** (Beck & Beck, 2013) teaches children to discriminate the sounds in words by manipulating one letter: "Here is the word *mat*. Watch me as I can change the last letter *t* (teacher pronounces the sound /t/) to the letter d (teacher pronounces the sound /d/). The new word is mad."

○ **Phoneme/grapheme mapping** teaches children to map the sounds in a word to their correct orthographic patterns. Here, the teacher explains how written language functions (e.g., explaining how a silent e makes a vowel sound long). Children might use sound boxes to count the sounds in a word and then map those sounds to the orthographic patterns in the word. Finally, the child spells and pronounces the word and continues practice with similar patterned words.

• **Teaches multisyllable word analysis:** As students advance in the grade levels, instruction should provide strategies for word recognition through morphological analysis (roots and affixes), as well as syllable patterns.

• **Uses writing and connected texts:** A strong phonics program will not teach patterns in isolation. Rather, students will learn a pattern, practice reading the pattern in a sentence or connected (decodable) text, and write words with the pattern. See later for information about text types and their appropriate use. Merely providing a worksheet on a phonics pattern is *not* effective instruction.

• **Practice high-frequency words:** High-frequency words are words that cannot be decoded through common phonics patterns yet are common in the English orthography. Words like *the*, *where*, *their*, etc., are considered high-frequency words. High-frequency words should be taught through explicit instruction that provides the word in isolation, as well as in continuous text. Many books with predictable patterns provide repeated exposure to high-frequency words in authentic contexts. Additional instructional strategies include mapping irregular words, oral decoding, and spelling strategies (see Kilpatrick, 2016).

Aligned Instructional Practices for Spelling

Spelling is an important aspect of any word recognition program. Spelling instruction develops a reader's ability to correctly store and retrieve mental orthographic representations (MOR) (Apel, 2009), or the image of a word. Complete and accurate MOR's support a reader's ability to fluently read and write and are necessary for literacy proficiency. Following are practices that support spelling instruction:

- **Part of a comprehensive word study program:** Spelling instruction should be explicit and included within a dynamic word study program that includes decoding and word recognition. Thus, spelling should be taught in concert with phonics instruction. A comprehensive word study program includes practice with phonology (phonemic awareness and phonics), orthography (spelling), and morphology (vocabulary). Thus, effective spelling instruction is not teaching children to memorize a list of words.
- **Incorporates knowledge of phonology:** Emergent readers and writers benefit greatly from applying invented spellings when they are writing stories or informational pieces. This practice sharpens phonemic awareness and helps develop alphabetic knowledge. However, during word study instruction, children can be provided with explicit teaching that guides them to correctly map phonemes and graphemes to learn to spell words correctly. As children's reading and writing develop, children should be expected to apply the traditional spellings of words and not solely rely upon phonological knowledge to spell words.
- **Focuses upon morphology:** Morphology refers to the units of meaning within words. Knowing the spelling of morphemes is important, as they are generally consistent. For example, the morpheme "ed" (which is used to show past tense) is pronounced differently in the words talked and stunted, yet the spelling remains the same. Using pictures to teach plural concepts can also help with morphological awareness—for example, teachers can demonstrate how adding an "s" to a word makes it plural and use pictures to conceptually illustrate this to students (e.g., cat and cats or bird and birds). A well-designed word study program will include morphology instruction as a key component.
- **Teaches orthographic conventions:** Spelling instruction can focus on common orthographic conventions that are applied when spelling words. For example, changing the y to an i before adding the suffix es, is a useful spelling strategy. Instruction should focus on the most common spelling conventions.
- **Assessment:** Weekly spelling tests are a poor measure of a student's spelling abilities. The most useful assessment will evaluate spelling through a diagnostic spelling assessment that explores the student's use of phonology, morphology, and orthography. This can be completed by evaluating a student's authentic writing and/or through a spelling inventory. Both can be used to guide spelling instruction.

Frequently Asked Questions About Phonics and Word Recognition

How often should phonics instruction occur?

Based on the needs of the students, small-group phonics instruction can be anywhere from 15 to 20 minutes per day for typically developing readers to up to 45 minutes every day for children who need more support. Learning how to decode written language can be cognitively exhausting – especially for a child with a reading disability such as dyslexia (a specific learning disability that affects phonological processing and/or naming speed). Thus, it is imperative that we are empathetic to the effort that that word learning requires. Phonics instruction can be overdone, so we need to make sure that our teaching is meaningful, engaging, and relevant to the needs of our learners.

In which grades is phonics taught?

Typically, phonics is taught daily in grades K–3 (although this can vary based on the children). In grades 4–5, students advance their understanding of morphology, spelling, and multisyllable word analysis. Educators should be responsive to the needs of their readers and provide appropriate phonics instruction based on the child's current level of word recognition ability.

To ensure fidelity to the reading program, should all teachers be required to be on the exact same page of the reading program every day?

No. Strong instruction is responsive to the needs of readers. Phonics instruction can be systematic and yet still be designed around what children need and how quickly they are or are not developing phonics knowledge. Assessment should guide the work that children need—not a lock-step calendar.

Should the phonics program be scripted?

No. There is no research to suggest that a scripted program is more effective than one where the teacher designs the lesson using a scope and sequence and research-based principles that support word-recognition. The key is deep teacher knowledge and expertise coupled with useful instructional materials and engaging instruction. All teachers need to understand how orthographic mapping works and should be provided professional learning on this topic.

Is guided reading an appropriate method for phonics instruction?

Common practices like guided reading (Fountas & Pinnell, 2016; Richardson, 2016) or strategy groups (Serravallo, 2015) do not emphasize phonics in a systematic or robust manner. In a guided reading framework, word study might be conducted at the end of the lesson for a brief amount of time. In a strategy group approach, phonics is approached incidentally, as one of many problem-solving strategies. There is no research to suggest that guided reading or strategy groups improves phonics ability. Thus, a dedicated time to phonics instruction is essential in all primary classrooms.

When my students practice reading in connected texts, should I use decodable texts or leveled texts for instruction?

Just as guided reading is not hearty enough to singularly teach phonics, word study programs are not independently strong enough to teach continuous reading. For children to become fluent readers, they need to practice decoding and blending within connected text. A variety of text types are available for teaching emergent readers, yet not all of them are created equally.

Predictable texts have a highly repetitive pattern, often contain only one line of print per page, and include plenty of picture support so children can memorize the text. These books are useful for developing directionality, finger pointing, and concept of word. Readers who are in the partial-alphabet phase (Ehri, 1994) and are learning initial letter sound correspondence can practice reading with a text that is patterned. They can be prompted to point to each word as they "read" and look at the letter and picture to assist in word identification. This instruction develops initial consonant letter/sound identification and teaches *concept of word*, which is needed for automatic reading (Bowling & Cabell, 2018).

As children progress into full alphabetic reading, *decodable texts* are a useful instructional tool. In these text types, the language is determined by a specific phonics pattern (e.g., "Pat the cat sat on his mat. Next, he took a nap"). Decodable texts allow children to practice decoding skills using phonics patterns that were recently instructed; this helps create the connection-forming process that is needed for orthographic mapping (Ehri, 1994). Decodable texts should be used with children who have a well-developed concept of word, know several high-frequency words, know most consonants and a few short vowel sounds, and are able to blend a CVC word together (Mesmer, 2019). The key for instruction is using *quality* decodable texts that provide repetition and targeted practice; various poems with decodable patterns can also provide practice for readers. Importantly, decodable texts are meant as a short-term scaffold. Once children have strong grapheme-phoneme correspondence (GPC) knowledge and are smoothly decoding and blending single syllable words, decodable texts lose their potency and teachers can move on to other text types (Castles, Rastle, & Nation, 2018). Additionally, as children are learning with decodable texts, they should not be limited to reading only those text types.

Sight word readers are another type of text that can help children learn to identify high-frequency words such as "the," "when," "where," etc. These words are often nondecodable, and some children may need additional support learning to recognize them. However, like decodable texts, sight word readers should be used cautiously. Due to their predictable structure, they may limit how much a reader attends to the high-frequency word(s) under study.

Leveled texts are another type of text that is typically used in guided reading lessons. The stories in leveled readers follow a natural syntax, have diverse vocabulary, and have engaging storylines. Leveled readers use predictable patterns during the early levels and focus children on using picture or context clues to assist in word identification. However, like decodable texts, leveled texts have drawbacks. To begin, phonics patterns are not controlled for in leveled books, and children may not get practice with the patterns they are learning during word study. Moreover, an overuse of predictable patterns found in many of the beginning levels can be detrimental, especially for readers who struggle (Chapman & Tunmer, 2003). Research indicates that readers who acquire phonics knowledge more slowly may compensate for weak decoding skills by over-relying on context (Perfetti & Roth, 1981; Stanovich, 1986). Since pictures and context are the primary means for word identification at the beginning text levels, higher-leveled readers can be used to teach typically developing readers in the consolidated alphabetic phase of word learning.

Text Types: Key Take-Away!

Selecting the right text for phonics instruction is essential. However, all emergent read-ers should have opportunities to access, explore, and read a wide variety of text types each day, including nonfiction texts, picture books, audio books, decodable and leveled texts, and books that represent diverse cultures and communities. Not only should the texts we provide help teach children to read, but they should positively support chil-dren's development as lifelong readers. Thus, when evaluating instructional materials, a robust and healthy classroom library is an essential consideration. See Chapter 8 for information on evaluating the classroom library.

How should teachers prompt readers when they are struggling with a word?

When children are stuck on how to pronounce a word, teachers sometimes strive to facilitate word recognition by using a context prompt such as "think about what makes sense." Stanovich (1986) explained that to understand the role of context during reading, it must be distinguished by its purpose, which is either (1) as an aid to word recognition or (2) as an aid to reading comprehension. Unfortunately, when viewed as an aid to word recognition, context is an unreliable mechanism for orthographic mapping.

Ehri (1994) explained that children learn to automatically recognize a word by sight by utilizing a *connection-forming process* that is responsible for storing words into long-term memory. Knowledge of the alphabet system, not context, is the driver for making these connections stick. Instructionally, this implies that as full-alphabet readers are practicing in connected texts, we should prompt them to identify an unknown word by blending the phonemes and graphemes together. At this delicate phase of word learning, we should be emphasizing the use of decoding, not context. Emergent readers need to store alphabet patterns into long-term memory so words can eventually be recognized by sight. Relying on context as the primary strategy (and prompt) will not create this necessary foundation.[2]

Although context prompts that ask children to "think about what makes sense" are inadequate for developing automatic word recognition, context (e.g., semantics) does play a role when a reader must "recode" a word that was incorrectly pro-nounced. For example, if a child reads the word "hus" for "house," they might draw upon their semantic lexicon to recode the word into a correct pronunciation. This process is known as the *set for variability* (Tunmer & Chapman, 2012) and explains how readers use orthographic and phonological information to identify a word, yet they draw upon their semantic knowledge to recode the word if it was incorrectly pronounced. The set for variability also explains why some readers with a strong oral vocabulary can compensate for weak decoding skills by relying on their vocabulary knowledge and context to identify some unknown words.

Unfortunately, most texts do not provide enough context for readers to identify an unknown word. Thus, when a reader miscues during oral reading (on a word where the phonic pattern was taught), we should provide space for self-monitoring and self-correcting. If the reader does not self-correct the error by the end of the sen-tence, we can prompt the reader to go back and attend to the graphophonic infor-mation in the word. The prompt "does that make sense?" is a useful confirmation strategy once the word has been successfully decoded, blended, and correctly pro-nounced. This also reinforces reading as a meaning-making activity.

Should professional development be required?

Research (Ehri & Flugman, 2018) has suggested that teachers who receive ongoing (e.g., year-long) professional development on how to implement explicit, systematic phonics instruction can positively affect reading outcomes for K–1 students. Given the complexity and enormity of reading instruction, research (Brady et al, 2009) has suggested that both new and experienced educators have a need for understanding how to deliver effective phonics instruction.

Guiding Questions for Discussion

- Is phonics knowledge assessed?
- Are data used for grouping and differentiation?
- Do teachers use a shared scope and sequence for phonics instruction?
- Do teachers plan and deliver daily phonics lessons that incorporate explicit instruction and opportunities for students to practice learning phonics patterns in both writing and reading?
- Are children practicing taught phonics patterns within aligned connected texts?
- Are a variety of high-quality text types available for instruction?
- Are other instructional materials available to teachers?
- Are teachers well trained in both analytic and synthetic approaches to phonics?

Further reading

To extend your knowledge of the ideas presented in this section, read the following:

→ Ehri, L.C. (2000). Learning to read and learning to spell: Two sides of a coin. *Topics in Language Disorders, 20*(3), 19–36.

→ Mesmer, H. (2019). *Letter lessons and first words: Phonics foundations that work.* Portsmouth, NH: Heinemann.

→ Stahl, S.A., Duffy-Hester, A.M., & Stahl, K. (1998). Everything you wanted to know about phonics (but were afraid to ask). *Reading Research Quarterly, 33*(3), 338–355.

⚠ STOP AND EVALUATE PHONICS

Fluency

What Is It?

Fluency is often referred to as the bridge between decoding and reading comprehension (Pikulski & Chard, 2005). An erroneous belief is that fluency refers to the speed of the reader; the construct is more complex and involves elements of automaticity, accuracy, and prosody (expression). Fluency is defined as the following:

> *Fluency combines accuracy, automaticity, and oral reading prosody, which taken together, facilitate the reader's construction of meaning. It is demonstrated through oral reading through ease of word recognition, appropriate phrasing, pacing, and intonation. It is a factor in both oral and silent reading that can limit or support comprehension. (Kuhh, Schwanenflugel, & Meisinger, 2010, p. 242)*

What Is Automaticity?

This refers to the rate, or speed of reading. Emergent readers are typically less automatic than more advanced readers because their attention is heavily focused on decoding the words. Therefore, they are less apt to be quick. Although decoding is important for developing fluency, it is insufficient on its own. To become fluent, readers need to practice in connected texts.

An older model of reading that helps explain the role of automaticity in fluency was crafted by La Berge and Samuels (1974). Their model suggests that successful reading requires accurate, automatic word recognition *and* comprehension. When low-level subskills of reading become both accurate and automatic, then attention is freed to allow for the ease of comprehension. According to this model, readers who are disfluent have their attentional resources drained by *poor decoding*, which results in a lack of automaticity and ultimately poor comprehension. Viewed this way, disfluency is often due to poor decoding. This can be the result of an underlying phonological deficit, which impedes the automaticity of the reader. Therefore, it is hypothesized that when accuracy (and subsequently automaticity) improve, so does overall reading comprehension.

Another aspect related to automaticity is *naming speed*. Naming speed refers to an individual's ability to automatically retrieve the name of a symbol (e.g., a number, color, object). Naming speed is suggested to be separate from phonological processing and an independent contributor to reading difficulty (Wolf & Katzir-Cohen, 2001). Thus, a child could be disfluent because of poor decoding *and/or* weak naming speed. Wolf and Bowers (1999) have used the term "double-deficit hypothesis" to suggest that children with severe reading difficulties are challenged by both naming speed and phonological processing.

What Is Prosody?

Prosody refers to the expression, intonation, and purposeful phrasing that a reader uses to provoke meaning (Kuhn et al., 2010). There are four components to prosody: intonation, rhythm, stress, and pacing. Readers who use *intonation* rely on pitch to facilitate meaning. For example, questions often have a rising pitch, exclamatory sentences can reveal excitement through pitch, and declarative sentences can be expressed flatly or with intonation, depending on the intended meaning. Readers that demonstrate intonation generally have decent fluency. In addition, prosodic reading occurs when readers stress certain sounds in words, monitor their pace, and read in a rhythm that fosters meaning. Collectively, these components allow the reader to give meaning to the text.

What Is Accuracy?[3]

Accuracy differs from automaticity because it centers around accurate reading and not reading rate. Thus, accuracy refers to the ability to recognize and read words correctly. Readers can be accurate but not quick. Likewise, readers can be quick but not accurate. Inaccurate readers typically have issues with decoding. Readers who struggle with decoding will be disfluent.

Why Does It Matter?

Fluency is an important skill for reading, as it has been shown to be correlated to reading comprehension (although this relationship is not linear or causal) (Fuchs, Fuchs, Hosp, & Jenkins, 2001; Pikulski & Chard, 2005; Sabatini, Wang, & O'Reilly, 2019).

Fluency is the bridge that links decoding to reading comprehension (Kuhn, et al., 2010). The NRP (2000) considered it important enough to recognize it as one of the five pillars of reading instruction. A significant body of research has suggested that fluency instruction improves reading outcomes (Chard, Vaughn & Tyler, 2002; Kuhn & Stahl, 2003; Rasinski, Reutzel, Chard, & Linan-Thompson, 2011).

How Is It Assessed?

It is important not to begin fluency assessments until a reader has developed efficient word recognition abilities and has accrued several words that are recognized by sight (Perfetti, 1985). For example, before fluency assessments begin, readers should be able to use decoding skills to read basic CVC words accurately. Thus, it is not recommended to begin oral reading fluency (ORF) measures until the reader has accrued a bank of approximately 50 to 60 words that are automatically recognized by sight (Hasbrouck & Tindal, 2017). Given the developmental nature of reading acquisition, this can be late kindergarten for some readers and early second grade for others. Learning to read is a delicate process, and *speed should not be forced* upon emergent readers who are giving complex cognitive attention to accurate word reading.

Each aspect of fluency can be individually assessed. In this section, I break down ways to measure fluency.

Measuring automaticity: Automaticity can be best measured by listening to the reader and documenting the correct words per minute (CWPM). You can rely upon a selection from the present curriculum, referred to as a curriculum-based measure (CBM), to time the reading.

To measure rate, you will need a stopwatch, a pencil, and a passage from a text at the reader's grade level. The text should be something the reader has not seen before (a cold read). Have the student read aloud for one minute. To calculate the CWPM, subtract the total number of errors from the total number of words read. An error is a word that is omitted, incorrectly read, or substituted. Words that are repeated, self-corrected, or inserted do not count as errors. Table 3.6, based on Hasbrouck and Tindal (2017), can help you determine if your student is within the range of fluency proficiency.

A note of caution: Although CWPM provides a window into a child's orthographic processing and speed of reading, it can also give false positives or not identify children who need help with other aspects of reading (Kuhn & Levy, 2015). Research suggests that although there is a correlation between reading rate and reading comprehension, when reading rate is coupled with a measure of reading prosody, then the measures are more precise. Thus, when exploring implications for assessment, practitioners must be careful when deciding upon interventions based upon reading rate alone (Troia, 2004). Qualitative aspects *must always* be taken into consideration, including oral prosody measures.

Measuring prosody: Prosody is an equally important construct to measure but is also more difficult because it is not quantifiable like automaticity. Rather, prosody is typically assessed through a rubric, like the one developed by the National Assessment of Educational Progress (NAEP) Oral Reading Fluency Scale (Daane et al., 2005) (Table 3.7). Additional prosody rubrics can be found within standardized reading assessments like the Qualitative Reading Inventory-VI (Leslie & Caldwell, 2017). In the NAEP fluency scale in Table 3.7, readers progress through the levels as they develop. For example, in the beginning of grade 1, students' reading aligns to level 1 and moves to level 2 throughout the year. As children move up the grades, their reading prosody should develop accordingly. By fourth grade and beyond, all children should be at a level 4.

Table 3.6 Fluency Norms

Grade	Percentile	Fall WCPM*	Winter WCPM*	Spring WCPM*
1	90		97	116
	75		59	91
	50		29	60
	25		16	34
	10		9	18
2	90	111	131	148
	75	84	109	124
	50	50	84	100
	25	36	59	72
	10	23	35	43
3	90	134	161	166
	75	104	137	139
	50	83	97	112
	25	59	79	91
	10	40	62	63
4	90	153	168	184
	75	125	143	160
	50	94	120	133
	25	75	95	105
	10	60	71	83
5	90	179	183	195
	75	153	160	169
	50	121	133	146
	25	87	109	119
	10	64	84	102
6	90	185	195	204
	75	159	166	173
	50	132	145	146
	25	112	116	122
	10	89	91	91

Note: * denotes Words Correct Per Minute

Table 3.7 Oral Reading Fluency Scale for Prosody

Fluent	Level 4	Reads primarily in larger, meaningful phrase groups. Although some regressions, repetitions, and deviations from the text may be present, these do not appear to detract from the overall structure of the story. Preservation of the author's syntax is consistent. Some or most of the story is read with expressive interpretation.
	Level 3	Reads primarily in three- or four-word phrase groups. Some small groupings may be present. However, the majority of phrasing seems appropriate and preserves the syntax of the author. Little or no expressive interpretation is present.
Nonfluent	Level 2	Reads primarily in two-word phrases with some three- or four-word groupings. Some word-by-word reading may be present. Word groupings may seem awkward and unrelated to the larger context of the sentence or passage.
	Level 1	Reads primarily word by word. Occasional two-word or three-word phrases may occur, but these are infrequent and/or they do not preserve meaningful syntax.

Some researchers (Rasinski, 2006) have developed more nuanced fluency scales. These include dimensions of fluency such as expression and volume, phrasing, smoothness, and pace. For readers who are exhibiting little prosody during reading, a more complete analysis of where prosody is breaking down is warranted. Lastly, as you assess readers' prosody, you may consider audio-recording their reading to allow you to correctly gauge where they correspond to the fluency scale.

What Should Fluency Instruction Look Like?

Timothy Rasinski (1989) designed a set of principles to guide educators as they develop their readers' fluency. He suggests readers engage in the following practices:

➢ **Students are provided exemplary models of reading:** Children should be provided read-alouds that allow them to hear how good reading should sound. This should be provided to children in both narrative and nonfiction text.
➢ **Students receive oral support:** Educators should work alongside children as they read orally. Rasinski stresses this should not be "round robin style" reading but rather should incorporate practices such as echo reading, choral reading, and partner reading (see later).
➢ **Students practice:** Readers should be allowed time during the school day to practice their fluency. This happens during independent reading, partner reading, and teacher-directed instruction.
➢ **Students learn strategies for phrasing:** Readers should be provided clear instruction in how to parse texts into meaningful phrases that imbue meaning. This supports reading comprehension.

Aligned instructional practices: These practices promote fluency and should be used for that purpose. Thus, if the main intent is to develop decoding, these strategies are not recommended as effective practices. See the phonics section earlier.

- **Echo reading:** In this practice, the teacher provides a correct oral reading of a short section of text. In small groups, students silently follow along in their own copy of the text as the teacher reads aloud. After the teacher has read and modeled automaticity, accuracy, and strong prosody, students then reread the short section aloud with the teacher. In time, the sections can become increasingly longer, and the teacher's support can become less and less (Kuhn, 2009). Throughout echo reading, children should be reading texts at their instructional level and the teacher should periodically be checking for reading comprehension. It is essential that echo reading be stressed as a meaning-making process and not an exercise in mindless mimicking.
- **Choral reading:** This instructional routine provides less scaffolding than echo reading (Kuhn, 2009) as the teacher provides less initial support and more is demanded of the readers. In choral reading, the teacher and a small group of students read a passage of text in unison. Readers should be prompted to "read like the teacher" and mimic her expression, rate, and pacing. Readers can use short texts such as poems, songs, and speeches. Readers can also use poems that incorporate multiple voices.
- **Partner reading:** In this practice, students practice fluency exercises with another reader. To begin, the teacher provides clear directions for how to engage in partner reading. Each child uses their own text and is reading with another student who has a reading level slightly below or above them. They take turns, reading one page or paragraph/section at time and are prompted to read with expression and give feedback to one another.
- **Repeated Readings:** This activity requires a reader to practice a passage (such as a poem, song, or limerick) several times over a few days. Readers can practice individually or with a partner. It has been shown that repeated readings improve overall reading performance both for passages that are practiced as well as for novel ones (Troia, 2004), suggesting repeated readings help with overall word retrieval.
- **Wide reading:** Wide reading refers to uninterrupted reading within connected texts, such as books for independent reading. Prolonged engagement in reading has been shown to be a critical element in developing a reader's fluency (Kuhn et al., 2010). Thus, practitioners should closely examine the quantity of independent reading that their students are completing. This is extremely important for students with a fluency deficit, as practice with reading texts will strengthen their overall fluency ability. However, wide reading is only effective when the child has the foundational skills needed for sustained amounts of reading.
- **Readers' theater:** This activity allows students to simulate a play without memorizing the words. Akin to repeated reading, the student reads a play, poem, famous speech, lyrics, or other prose to practice for presentation to the class. Each practice provides the exercise of repeated reading while also serving as an activity to develop prosodic reading. It has been shown that readers' theater improves reading rate and prosody (Raskinski, 2006).

Guiding Questions for Discussion

- How do we assess fluency?
- How are results used?
- Are fluency assessments emphasizing rate over prosody? If so, how can we address this?
- Is fluency instruction meaningful and joyful? Are we honoring the integrity of the student with our fluency instruction?
- How is fluency addressed beyond decoding instruction?
- Is comprehension and making meaning recognized as the goal of fluency instruction?
- Where could fluency practice be built into the reading block?

Further reading

To extend your knowledge of the ideas presented in this section, read the following:

→ Kuhn, M.R. & Levy, L. (2015). *Developing fluent readers: Teaching fluency as a foundational skill.* New York, NY: Guilford Press.

→ Rasinski, T.V. (1989). Fluency for everyone: Incorporating fluency instruction in the classroom. *The Reading Teacher, 42*(9), 690–693.

⚠ STOP AND EVALUATE FLUENCY

Notes

1. Although seemingly unnatural, pseudo-word assessments facilitate teachers' understanding of which phonics patterns are fully recognized and memorized by a child. Nevertheless, any pseudo-word assessment should be used sparingly and with caution; children should never be instructed using pseudo-words.
2. If your school district currently only has guided reading books or leveled texts, you will be forced to prompt readers to use context, since some of the words are well beyond the child's current phonics ability. Therefore, as you select reading materials, be mindful of how important the text types are to supporting phonics acquisition (text types are discussed earlier).
3. Accuracy was heavily discussed in the word recognition section, the section on fluency primarily focuses upon the constructs of automaticity and prosody.

4

Evaluating Comprehension Grades K–3

Chapter Preview

In this chapter you will review comprehension instruction for K–3 readers. The constructs reviewed in this chapter include:

- Oral Language
  - Oral Language Considerations for Bilingual Learners
- Read-Alouds with Discussion
- Content-Based Approaches
- Cognitive Strategy Instruction
- Writing to Learn

Evaluation: A three-part rubric is used to evaluate all constructs:

Phase One Rubric:
Evaluates alignment of current instructional practices

Phase Two Rubric:
Rates the quality of the current reading program provided to teachers

Phase Three Rubric:
Rates the quality of the program up for adoption

Anchor Standards: The following Common Core Anchor Standards are addressed by this chapter.

Reading: Literature (K–3)
Reading: Informational Text (K–3)
Speaking and Listening (K–3)

Introduction

Kindergarten through third grade is a critical time for emergent readers. Children are tasked with cracking the code of written language while concurrently developing background knowledge and cognitive strategies for comprehending text. The outcome of this work is positively shaped by meaningful instruction that both motivates and engages readers. In this chapter, you will explore the construct of reading comprehension and consider how the materials you select must engage and motivate young children while also supporting their development as critical thinkers about text.

The Reading Rope

The Reading Rope metaphor (Scarborough, 2001) (Figure 4.1) is a helpful way to recognize how comprehension is comprised of many strands that are woven together to produce strategic and automatic reading.

The Reading Rope is an extension of the simple view of reading (Gough & Tunmer, 1986: Hoover and Gough, 1990), which states that reading comprehension equals the product of decoding and language comprehension: $D \times LC = RC$. An individual can read proficiently if they have average decoding skills and average language comprehension skills. Yet an individual will struggle with reading comprehension if they have one of the following: (1) weak decoding and average language comprehension, (2) weak decoding and weak language comprehension, or (3) average decoding and weak language comprehension. Table 4.1 illustrates these reading profiles.

The Reading Rope deconstructed language comprehension into specific threads to illustrate how background knowledge, vocabulary, language structures, and literacy knowledge contribute to the comprehension process. As such, curriculum and instruction will develop each of these strands. Nevertheless, developing a reader's comprehension cannot be severed from affective factors of engagement and motivation. Ultimately, we must understand how the cognitive process of reading

THE MANY STRANDS THAT ARE WOVEN INTO SKILLED READING

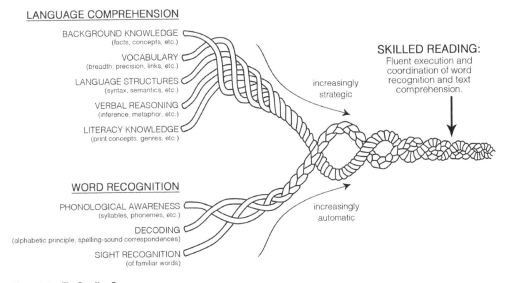

Figure 4.1 The Reading Rope.

Table 4.1 The Simple View of Reading

	Adequate Language Comprehension		
Weak Decoding	Reading Difficulty	Typically Developing Readers	Adequate Decoding
	Reading Difficulty	Reading Difficulty	
	Weak Language Comprehension		

comprehension unfolds and align our instruction accordingly—this is best accomplished within a context that inspires and engages the reader.

Note: *Vocabulary is a critical aspect to comprehension and will be discussed in its own chapter.*

How Comprehension Occurs: The Construction-Integration Model

The construction integration (CI) model (Kintsch, 2004) allows us to fully understand how each of the language comprehension strands of the Reading Rope are woven into the comprehension process. As an educator, the CI model can serve as a useful tool for understanding the invisible process of reading comprehension and help us support readers when text processing becomes difficult. In the CI model, reading comprehension is constructed and integrated through these levels:

1 **Surface level:** This is the most basic level of text processing; the reader decodes and recognizes basic words and phrases of the text and holds them in working memory.
2 **Text base:** The reader then connects sentences and ideas together and begins to get the gist of the passage. To do this, the reader relies on their knowledge of vocabulary, language structure, and literacy knowledge (key strands of language comprehension in the Reading Rope). To support development of the text base, students must learn various genre and text structures and develop vocabulary knowledge. Additionally, the text base can be strengthened by applying cognitive strategies such as questioning, retelling, and summarizing.
3 **Situation model:** At this level, true learning occurs as the reader combines the text base with their background knowledge, which results in full comprehension of the text. The situation model is retained in long-term memory. It is notable that rich background knowledge on a topic results in a more complete situation model. Thus, to develop a situation model, we need to continually develop students' deep and wide content and literary knowledge.

In this chapter, we will focus on instructional strategies that develop a rich situation model in children. Since background knowledge is a key element of language comprehension and necessary for a full situation model, you will find that this chapter emphasizes the importance of knowledge-building activities. However, readers also need to understand the gist of what they read and develop a text base; thus, cognitive strategies for developing the text base (Kintsch, 2004) are also described.

Oral Language: Where Literacy Begins

What Is It and Why Does It Matter?

Children's oral language experiences, which begin at birth, provide the foundation for all literacy acquisition. Oral language can be defined as "the ability to produce or comprehend spoken language, including vocabulary and grammar" (National Early Literacy Panel, 2008, p. viii). Unlike learning to read, oral language development is a natural process—typically developing children don't need explicit instruction to learn how to speak. However, learning to read requires direct teaching and is not something people are born to do. And yet even though language is innate, there are instructional practices that educators can do to help develop children's oral language skills.

For example, when children interact with parents, caregivers, and educators, they develop an awareness of how language (grammar, phonology, semantics, and pragmatics) operates. Parents and caregivers can positively shape children's oral language development through talk, storybook reading, and play. Children who enter kindergarten with weak oral language skills are at a greater risk for future reading difficulty (Fielding, Kerr & Rosier, 2007). This finding is unsurprising, as oral language skills mirror and shape reading acquisition in distinct ways.

To begin, oral language supports children's early awareness of how *grammatical systems* in written language work. Through talk, children acquire an understanding of how words and phrases string together to construct meaning. For example, children progress from using simple phrases such as "Blanket want" to using functional words such as pronouns, prepositions, articles, and conjunctions and state: "I want my blanket." This developing knowledge of syntax provides a schematic reference for how written language should flow during reading.

Through oral language, children also develop an understanding of the *phonology*, or sound, of spoken language. They learn to detect distinct sounds in words that separate them in meaning from one another, such as the words cat and bat. This awareness of phonology is critical for acquiring phonological awareness and eventually phonics skills.

Through oral language experiences, children develop *semantic* knowledge such as vocabulary and inferencing abilities (Kendeou, van den Broek, White & Lynch, 2009). Vocabulary knowledge has a strong correlation to reading comprehension and further supports children's ability to decode and identify words. Oral language also contributes to children's semantic understandings by fostering their ability to make inferences. As early as age four, children can listen to a story and begin to make inferences about character actions, thoughts, and future behaviors. This, in turn, promotes inferencing ability as the child reads a book.

Lastly, through oral language, children learn the *pragmatic* use of language, also called social language. For example, through a variety of interactions within different settings, children learn how to engage with others in a specific context (Byrnes & Wasik, 2009) such as home, church, school, or during play. Given the wide cultural variations in communication, it is important that educators recognize how culture can shape pragmatic use—and how our own biases can influence our perceptions of what is pragmatically appropriate. We should observe children's communicative practices in informal settings to understand the language practices that they employ in academic ones. We should not perceive differences as deficits. Rather, we need to learn how to leverage children's rich linguistic practices and bridge them to academic language settings.

Each child's early experiences with oral language vary. For example, children with a history of ear infections or children who experience trouble acquiring critical language skills such as articulation (the ability to make speech sounds) and/or language processing skills are at a greater risk for reading difficulty. Indeed, 40 to 75 percent of young children who are identified as having a speech and language disability will go on to have difficulty learning to read (Catts, Fey, Zhang, & Tomblin, 2001).

Given this relationship, as educators we can partner with our school speech and language therapist to help us identify children at risk. Children who have difficulty following directions, asking questions, and producing proper grammar either orally or in writing should trigger concern (bilingual learners should be evaluated in their native language). Moreover, as teachers of young children, we should know our students' health histories with regard to ear infections and speech delays. There is a possibility that any of these concerns will manifest as a speech and/or language disorder, which in turn can affect the child's ability to learn to read.

How Is Oral Language Assessed?

Educators can rely upon a rudimentary informal assessment, like the following checklist, to assess monolingual, English speaking children's oral language (emergent bilingual learners should be assessed in their native language). Teachers should partner with a speech and language therapist if a child exhibits difficulty with any of these tasks. The speech and language therapist can collaborate with you and the child's caregiver to decide if additional, more standardized assessments need to be administered.

Informal Observation of Oral Language			
Expressive Language	**Always**	**Sometimes**	**Never**
Has correct sound pronunciation			
Has correct word pronunciation			
Uses developmentally appropriate vocabulary			
Uses correct syntax			
Speaks in complete sentences			
Asks questions			
Retells basic story			
Receptive Language			
Recognizes familiar sounds			
Follows directions			
Engages with and understands stories that are read aloud			
Engages in back-and-forth conversations with peers and adults			
Follows classroom procedures			
Understands prepositions (over, under, above, beside)			

Retelling rubrics: Another way to assess receptive oral language, or listening comprehension, is through a retelling rubric. Assessing a child's listening comprehension can help you determine a reason (or potential) for weak reading comprehension. Following is an example of a retelling rubric that can assess emergent readers' understanding of narrative text structure.

Basic Retelling Rubric Say to the child: Tell me about the story you read.		
	With Prompting and Support	**Voluntary Response**
Identified characters		
Provided setting		
Sequenced events		
Problem stated		
Solution stated		
Gist of the story provided		
Comments about the retelling and notes for future instruction:		

Inferencing tasks: The ability to infer is a key skill for effective reading comprehension (Kintsch, 2004). Children who struggle to make inferences in oral language will most likely struggle to make inferences while reading, which will result in poor reading comprehension. If you are concerned about a child's listening comprehension, you may want to complete a retelling rubric as well as a brief inferencing task to understand how they are processing oral language. Your school district's speech language pathologist can direct you to screeners to use for this purpose.

Aligned Instructional Practices

- **Model language use:** When children are developing as proficient users of language, invariably they will make syntax errors as they develop an understanding of the language. Instead of correcting errors, rephrase what they stated by using correct grammar. For example, if the child states "I wented to the drinking foundation" you would respond "You went to the drinking fountain. Thanks for letting me know."
- **Embrace dialect:** Different regions of the world and country shape a person's dialect. In the classroom, it is important to embrace all dialects as children communicate. We want children to use language to exchange ideas, communicate needs, and ask questions as it develops cognition.
- **Sharing time:** This is an excellent way to allow all children the opportunity to use expressive and oral language features. Teachers can use a morning community builder or prompt that allows children the opportunity to listen and respond to their peers. Sharing time should be done in a circle where children learn to take turns (and not raise their hands). Sharing time should honor authentic language use. See later for suggestions on how to teach classroom ground rules of talk to support student-centered talk.

- **Meaningful play:** PK–1 teachers can provide opportunities for oral language development through dramatic play centers. Children can host puppet shows; dress up and pretend; use writing materials to create signs, labels, and mail; etc. There are numerous ways that play can foster rich language and literacy use.
- **Dialogic reading (grades PK–1):** Dialogic reading (Whitehurst, et al., 1988) is a shared reading method that utilizes engaging picture books and intentional discussion prompts; it is specifically intended for young children. Research suggests that dialogic reading can have a positive effect on young children's oral language (Lonigan, Bloomfield, Anthony, Dyer, & Samwel, 1999; Wasik & Bond, 2001). Moreover, dialogic reading develops children's ability to learn how to engage in academic conversations, understand that reading is meaning-making process, and develop listening comprehension.

Dialogic reading is guided by a sequence of instruction using the PEER acronym:

Prompt the reader to say something they observed in the book
Evaluate, or affirm, the reader's response and then
Expand on the response by summarizing it and finally
Repeat the prompt to facilitate understanding of what was expanded upon

A basic example of this exchange might proceed as follows as the teacher works to develop vocabulary knowledge in the text. In this example, the teacher is reading aloud a page from a book that has a school bus on it.

TEACHER: What is that called?
CHILD: A bus.
TEACHER: Yes, that is a yellow school bus. Can you say school bus?

The PEER sequence can also be applied with different prompts and purposes. One way to remember these prompts is through the CROWD acronym:

Completion prompts ask the reader to complete the sentence in a patterned book: "I'll huff and I'll puff, and I'll blow your house ____."
Recall prompts help the reader state literal information that was read. "Did Max go to bed without eating his supper?"
Open-ended prompts allow for various responses to an open-ended question: "I wonder why Max wanted to be the king of the wild things?"
Wh-prompts ask who, what, why, and when questions: "What did Goldilocks eat?"
Distancing prompts ask the reader to connect the book to their own life: "Do you ever get angry?"

Dialogic reading can also occur in small groups for children who need more experience with oral language. For it to be effective, the stopping points must be well planned. Teachers should use a variety of prompts and make sure that dialogic reading does not become a rote question-and-answer session. As children become more versed in this discourse structure, teachers should move to more open-ended discussions that allow many voices to discuss critical explorations of the picture book being read (see "Read-Alouds with Discussion" later).

Additional Considerations for bilingual learners: In the United States there are over 4 million bilingual students attending public schools (U.S. Department of Education, 2015). Since our primary role as educators is to effectively asses and teach all children, it is important to recognize the breadth and depth of bilingual children's language skills and build upon them within instruction Following are some important considerations to remember when working with emergent bilinguals:

- **Differentiate instruction:** Bilingual learners are a heterogenous group with each child having diverse literacy needs, strengths, and background knowledge (Ford et al, 2013). As such, instruction should be guided by assessments and planned accordingly We should assess our reader's strengths in listening comprehension in their native language. This will help us understand if the child may have listening comprehension needs that are not due to learning a second language. If a child struggles with listening comprehension in their native language, chances are they will struggle with reading comprehension, whether or not they are learning a second a language. Learning a second language may make reading comprehension more onerous if receptive language is a concern. Work with your school district's English language learner (ELL) teacher to provide guidance on how to assess listening comprehension in a native language.
- **Leverage funds of knowledge:** Researchers (Moll, Amanti, Neff & Gutierrez, 1992) have suggested that learning environments capitalize on the familial and cultural "funds of knowledge" (p.133) that students possess as this knowledge can be used as a form of currency within academic settings. For example, children can be prompted to make connections about their lives to literature being read; this is a strategy than can strengthen text comprehension.
- **Explicit instruction in the sounds of English:** Educators must develop bilingual learners' alphabetic knowledge. Alphabetic learning also supports phonemic awareness, which is necessary for decoding and blending words. For bilingual Spanish-speaking students, educators can build upon the similarities between English and Spanish for cross-language transfer. Several phonemes and graphemes are identical in Spanish and English and can be leveraged for instruction.
- **Small-group learning:** Meaningful and flexible small groups can encourage social language use and allow bilingual leaners the opportunity to leverage their rich linguistic skills; this is important to literacy development (Tharp & Entz, 2003). Small groups should be designed with meaningful activities that build on learners' interests, scaffold oral language use through sentence stems, visuals, and turn taking that provides comfortable spaces for participating in the discussion.
- **Pre-reading activities:** Prior to a lesson, relevant content information can be discussed or front-loaded. For example, we can ask students to discuss what they know relating to a read aloud and leverage their background knowledge on the text (García & Kleifgen, 2019). We can also provide definitions that are necessary for comprehending a text, use outlines with visuals to support tracking of the instruction, and provide visual and hands-on examples that will facilitate knowledge building throughout a lesson.

- **During listening activities:** There are various scaffolds we can rely upon to support listening comprehension during the lesson. For example, during a read aloud, we can ask learners to make connections to the text, and again, leverage their background knowledge to deepen comprehension. During instruction, we can provide visual clues or pictures, speak slowly and expressively, engage in frequent checks for understanding, and provide access to information in another modality (e.g., a digital recording or video).
- **Mentor texts:** To support reading comprehension and engagement, we can utilize mentor texts (García & Kleifgen, 2019) which are books that are read and reread by the teacher (and students) and become familiar to children. Our mentor texts should include books by bilingual authors whose themes support children as they make meaningful connections to their own lives and the books being read.
- **After listening activities:** After we have instructed, we can support our learners with specific cognitive strategies that support retention of the content. For example, we should provide higher order questions (not merely literal, low-level questions) and use sentence stems to support student responses. We can ask students to make connections to their own lives. We can provide choice for how students respond to their learning – allowing them to utilize both writing and pictures to document their thinking (García & Kleifgen, 2019).
- **Language experience approach (LEA)** (Bezdicek & García, 2012): This approach leverages children's background knowledge and promotes listening, speaking, reading, and writing. In LEA, children discuss an event that took place, for example, a field trip. The teacher provides photographs or visuals to prompt the discussion. Each child then orally dictates a sentence to the teacher about the experience. The teacher transcribes the sentence on paper, and the child illustrates it. Once the story is illustrated, the teacher reads the sentence to the child and asks the child to practice reading it independently. Several children can each create their own illustrated sentences, and the teacher can staple these into a book for children to read.
- **Dialogue journals:** Interactive dialogue journals are a risk-free way to respond to literature. In a dialogue journal, the child listens to a story and draws a picture and/or writes a response to the teacher (in either their native or English language). The teacher responds to the child by writing or drawing. After a few exchanges, the teacher confers with the child about the journal.

Guiding Questions for Discussion

- Is oral language assessed in preschool and kindergarten?
- How is oral language developed in our emergent readers? What practices do we employ?
- How are teachers supporting children with language and/or speech impairments?
- Are young children provided adequate time for play?
- Are the needs of bilingual learners being met with the current curriculum and instructional approaches?

Further reading

To extend your knowledge of the ideas presented in this section, read the following:

→ Snow, C.E. (1991). The theoretical basis for relationships between language and literacy in development. *Journal of Research in Childhood Education*, 6(1), 5–10.

→ Whitehurst, G.J. (n.d.). "Dialogic reading: An effective way to read to preschoolers." Retrieved from www.readingrockets.org/article/dialogic-reading-effective-way-read-preschoolers.

→ Olivia-Olson, C. Espinosa, L.M., Hayslip, W., & Magruder, E.S. (2019). Many languages, one classroom: Supporting children in superdiverse settings. *Teaching Young Children*, 12(2), 8–12.

⚠ STOP AND EVALUATE ORAL LANGUAGE

Read-Alouds with Discussion

What Is It?

Read-alouds with discussion (RAD) are sometimes referred to as interactive read-alouds. Unlike a traditional read-aloud, where the purpose is listening to a story for pure enjoyment, the RAD approach relies upon (1) high-quality texts, (2) metacognition, (3) teacher questioning, and (4) dialogic discourse.

Why Does It Matter?

As early as kindergarten, students are expected to engage in discussions where ideas and questions are exchanged between learners. For example, the Common Core State Standards (CCSS) includes the following speaking and listening standards for kindergarten students:

1 Follow rules for discussions, such as listening to others and taking turns.
2 Continue a conversation through multiple exchanges.
3 Ask and answer questions orally about key details of a text that is read aloud or information presented through other auditory/visual media.
4 Ask and answer questions for a variety of purposes, such as to get information or to clarify what is not understood

These standards only increase in complexity as students advance in the grades. The CCSS is aligned with research that suggests reading comprehension can be elevated through discussion-based approaches where teachers execute high-level questions (Nystrand, 2006; Wolf, et al., 2005) and rigorous thinking questions (Michaels, O'Connor, Hall & Resnick, 2010) that press learners to say more and expand on their thinking.

As such, the discourse patterns in a RAD are critical to its effectiveness. For example, research has revealed that specific teacher discourse patterns can limit children's ability to engage critically with a text. An *initiate, respond, and evaluate or feedback* (IRE/IRF) pattern (Mehan, 1979) is suggested to limit a reader's ability to think deeply about a text (Applebee, et al., 2003; Nystrand, 2006). In this discourse pattern, the teacher does the bulk of the talking and asks questions in a quiz-like fashion:

Initiate (Teacher): What year does the story take place?
Respond (Student): In the 1980s.
Evaluate/Feedback (Teacher): Yes, in 1985.

Notice how the IRE limited discussion and exploration of the topic as the teacher closed the exchange once the correct answer was stated. However, in a *dialogic exchange*, such as the one next, comprehension is strengthened as the teacher serves to enrich the students' thinking through her questioning repertoire (Fall, Webb, & Chudowsky, 2000; Kucan & Beck, 2003; Saunders & Goldenberg, 1999).

TEACHER: When did this story place?
STUDENT: In the 1980s.
TEACHER: How do you know that?
STUDENT (1): Because she had just bought the new Michael Jackson album, *Thriller*, and was wearing a Michael Jackson t-shirt.
TEACHER: Can anyone add on?
STUDENT (2): And, remember, Reagan was president and the author described how her mom had a "Just Say No" bumper sticker on her car.
STUDENT (3): That's right, and they didn't have cell phones. Remember, her mom always made sure she had two dimes for the pay phone. Her mom was kind of overprotective.
TEACHER: Does anybody else believe that the mom was overprotective?
STUDENT (4): I do.
TEACHER: Say more. Why do you believe that? What in the text makes you think that?

Notice how the teacher intentionally used questions to get students to expand on their thinking and defend their statements. She also prompted readers to cite evidence from the text to support their thinking. RADs are fertile ground for these types of dialogic exchanges and are an effective way to promote comprehension and content knowledge.

How Is It Assessed?

Formative assessment tools such as anecdotal record-keeping forms can provide you with valuable information about a reader's interaction during a read-aloud.

Aligned Instructional Practices

RADs should be conducted daily with a wide variety of texts, both fiction and nonfiction. Not only does this practice allow children to engage in high-level discussions, it also develops background knowledge. Specific areas to focus on include:

- **Ground rules for talk:** One reason a teacher may avoid a discussion that relies on more student voices than teacher voice is the fear that the discussion will get out of control. To ensure a healthy and respectful discussion, it is important to establish ground rules of talk early in the school year. As you practice how to engage in dialogic discussions, ask students to work in small groups and come up with basic rules for a quality discussion. Chances are the following rules might be what they come up with:

- Listen to others who are talking.
- Share your idea (or add on to someone else's) and provide reasons to support what you are saying.
- Ask questions.
- Take turns and let other people talk.
- Agree or disagree but be open to changing your mind when ideas are presented.

Write these rules on an anchor chart and laminate. Refer to these rules during a discussion, especially if students stray from accountable discussions. They are also a helpful scaffold for your own teacher talk.

- **Talk lessons:** Before we can expect readers to engage in open-ended discussions, we need to provide them with lessons on how to engage in academic discussions where hands are not raised, and students help control the flow of the discussion. We can model for students how to use academic discourse statements during a discussion, such as:
  - "I agree."
  - "So, are you saying?"
  - "Why do you think that?"
  - "I am wondering…"
- **Teacher questioning:** Questioning is integral to facilitating a deeper understanding of the text. However, not all question types are created equal; some are much better at promoting critical thinking than others. Research on the role of teacher questioning suggests that the following questioning moves can strengthen comprehension (Michaels, O'Connor, Hall & Resnick, 2010; Soter et al., 2008):
  - High-level questions: These are characterized by the teacher asking a text-dependent question that cannot be answered through literal information. They require a student to analyze the text: "What is the theme of the text?" "What do the character's actions tell us about him as a person?"
  - Rigorous thinking question that builds on student response: These sorts of questions press students to defend their thinking and remain accountable to the knowledge shared: "How do you know that?" "What do you mean?" "Where did you find that information?"
  - Authentic questions: These are open-ended questions where the teacher doesn't know the answer. "If you were in that situation, what would you do?"
  - Linking questions: These ask readers to rephrase or add on to what a peer said: "Who agrees or disagrees with what…said?" "Who wants to add on to what…said?"
- **Student-centered discourse:** High-level teacher questions guide a RAD; however, the students should be doing the bulk of the talking. Thus, in the RAD the classroom talk structure will look like this: Teacher – Student – Student – Student – Teacher and so on.
- **Range of high-quality text:** In a RAD the texts should be (1) culturally relevant and accurate, (2) fiction and nonfiction, (3) high quality, and (4) complex.
  - Culturally relevant texts include histories and experiences of culturally and linguistically diverse communities; the texts do

not reinforce stereotypes, biases, or mistruths (Souto-Manning & Martell, 2016).

- Fiction texts should be studied and can be compared and contrasted in various ways (e.g., characters, authors, themes, and plots). Nonfiction texts should support students as they build knowledge within and across the grade levels.
- The curriculum materials should include high-quality texts that provide engaging storylines, are culturally relevant, and include eye-catching illustrations and visual features (see Chapter 8 for more information on quality texts).
- Complex texts can be read aloud and discussed. Complex texts are above grade level; children cannot read them independently but can understand them while listening.

- **Read aloud, think aloud, and discuss:** In a RAD, the teacher should intentionally engage in a think-aloud to demonstrate how to analyze aspects of the text. By thinking aloud while reading, the following can be modeled and discussed:
  - How point of view is used in the text
  - How character actions contribute to the plot
  - How the author intentionally uses certain words and phrases to provide meaning
  - How to compare and contrast characters, texts, themes, and authors
- **Small or whole group:** RAD are often conducted in a whole group, but for some students, such as bilingual leaners or children with language needs, a small group can provide enriched discussion opportunities. As readers progress and are independently reading longer texts, some of the discussion-based approaches described in Chapter 5 can also be utilized.

Guiding Questions for Discussion

- Do children regularly engage in dialogic discussions during a read-aloud?
- Have students been provided with instruction on how to ask and answer questions, how to challenge ideas, and how to welcome others into the discussion?
- Are teachers reading aloud a wide variety of fiction and nonfiction texts during read-aloud time?
- Are read-alouds culturally responsive?
- Does each classroom have agreed-upon rules for talk, or ground rules for talk?

Further reading

To extend your knowledge of the ideas presented in this section, read the following:

→ Alexander, R. (2009). *Towards dialogic teaching: Rethinking classroom talk* (4th ed.). Thirsk: Dialogos.

⚠ **STOP AND EVALUATE READ-ALOUDS WITH DISCUSSION**

Content-Based Approaches

What Is It?

This refers to developing knowledge of the content of the text and improving comprehension of informational text.

Why Is It Important?

Content-based approaches teach readers to acquire deep knowledge about a topic. Additionally, they support readers as they navigate informational text. In a landmark study, Nell Duke (2000) uncovered a scarcity of exposure to informational texts in first-grade classrooms. Through her investigation she learned that approximately 3.6 minutes of a day were spent teaching and learning about information texts. Moreover, this exposure was even less for children from school districts with lower socioeconomic status (SES).

The CCSS devote an entire set of reading standards to nonfiction, and in the elementary grades, the balance between fiction and nonfiction text standards is equal. However, by middle school, the expectations for comprehending nonfiction increase, and the bulk of comprehension instruction should be spent on nonfiction teaching.

How Is It Assessed?

Learning can be defined as a change in long-term memory (Sweller, 1998). To assess whether a reader has comprehended, or learned, you will need to assess their changing knowledge on a topic, as well as their understanding of text structure. Frequent formative assessment will assist you in this process. Projects, writing, and discussion are additional ways to check for learning. To assess student understanding of nonfiction components like text features, you would need to evaluate how the reader was able to use the components to enhance his or her understanding of the nonfiction text.

Aligned Instructional Practices

- **Read-alouds with text sets:** Teachers must provide frequent fiction and nonfiction read-alouds with discussion (see RAD above). However, it is important to be intentional with the texts you provide. Read-alouds can be more meaningful if they are conducted in a text set on a specific topic. For example, in kindergarten, a text set on the topic of spiders might be read across several days. Students might then compare and contrast the difference between spiders and insects or different types of spiders. Text sets allow readers to go deeper into a content and develop rich content knowledge. A comprehension scope and sequence should include knowledge development of specific themes. Text sets are integral to this process.
- **Teaching graphical devices:** Emergent readers are not always familiar with the many graphical devices that comprise a nonfiction text, such as bolded words, graphs, captions, flowcharts, maps, headings, indexes, tables, and diagrams (Roberts et al., 2013). Instructional materials should include lessons on how to read and understand text features that support

nonfiction reading comprehension. Specific practices include discussion about graphics during read-alouds and shared reading, reading and writing with graphics for authentic contexts, selecting texts with easy-to-read and eye-catching graphics, discussion of why graphics matter to the text, providing a graphic-rich classroom, and making sure students read books that contain graphics.

- **Teaching informational text structures:** Emergent readers can begin to learn how to identify the different types of text structure: description, sequence, problem/solution, compare and contrast, cause and effect (Meyer, 1975). This instruction can be embedded during expository text instruction. Students can learn key words for identifying specific text structures and use graphic organizers to visually represent the unique structure of a passage.

- **Compare and contrast texts on a similar topic:** Just as we read at the onset of this chapter, we want to develop a rich situation model in readers. One way we can achieve this is to help readers compare and contrast two topics presented within a text or compare and contrast two texts on a similar topic. For example, we might read a book about insects and spiders and compare and contrast their similarities and differences. The following day, we might read a book about tarantulas and the next day a book about black widow spiders. These texts offer up great opportunities for readers to compare and contrast and develop a rich situation model.

- **Text analysis/close reading of complex texts:** As readers advance in the grades, they are expected to analyze complex texts closely. K–3 readers can begin to learn close reading strategies by exploring and analyzing author's purpose and point of view. This work can be connected to the content writing that the student is learning during writing instruction.

- **High-quality, project-based learning:** An effective way to build content knowledge is to provide explicit teaching on a concept and then support the learner as they continue to develop deeper knowledge through guided, independent research and discovery. In a high-quality, project-based approach, learning is centered on a content area theme, such as geography. The project is designed so the learning is purposeful and collaborative and a tangible outcome is derived (and assessed). For example, a project-based theme might include lessons on geography, with the end goal being a visitors' guide that the students create (Halvorsen, Duke, Strachan & Johnson, 2018. Teachers might introduce local geography and provide lessons that systematically build on one another so the knowledge of understanding the key concepts and vocabulary related to the unit are explicitly taught. After these content-building lessons, students can collaborate in guided discovery and apply the content knowledge taught by the teacher within their own project.

- **Access/classroom libraries:** K–3 readers need access to a wide variety of quality, informational texts in a well-stocked classroom library. Informational texts include biographies; reference texts; explanatory texts about history and science; newspapers and magazines; technical texts, including texts that provide directions, display graphs, and charts; and digital sources. Texts must be culturally relevant and represent the diversity of the students in the classroom and the world. See Chapter 9 for additional information on the classroom library.

Guiding Questions for Discussion

- Is knowledge building a focus of our comprehension instruction?
- Are texts sets routinely used for comprehension instruction?
- Are nonfiction text structures and features explicitly taught?
- Do classroom libraries contain an abundance of nonfiction text?
- Is project-based learning included within content area or reading instruction?

Further reading

To extend your knowledge of the ideas presented in this section, read the following:

→ Cervetti, J.N. & Heibert, H. (2015). The sixth pillar of reading: Knowledge development. *The Reading Teacher 68*(7), 548–551.

⚠ STOP AND EVALUATE INFORMATIONAL TEXT/CONTENT KNOWLEDGE

Cognitive Strategy Lessons

What Is It?

A cognitive strategy lesson provides readers with a procedure to remain actively involved in the reading process. Learning these procedures facilitates increased understanding of the text being read. The main comprehension strategies are summarizing, questioning, monitoring, and story structure. Through teacher modeling, cognitive strategy instruction teaches the reader how to be metacognitive and apply the strategy independently. Cognitive strategy lessons can be done as either a whole- or small-group lesson and in both fiction and most nonfiction texts. The following strategies are often focused upon in lessons:

- How to reread to clarify information
- How to summarize important points
- How to make inferences while reading
- How to ask and answer questions and make or confirm predictions
- How to retell what was read

Why Does It Matter?

The National Reading Panel (NRP) (2000) identified cognitive strategies instruction as an effective practice for *supporting* text comprehension. Cognitive strategies should be used as a scaffold for developing deeper knowledge about the text being read and should not be used as a means to an end. Thus, it is critical that educators recognize that background knowledge on a text is necessary for comprehension. If a reader lacks background knowledge on a text and/or the text is filled with complex vocabulary, the comprehension process might be onerous, even if the reader is intentionally using cognitive strategies for support. Therefore, it is important that a well-rounded reading curriculum combine cognitive strategy instruction within a knowledge-rich curriculum.

How Is It Assessed?

Cognitive strategy use can be assessed with formative tools such as exit slips, written responses, and individual reading conferences. Additionally, some of the aligned practices can serve as a form of assessment. For example, a graphic organizer is a tool for strengthening reading comprehension. However, it can also help the teacher assess how the child is processing written language and developing understanding of a topic.

Aligned Instructional Practices

A well-rounded reading curriculum will provide opportunities for teachers to apply the following instructional practices:

- **Gradual release of responsibility:** Cognitive strategy use is best taught through a gradual release model where the teacher models how to use the strategy (and includes instruction as to why it matters), then supports readers as they work together to use the strategy together, and then gradually releases full responsibility to the reader to apply the strategy independently. Using a read aloud with discussion (RAD) is an effective way to model strategies to readers. However, merely giving readers a worksheet to complete will not support meaningful strategy use.
- **Story mapping/narrative text structure:** This strategy promotes retelling and understanding of narrative text structure. Story mapping can help readers remain active in a fiction text, monitor their reading, and analyze the elements of a story (characters, setting, problem, solution); this supports deeper comprehension of the text and also helps children as the learn narrative writing techniques (see Chapter 7).
- **Summarizing:** This is an integral strategy for developing retelling and is important to use when writing about a topic. Lessons can be provided that demonstrate how to effectively summarize a text and provide the main idea.
- **Graphic organizers:** Graphic organizers (semantic organizers) are an effective tool for reading comprehension. Graphic organizers help readers remain active throughout the reading process, sequence and summarize information, and construct new understandings about what was read.
- **Text-based questioning:** The NRP (2000) also suggested that question answering and question generating can support comprehension of a text. Providing brief mini-lessons that allow readers to ask who, what, when, where, why, and how, and prediction questions are a useful way to develop a reader's surface level and text base level reading comprehension.
- **Comprehension monitoring:** Readers need to be provided with strategies to be metacognitive as they read and know how to apply fix-up strategies when reading breaks down. Brief lessons on how to be an active reader by using sticky notes, graphic organizers, or jotting down thoughts help readers monitor their comprehension as they read.

Guiding Questions for Discussion

- Are children provided lessons on how to use comprehension strategies to support deeper thinking and active engagement while reading?
- Are strategies taught with intention and not disconnected from their purpose (which is to support active involvement and memory for what was read)?
- Are readers taught to monitor their comprehension?

> **Further reading**
> *To extend your knowledge of the ideas presented in this section, read the following:*
>
> → Shanahan, T. (2018). Comprehension skills or strategies: Is there a difference and does it matter? Retrieved from https://shanahanonliteracy.com/blog/compre-hension-skills-or-strategies-is-there-a-difference-and-does-it-matter

⚠ STOP AND EVALUATE COGNITIVE STRATEGIES

Writing to Learn

What Is It?
Writing to learn is simply comprehension through writing. Readers can do this by summarizing, reflecting, and completing graphic organizers. Writing and reading are symbiotic and leverage the same cognitive processes.

Why Does It Matter?
Graham and Hebert (2010) conducted a meta-analysis of studies pertaining to writing about reading and found that the following three writing practices are most effective: (1) students should write summaries about what they have read in literary and content area texts, (2) students should learn the writing process as well as spelling and sentence construction skills, and (3) students should write their own texts. It is important to note that these suggestions do not mean that children should be writing laborious book reports after each text they've read. Just like cognitive strategies, writing about reading works in the service of deepening knowledge and fostering reading comprehension.

How Is It Assessed?
Writing to learn can be assessed formatively by observing student learning and providing feedback to learners. Writing to learn is a tool for better comprehension, and assessment should be used to guide further instruction.

Aligned Instructional Practices

- **Reader's notebook:** Students can use reading response notebooks to track their thinking and reflect on what was read. Kindergarten and first-grade readers might use pictures with labels to respond to a text; as readers progress, they can transition to more detailed written responses.

- **Content area summary writing/quick writes:** Writing in the content areas is suggested to strengthen student learning and develop content knowledge. Beginning in grade 1, students can be taught to summarize a text or parts of a content area text. For emergent readers, this summary might be a picture with captions or a sentence or two. As children progress in the grades, summaries can become more detailed. Instructionally, teachers must model how to do this and scaffold this process for them.

Guiding Questions for Discussion

- Is writing used to support comprehension?
- Do readers reflect on text through writing?
- Is writing to learn used across the content areas?

 **STOP AND EVALUATE WRITING TO LEARN**

5

Evaluating Comprehension Grades 4–12

Chapter Preview

Reading comprehension is explained and evaluated in this chapter. The constructs reviewed include:

- Discussion-Based Approaches
- Content-Based Approaches
- Cognitive Strategy Instruction
- Disciplinary Literacy
- Writing to Learn
- Online Reading Comprehension

Evaluation: A three-part rubric is used to evaluate all constructs:

Phase One Rubric: Evaluates alignment of current instructional practices

Phase Two Rubric: Rates the quality of the current reading program provided to teachers

Phase Three Rubric: Rates the quality of the program up for adoption

Anchor Standards: The following Common Core Anchor Standards are addressed by this chapter:
Reading: Literature (4–12)
Reading: Informational Text (4–12)
Speaking and Listening (4–12)
Grades 6–12 Literacy in History/Social Studies, Science, and Technical Subjects

Reading Comprehension Instruction in the United States: A Brief History

This chapter begins with an historical overview of reading comprehension instruction in the United States. The theoretical frameworks that shape our understanding of how comprehension occurs and the research-aligned instructional practices are also described.

As teachers of middle and high school students, the crux of your literacy instruction is reading comprehension. Yet did you know that prior to the 1970s, reading comprehension instruction was negligible in American classrooms? Comprehension *assessment* was disguised as instruction (Durkin, 1978) as students completed multiple-choice workbook pages contained in the ubiquitous McGuffey Readers (Barry, 2008). Exceptions to this practice occurred in high school classrooms where students were taught to analyze poetry and closely read a text.

In the 1980s, a shift occurred as cognitive models of comprehension and literary theories of interpretation were introduced to educators (Pearson & Cervetti, 2015). *Schema theory* (Anderson & Pearson, 1984), which suggests that the text is devoid of meaning until a reader actively integrates their prior knowledge and constructs meaning from it, became a driving explanation for how comprehension occurs. As such, reader-centric and schema-driven instructional practices such as K-W-L charts and picture walks became popular.

Around the same time, cognitive strategy instruction (Palinscar & Brown, 1984; Pressley et al., 1992) began to pervade literacy learning as readers were taught metacognitive strategies for supporting comprehension such as clarifying, summarizing, questioning, and activating prior knowledge. In addition, reader-centric (Rosenblatt, 1978) and sociocultural-based (Freebody & Luke, 1990) literary theories emerged that complemented both schema theory and strategy-based instruction. Instructionally, teachers focused upon students' personal responses to texts, and various discussion-based approaches become popular in English language arts classrooms.

The Construction Integration Model

In the following years, schema theory (Anderson & Pearson, 1984) was overshadowed by the more text- and reader-balanced *construction integration model* (CI model) (Kintsch, 2004). This model considers prior knowledge integral to the comprehension process but suggests that a reader can form a surface-level understanding by extracting basic ideas and details from the text. Background knowledge plays a more important role in subsequent phases of comprehension when the reader integrates their prior knowledge with the information in the text and stores it into long-term memory. This results in the reader forming *a situational model*, or full mental representation of the text. The CI model suggests that reading comprehension is constructed and integrated through these levels:

1   Surface level: This is the most basic level of reading and is where the reader extracts basic words and phrases of the text and holds them in working memory.
2   Text base: The reader then connects sentences and ideas together and begins to get the gist of the passage. To do this, the reader relies on their knowledge of word meanings, syntax knowledge, genre, and text organization.
3   Situation models: At this level, the reader combines the text base with their background knowledge, purpose for reading, interests, and beliefs to fully comprehend the text. The combination of the text base with background knowledge results in a complete situation model, which is retained in long-term memory.

The National Reading Panel: An Emphasis on Strategies

In 2000, the National Reading Panel (NRP) (2000) relied upon the CI model (Kintsch, 2004) to demonstrate the importance of cognitive strategies in the reading process. In doing so, the NRP recommended that comprehension instruction include an emphasis upon seven strategies: asking questions, answering questions, monitoring, summarizing, story mapping, graphic organizers, and cooperative grouping. These strategies were meant to help readers remain active during the comprehension process. Unfortunately, throughout the next decade (and more), instruction of these strategies often strayed from their original metacognitive intent and were criticized for being overtaught (Willingham & Lovett, 2014). Additionally, researchers have suggested that cognitive strategies are best taught in tandem (multiple strategies at a time) and not in a single strategy approach (Reutzel, Smith, & Fawson (2005).

The Common Core State Standards: Close, Analytic Reading

By 2011, many states began to adopt the Common Core State Standards (CCSS), which pivoted away from the explicit application of strategies discussed in the NRP. Instead, the CCSS focused learners on closely reading and rereading a complex text by micro-analyzing its organization, structure, and author's craft. Additionally, the standards also emphasized the importance of readers developing broad and deep topic and cultural knowledge through reading fiction and informational texts (National Governors Association, 2010):

> By reading texts in history/social studies, science, and other disciplines, students build a foundation of knowledge in these fields that will also give them the background to be better readers in all content areas. Students can only gain this foundation when the curriculum is intentionally and coherently structured to develop rich content knowledge within and across grades. Students also acquire the habits of reading independently and closely, which are essential to their future success.
> http://www.corestandards.org/ELA-Literacy/CCRA/R/

Present Day: Knowledge Building and Reading Comprehension

In the past several years, there has been an increased emphasis upon knowledge development as means of effective reading comprehension instruction (Hirsch, 2006; Wexler, 2019; Willingham, 2006). The roots of these ideas are aligned with the CI model (Kintsch, 2004) which suggests a rich knowledge base supports our ability to make inferences, provides traction for our working memory, and ultimately helps us retain ideas long term. As part of a knowledge development focus, schools are being called upon to maintain a strong science and social studies curriculum; content learned in these disciplines directly correlates to how well an individual comprehends what they read across *all disciplines*.

As you evaluate how comprehension is approached in reading programs and practices, you will note that reading text sets across a topic is described as an evidence-based practice that facilitates knowledge development. However, you will also notice that cognitive strategies can support this work. The key for success is intent: Do not over-teach strategies, and always ensure that your instructional goal is to help readers become metacognitive and active comprehenders as they develop deep knowledge across a topic.

In closing, this summary does not capture the breadth and depth of comprehension research, theory, and practice. Nevertheless, it underscores how comprehension research has continually evolved and caused instructional practices to shift. It also helps you understand the recommendations provided in this chapter. Although literacy education seems to continually follow new trends, it is important that we do not abandon evidenced-based practices but adjust as research provides us with new insights on how to improve student learning. This chapter is written with those ideas in mind.

How This Chapter Is Organized

Following are the topics covered in this chapter. Table 5.1 provides clear definitions of each approach that is reviewed. Since comprehension is a complex construct and terms and approaches are sometimes confused, this table should help explain how these approaches differ. Moreover, as this is a thick chapter, your expert group can be divided into two teams: grades 4–8 and grades 9–12.

1. Content-Based Approaches
2. Cognitive Strategy Instruction
3. Discussion-Based Approaches
4. Disciplinary Literacy
5. Writing About Reading
6. Online Reading Comprehension

Table 5.1 Definition of Comprehension Approaches in This Chapter

Approach	What Is It?
Discussion Based	Instruction that uses discussion (speaking and listening) as the vehicle for building comprehension of the text. Discussion-based approaches focus on deepening knowledge of the text as well as reacting to the text personally and critically, as a reader.
Content Based	Instruction that focuses upon deepening knowledge about the content within texts.
Cognitive Strategy	Instruction that teaches procedures for supporting comprehension of any text (content or English Language Arts [ELA]). Used in the service of building understanding of the text being read.
Disciplinary Literacy	Instruction that teaches specialized approaches to reading and writing in discipline-specific ways. For example, "read like a historian" and "write like a scientist."
Writing About Reading	Instruction that focuses on the specific ways writing can be used to support comprehension.
Online Reading Comprehension	Instruction that teaches specific strategies for comprehending online text.

Before You Begin…Overview of Effective Classroom Discourse

Following are some guidelines to remember for effective classroom discourse. These guidelines can also be applied across all content areas during most lessons in your classroom.

Teacher questioning: The following types of questions are shown to have a positive effect on student reasoning and thinking about a text.

- High-level questions: Characterized by teacher asking a text-dependent question that cannot be answered through literal information. Requires a student to analyze the text: "What is the theme of the text?" "What do the character's actions tell us about him as a person?" Use text evidence to support your response.
- Authentic questions: The teacher doesn't know the answer to the question—it is open ended, as the answer cannot be found in the text. For example, "If you were in that situation, what would you do?" Although these are appropriate for analytic reading, they are helpful once a critical reading and interpretation of the text has been discussed.
- Rigorous thinking questions (Michaels, O'Connor, Hall & Resnick, 2010): These are uptake questions where the teacher builds on a student's response by pushing the student to defend their reasoning: "Why do you think that?"

Talk lessons: Before we can expect readers to engage in rich discussions, we need to reinforce strategies for high-level talk. Readers can practice with fishbowl discussions centered around a controversial topic (e.g., Do you think cell phones should be allowed in school?) and provide feedback to one another on their discussion techniques.

- I agree…
- So, are you saying?
- Why do you think that?
- I am wondering…
- What do you think?
- I disagree…

Ground rules for talk: To ensure a healthy and respectful discussion, it is important to establish ground rules of talk early in the school year. After you have practiced how to engage in dialogic discussions, ask students to create the rules for a quality discussion. Chances are the following rules might be what they come up with:

- Listen and give eye contact when others are speaking
- Share your idea and provide reasons to support your thinking.
- Ask questions.
- Take turns and let other people talk.
- Agree or disagree yet be open to changing your mind when ideas are presented.

Write these rules on an anchor chart and laminate. Refer to these rules during a discussion, especially if students stray from accountable discussions. They are also a helpful scaffold for your own teacher talk.

Discussion-Based Approaches

What Is It?

Discussion-based approaches use dialogue between students and the teacher to build understanding of the text and allow readers to respond personally and critically to what they read. Discussion-based approaches emphasize idea building, open-ended questions, building on other people's thinking and not merely relying on the teacher as the sole arbiter of knowledge. Most of these approaches are specific to the ELA classroom, but some can be coupled with content area learning.

Why Does It Matter?

Classroom discourse is important for helping students develop a deeper understanding on a topic. Although you will spend important instructional time using direct instruction—even lecture—you will also want to devote time to rich classroom talk, often referred to as dialogic discourse. Classroom discourse in a dialogic environment removes the teacher as the locus of information and places learners (including the teacher) as a key participant in meaning construction. In this context, classroom discourse aims to provide a critical and active thinking relationship between teacher and student, as well as between students. Research has suggested that students who are in dialogic classrooms make significant gains in reading comprehension (Applebee, et al., 2003; Chinn et al., 2001; Nystrand & Gamoran, 1991; Soter et al., 2008).

How Is It Assessed?

Classroom discourse can be assessed formatively, through teacher self-assessment, and reflected upon by the students. Some specific discussion-based methods, like the Socratic Seminar, give points to students based upon the quality and quantity of the talk. However, as an overall construct, classroom discourse should be reflected upon by the teacher with the following prompts:

- Did most of the students participate?
- Did I add on to student thinking, rephrase their ideas, and push for alternative explanations?
- Did I use good wait time?
- Did students challenge each other's thinking?
- Did students ask open-ended questions of one another?
- Were the bulk of my questions high-level?

Aligned Instructional Practices

- **Socratic/Paideia Seminar:** Socratic Seminars, sometimes referred to as Paideia Seminars (Billings & Fitzgerald, 2002), are conducted after a book has been read and used to deepen understanding of the text. They can be used in the ELA and history classroom. The teacher begins the seminar with an opening question, and then students take control of the discussion. However, the teacher does provide additional questions/ideas as necessary to push the thinking forward. Students ask and answer questions of the text and each other, challenge ideas, and defend their position. Students are expected to come to Socratic Seminars well prepared with text-based questions and ideas for discussion. After the seminar is complete, students reflect on their participation and learning. Reflection and observations of discussion can be used as an assessment.

- **Book Club:** These are used in the ELA classroom and are sometimes referred to as Grand Conversations (Eeds & Wells, 1989) or Literature Circles (Short & Pierce, 1990). They are like Socratic Seminars in that open-ended discussion is the heart of the learning. However, less emphasis is placed on critical analysis of the text and a greater focus is placed upon personal connections and aesthetic responses. Book clubs are organized around small groups of students who have chosen to read the same text. They discuss the text during and/or after the book has been read. Typically, the teacher is not part of a book club but can be present to observe and facilitate as needed.
- **Critical literacy discussions:** Critical literacy discussions pair well with a close reading lesson. In this approach students reflect, question, and engage in critical discourse around pertinent social issues. Thus, a central aspect of critical literacy is to help students view a text—or a series of texts—through a lens other than their own. As such, readers take on multiple perspectives on a topic and interrogate the content in the text by asking:
  ✓ Whose voice is represented?
  ✓ Whose voice is missing or silenced?
  ✓ How would _____ rewrite this story from his or her point of view?
  ✓ How does this text position people?
  ✓ Closely read the author's word choice—what does that tell you?
     In this regard, critical literacy moves beyond basic text analysis and requires readers to think critically about the role of the text and deconstruct the messages that may be implicit within them. In a critical literacy discussion, the teacher should select texts that have themes that lend themselves to critical consciousness and exploring bias and multiple perspectives.
- **Bilingual learner considerations:** For students developing proficiency in English, whole-group discussions should ensure that access is provided for all learners. Thus, teachers should leverage readers' background and cultural knowledge and provide texts that students can identify and connect with. Additionally, small-group discussions with bilingual learners should be used to promote inclusivity and access for all learners.

Guiding Questions for Discussion

- Are students frequently engaging in discussion-based approaches to comprehension in both ELA and content area classes?
- Are students taught strategies for effective classroom discourse? Do they view discussions as a way to build understanding as opposed to "being right" in a discussion?
- Are students reflecting on their own participation within a discussion?
- Do teachers feel confident leading high-quality discussions and asking high-level questions?
- Is the pattern of classroom discussions student driven, and does it look something like this: teacher (t) – student (s) – s -s -s -s -t -s -s- s- and so on?

Further reading

To extend your knowledge of the ideas presented in this section, read the following:

→ Nystrand, M. (2006). Research on the role of classroom discourse as it affects reading comprehension. *Research in the Teaching of English, 40,* 393–412.

⚠ STOP AND EVALUATE DISCUSSION-BASED APPROACHES

Content-Based Approaches

What Is It?

Content-based reading is focused on developing knowledge of content within the text. Both fiction and nonfiction texts can be used for this type of instruction.

Why Does It Matter?

Research suggests that content-based approaches more positively shape reading comprehension than strategy-focused approaches do (McKeown, Beck, & Blake, 2011). In content-based approaches, readers are asked to pay close attention to the text and engage in a learning routine wherein they question and deeply analyze the author's words to build knowledge of the text.

How Is It Assessed?

Formative assessment can provide teachers with an understanding of how students are processing the content they are reading. Educators should explore how students are responding to questions, the depth of their answers, and their ability to acquire knowledge as they read. Summative assessments can vary depending upon the purpose but could include written/short answer responses, projects, or research reports.

Aligned Instructional Practices

- **Close reading with text sets:** Close reading is the process of carefully analyzing a short text by exploring the author's word choice, use of literary devices, point of view, and text structure (Bressler, 2007). The purpose of close reading is to develop a deep understanding of the text. Close reading is embedded throughout the CCSS: *"Read closely to determine what the text says explicitly and to make logical inferences from it; cite specific textual evidence when writing or speaking to support conclusions drawn from the text"* (p. 10). Readers are also expected to *"delineate and evaluate the argument and specific claims in a text, including the validity of the reasoning as well as the relevance and sufficiency of the evidence. (p.10)"* Components of close reading include:
  - ○ *Short, complex, and culturally relevant text sets:* To build knowledge multiple texts, or text sets, about a specific topic should be used for instruction.

The texts provided to students should represent diverse cultures, communities, and perspectives and should not reinforce stereotypes, mistruths, and biases. Short, complex texts such as songs, poems, speeches, or short primary sources are typically used during close reading instruction (fiction texts can also be used). Since complex texts are being read, teachers will need to develop background knowledge on the text and scaffold tricky vocabulary words and complex sentence structures.

❍ *Differentiated lessons:* Close reading can be taught with both whole and small groups of students. To plan for a close reading lesson, teachers will want to begin by assessing their readers—analyzing comprehension needs, interests, and strengths—and planning from there.

❍ *Dialogic discussions:* A central aspect of close reading instruction is the discussion that takes place. Not only should readers analyze complex text, they should engage in meaningful dialogic discussions that push their thinking and allow them to critically analyze texts and topics.

• **Compare/contrast texts on a similar topic:** To extend close reading analysis and to develop deeper knowledge on a topic, curricula materials should provide opportunities for students to read many texts over several days (or weeks) about one topic and compare and contrast the knowledge learned. For example, when learning about the Civil Rights Movement, students could closely analyze primary sources, speeches by Martin Luther King Jr. and President Kennedy, and view and analyze news reports that occurred during the Civil Rights era. Students could compare and contrast the point of view of texts and how individuals were positioned by the author.

• **Access to nonfiction magazine, articles, and texts:** An authentic way to develop content knowledge is through nonfiction magazines, news articles, and high-quality texts. Several news organizations, including the New York Times, provide free online content for teaching current events. Additional websites can allow students to choose nonfiction content to read about.

• **Project-based learning coupled with content instruction:** An effective way to build content knowledge is to provide explicit teaching on a concept and then support the learner as they continue to develop deeper knowledge through independent research and discovery (Halvorsen, Duke, Strachan, & Johnson (2018). This learning can include instruction of text structure and graphical devices such as captions, headings, tables and graphs, etc.

In a project-based approach, learning is centered on a complex question that explores a content area theme such as "What type of birds live near our school?" The project is designed so the learning is purposeful and a tangible outcome is derived (and assessed). For example, in the bird unit, the teacher would provide explicit instruction so the knowledge and understanding of the key concepts and vocabulary related to the unit are learned. Several lessons might include topics on habitats of birds in North America (wetlands, grasslands, desert, etc.); key concepts and vocabulary would be taught in these lessons. Activities such as dissecting owl pellets, observing birds at feeders, and listening and identifying birds would be conducted. Throughout the unit, students are reading books and writing about their learning. Towards the end of the unit, students could create a field guide about birds that live near the school.

- **Bilingual learner access to content:** When possible, bilingual learners should be provided access to content in their native language. For example, during a Civil Rights unit, support content knowledge development by providing the presidential speeches in the native language as well as in English. Provide access through audio and video (see Chapter 4 for additional strategies for teaching bilingual learners).
- **Content-based methods:** Following are two examples of research-based approaches to developing content knowledge. A strong reading curriculum might embed these approaches for teaching comprehension.
  - **Concept-oriented reading instruction (CORI):** This approach emphasizes the importance of building scientific knowledge, motivation, and applying cognitive strategies to support comprehension of informational texts (Guthrie & Klauda, 2014). The CORI model is intended to be used with content areas such as history and science. Within a unit, a topic is explored, and students read texts with a range of reading levels about the topic. They will use cognitive strategies, for example, graphic organizers, to support their comprehension throughout the unit. Additionally, students can become experts on a subtopic of the unit. For example, a unit on weather will teach concepts about the weather but also include some students diving deep into an exploration of clouds; other students might read several books and write about the sun. In the CORI model, readers are engaged through choice, collaboration, and student-centered discussions. Research has suggested that the CORI framework enhances reading comprehension and is associated with an increase in intrinsic motivation and engagement.
  - **Questioning the author (QtA):** This approach can be used to build content knowledge on a topic within a text set. QtA can be used with fiction and nonfiction texts and works well with textbook passages. In a QtA lesson (Beck & McKeown, 2006), the teacher selects an engaging short text and provides regular stopping points that query the passage. Dialogic discussions are also used to construct understandings of the text. Teachers plan this lesson by thinking about what knowledge students need to acquire by the end of the lesson. Then, specific questions are planned and dispersed throughout the reading of the text. Some example of questions in a QtA lesson include the following:
    - What is the author trying to say here?
    - What did the author mean by…?
    - What does this tell us about…?

Guiding Questions for Discussion

- Are a variety of complex and culturally relevant texts used during instruction?
- Is close, analytic reading done in small groups and differentiated for learning?
- Are bilingual learners provided access to complex content?
- How is comprehension assessed?

Further reading

To extend your knowledge of the ideas presented in this section, read the following:

→ McKeown, M.G., Beck, I., & Blake, R.G.K. (2011). Rethinking reading comprehension instruction: A comparison of instruction for strategies and content approaches. *Reading Research Quarterly*, 44(3), 218–253.

⚠ STOP AND EVALUATE CONTENT-BASED APPROACHES

Cognitive Strategy Instruction

What Is It?

Cognitive strategies are actions readers take to support understanding of a text and build knowledge about a topic. Thus, strategies work *in service* of building knowledge. Reading comprehension strategies can be defined as "deliberate, goal-directed attempts to control and modify the reader's efforts to decode text, understand words, and construct meanings of text" (Afflerbach, Pearson, & Paris, 2017, p. 38). A central aspect of cognitive strategy instruction is the modeling and metacognition by the teacher to demonstrate how using the strategy supports comprehension of the text. For example, a strategy lesson would illustrate how summarizing a text helps a reader remember important points of the text/topic. The NRP (2000) suggested the following strategies can support memory for reading content:

- Comprehension monitoring
- Graphic organizers
- Asking and answering questions
- Summarizing
- Using text structure
- Integrating multiple strategies

It is important that cognitive strategy instruction be used judiciously. Content-based approaches are suggested to be more advantageous for developing comprehension than isolated strategy instruction (McKeown, Beck, & Blake, 2011) Thus, teachers can build knowledge on a topic by implementing strategy instruction across a series of texts on that topic. Strategy instruction should be used to support depth of knowledge on a topic/texts and not vice versa.

Why Does It Matter?

The NRP (2000) suggested that using comprehension strategies boosts comprehension. Specific research studies have found that strategies such as summarizing, questioning, visualizing, activating background knowledge, skimming, and paraphrasing support reading comprehension (Pressley, 2006).

How Is It Assessed?

The Qualitative Reading Inventory-6 (QRI-6) (Leslie & Caldwell, 2017) can provide teachers with information regarding how well students are comprehending what they read. The QRI-6 provides questions that explore a reader's background knowledge on a topic before reading, which can help teachers understand if background knowledge is limiting comprehension. If the assessment reveals that students are struggling, then cognitive strategy instruction can be used to support their learning. Use of cognitive strategies can then be assessed formatively. Teachers should monitor if students are relying on the strategies when needed and provide guidance when they are not.

Aligned Instructional Practices

- **Gradual release of responsibility:** Cognitive strategies are best taught through a gradual release of responsibility model. Multiple strategies are best taught together and within a content development approach (e.g., across text sets). In this approach, a teacher combines content knowledge instruction with integrated strategy instruction by reading aloud texts about a similar topic or theme (e.g., a text set). Comprehension strategies are modeled (asking questions, summarizing important information) while new knowledge is being developed on the topic of the text set. Throughout the read-aloud the teacher uses high-level questions and engages readers in a rich discussion about the text. As each text is read, new knowledge is learned and used as important background information in the next read-aloud.
- **Text structure:** Research suggests that instruction of expository text structure and text features can improve reading comprehension (Dickson, Simmons, & Kame'enui, 1995). Teachers should devote time to explicitly teaching (and reteaching as needed) the different text structures and text features that are found in content area texts that are being read: description, sequence, problem solution, cause and effect, and compare and contrast (Meyer, 1975).
- **Graphic organizers:** The NRP (2000) suggested that graphic organizers are an effective tool for supporting reading comprehension. They support active engagement throughout the reading process and allow readers to summarize, synthesize, and remember the information stated in the text.
- **Directed reading thinking activity (DRTA):** The DRTA integrates multiple cognitive strategies. Instructional materials for 6–12 content areas might utilize a thinking routine, like the DRTA, that facilitates cognitive strategy use. The purpose of DRTA is to help readers stay active and engaged throughout the text. In the activity, the student is guided to ask questions, make predictions, and then confirm or revise their predictions. This approach would work well for a student who needs more support to remain active in the text. However, once a text or passage is read, students should always be asked to summarize what they learned and/or engage in a meaningful discussion about what was read.
  - ○ **Direct:** Teacher directs student to preview the text and asks students to make predictions; teacher can document prediction on an anchor chart.
  - ○ **Reading:** Students read, often to a pre-selected spot (for young children, the teacher reads aloud to this spot). Students then confirm their predictions and revise them.
  - ○ **Thinking:** Teacher asks students to provide evidence to support their predictions or reasons why they will change their predictions.
- **Reciprocal teaching:** This approach also integrates multiple strategies and is rooted in teaching and applying four specific comprehension strategies

while reading a text: predicting, questioning, clarifying, and summarizing. This happens in the context of small-group reading as students engage in a routine where they apply these strategies. This approach is rooted in creating active and thoughtful readers. Just like in a DRTA lesson, once a text or passage is read, students should be asked to summarize what they learned and/or engage in a meaningful discussion about what was read.

- **Text quality, choice, and independent reading:** See Chapter 9.

Guiding Questions for Discussion

- How are cognitive strategies taught?
- Are cognitive strategies used to support comprehension in a meaningful way?
- Is a gradual release model used?
- Are students provide instruction in text structure?
- How are we assessing to determine who needs more support with cognitive strategies?

Further reading

To extend your knowledge of the ideas presented in this section, read the following:

→ Duke, N.K., Pearson, P.D., Strachan, S.L., & Billman, A.K. (2011). Essential elements of fostering and teaching reading comprehension. In S.J. Samuels & A.E. Farstrup (Eds.), *What research has to say about reading instruction* (4th ed., pp. 51–93). Newark, DE: International Reading Association.

 STOP AND EVALUATE COGNTIVIE STRATEGIES

Disciplinary Literacy

What Is It?

Disciplinary literacy refers to "literacy skills specialized to history, science, mathematics, literature, or other subject matter" (Shanahan & Shanahan, 2008, p. 44). It differs from content literacy instruction, which looks at how a strategy can be universally applied across all disciplines. Disciplinary literacy focuses upon the unique literacy habits within each discipline. For example, in history, readers must able to navigate and comprehend a primary source, analyze documents, and make claims. In an engineering course, readers must be able to document procedures, collect data, and write findings in an engineering notebook. Both require discipline-specific literacy skills that are not found in other disciplines.

Why Does It Matter?

Reading and writing are approached differently within discipline-specific contexts. Research suggests that disciplinary literacy instruction can support students as they navigate the nuanced literacy behaviors within different disciplines (Shanahan & Shanahan, 2012).

How Is It Assessed?

Content area teachers must collaborate and decide what discipline-specific skills and ways of thinking are necessary for the discipline. Tasks and assessments can be generated from this collaboration. Based upon those assignments and assessments, criteria for scoring the disciplinary aspects of the work can be designed.

Aligned Instructional Practices

- **Disciplinary texts:** Students read and write texts that are common in the discipline and teach readers the unique structure, vocabulary, and visual images that support comprehension. Teachers provide explicit instruction on how to navigate these texts as a disciplinary expert (Gabriel & Wenz, 2017). Specific instruction includes:
  - ○ Historical analysis of primary and secondary sources (grades 6–12)
  - ○ Analysis of science and technical texts (grades 6–12)
- **Reading from multiple sources:** Across the disciplines, students can be taught to read and synthesize information from multiple disciplinary sources, including primary sources, newspaper articles, and multimedia sources. This provides the opportunity to examine a topic from multiple perspectives beyond the textbook.
- **Academic vocabulary:** See Chapter 6.
- **Multimodal text sets** (Gabriel & Wenz, 2017): Teachers can create a text set on a common topic and provide students with multiple text types to support knowledge acquisition (e.g., visual images, video, newspapers, etc.). This practice ensures a deeper exploration of a topic and helps all students access the content.
- **Disciplinary writing:** Teach readers the specialized writing techniques for the discipline. For example, if a student is expected to write a lab report, teach proper third-person structure; don't assume students know how to write like a scientist or historian.
- **Data/document-based questions (DBQs):** These are used in secondary history classes and on Advanced Placement (AP) exams. DBQs teach students strategies for thinking like a historian to support a historical argument. The use of DBQs can also be taught as part of the writing process in a writing class (see Chapter 7). However, if DBQs are being used by a social studies or history teacher, explicit instruction in argumentative writing is needed.
- **The science writing heuristic:** This writing is specific to the discipline of science and uses a template to guide students through writing about a lab activity (Hand, Wallace, & Yang, 2004). The process begins with the research question and then focuses upon evidence and claims:
  1 Beginning ideas: What are my questions?
  2 Tests: What did I do?
  3 Observations: What did I see?
  4 Claims: What can I claim?
  5 Evidence: What evidence do I have to support my claims?
  6 Reading: How do my ideas compare with other ideas or texts?
  7 Reflection: How have my ideas changed?

Guiding Questions for Discussion

- How is disciplinary literacy infused into content area instruction?
- Do readers understand the different ways to approach texts depending upon the discipline being studied?
- Are students reading from multiple sources?

Further reading

To extend your knowledge of the ideas presented in this section, read the following:

→ Shanahan, T. & Shanahan, C. (2012). What is disciplinary literacy and why does it matter? *Topics in Language Disorders*, 32(1), 7–18.

 STOP AND EVALUATE DISCIPLINARY LITERACY

Writing to Learn

What Is It?

Writing to learn (WTL) is a way to deepen understanding of a text by writing about it. This sort of writing differs from the learning to write that is typically done for a term paper. Rather, the focus on WTL is quick and meaningful writing tasks that promote critical interaction with a text or concept. For example, in an engineering class, a teacher might use an engineering notebook where readers must document their design of a robot. In a history class, a student might have to write an annotated bibliography of various primary sources. Following is a chart illustrating the difference between writing to learn and learning to write.

Writing to Learn	Learning to Write
✓ Used to develop thinking on a topic ✓ Writing is not corrected or rewritten ✓ Also used as formative assessment ✓ Relies upon prompts for quick writes: 　• What? 　• How? 　• When? 　• Why?	✓ Prewriting ✓ Writing a draft ✓ Revising ✓ Editing

Why Does It Matter?

Graham and Hebert (2010) conducted a meta-analysis on research about WTL. Their analysis suggests that writing practices can foster reading comprehension and that students should write summaries in both ELA and content area classes. A study by Bangert-Drowns, Hurley, and Wilkinson (2004) suggested that content area writing is effective when frequent, quick-writes occur three or four times per week.

How Is It Assessed?

The purpose of writing to learn activities is *learning*. Thus, writing to learn activities are a type of formative assessment.

Aligned Instructional Practices

- **Reader's notebook:** Students can react to the text they have read. Responses can include personal reflections, questions for discussion, character analysis, and so on.
- **Cornell notes:** In this practice, students divide their note-taking page in half and provide the key ideas and details on the left-hand side and then provide a synthesis of the ideas on the right. Students will need explicit instruction in how to summarize for note taking. Applying lessons from cognitive strategy work can support this practice.
- **Exit tickets and admit slips:** These can be used as both an assessment and instructional tool. They allow readers to process content and allow the teacher to explore how readers are comprehending.
- **Low-stakes quick writes:** Like exit and admit slips, low-stakes quick writes allow students to process what they have learned without fear of a grade attached. Examples include drawings, and short response to a quote.

Further reading

To extend your knowledge of the ideas presented in this section, read the following:

→ Bangert-Drowns, R.L., Hurley, M.M., & Wilkinson, B. (2004). The effects of school-based writing-to-learn interventions on academic achievement: A meta-analysis. *Review of Educational Research, 74*(1), 29–58.

 **STOP AND EVALUATE WRITING TO LEARN**

Online Reading Comprehension

What Is It?

Online reading comprehension is the ability to use online reading strategies, identify important (and unimportant) information on a web page, evaluate online sources, discern credible websites found through a search engine, and read critically across multiple web pages.

Why Does It Matter?

Research suggests that online reading skills are unique. Some evidence suggests that readers who are proficient reading online may struggle with traditional text comprehension, while readers who struggle with online reading comprehension may be proficient at traditional text comprehension (Castek et al., 2011). Additionally, children and adolescents may be well versed in digital technology but may lack the skills needed for online reading comprehension (Bennett, Maton, & Kervin, 2008).

How Is It Assessed?

Interestingly, no states currently require online reading comprehension assessments or measure how students communicate in writing on digital platforms. However, given the ubiquitous nature of online reading, it would behoove school districts to investigate or create resources for online reading comprehension assessment.

Effective Practices

- **Locating credible sources:** Readers should be taught how to use search terms and evaluate the veracity of online sources.
- **Evaluating sources:** Students need explicit instruction on how to evaluate the trustworthiness of a website. The CRAAP test (see below) is a useful acronym to support this process.
- **Synthesizing sources of information:** Readers should learn how to synthesize information found on multiple websites or pages.
- **Internet reciprocal teaching:** This is derived from reciprocal teaching (Palinscar & Brown, 1984) but is intended for students to apply strategies to online learning. In this approach, the teacher provides a whole class lesson on a topic and models how to apply an online reading comprehension strategy. Next, students work collaboratively where they practice online reading comprehension skills by using the Internet to support a curriculum standard. In the last phase, students generate a research question, locate and evaluate sources, and present this information using a medium of their choice.

Evaluating Sources with the CRAAP Test

Currency

- How current is the information on the web page; is a date provided?
- When was the last time the website was updated?

Reliability

- Is the information provided fact or opinion?
- Are statements backed up with references to support claims?

Authority

- Who authored the content, and what are their credentials?
- How do you know the website isn't an advertisement?

Accuracy

- Is the information presented reliable?
- Is there evidence that statements have been researched with credible sources?

Purpose/Point of View

- What is the point of view of the information?
- What bias, if any, is included in the information?
- Is the website trying to market something or sell a product?

Guiding Questions for Discussion

- Are students taught strategies for online research?
- When do we begin teaching students how to evaluate the veracity of online sources?
- Do students know how to evaluate the credibility of information found online?

Further reading

To extend your knowledge of the ideas presented in this section, read the following:

→ Leu, D.J., Forzani, E., Rhoads, C., Maykel, C., Kennedy, C., & Timbrell, N. (2015). *The new literacies of online research and comprehension: Rethinking the reading achievement gap.* Reading Research Quarterly, 50(1). 1-23. Newark, DE: International Reading Association. doi: 10.1002/rrq.85.

 STOP AND EVALUATE ONLINE READING COMPREHENSION

6

Evaluating Vocabulary Grades K–12

Chapter Preview

The chapter begins with a research overview of how vocabulary knowledge develops. Research, instructional practices, and aligned assessments are also provided.

Evaluation: A three-part rubric is used to evaluate all constructs:

Phase One Rubric:
Evaluates alignment of current instructional practices

Phase Two Rubric:
Rates the quality of the current reading program provided to teachers

Phase Three Rubric:
Rates the quality of the program up for adoption

Anchor Standards: The following Common Core Anchor Standards are addressed by this chapter:

Language

Vocabulary Acquisition and Use (K–12)

Vocabulary is a construct that is often readily discussed but not consistently taught. Yet vocabulary knowledge is critical to student learning; correlational research has shown it has a positive relationship with reading comprehension (Anderson & Freebody, 1981; Nagy & Scot, 2000). Logically, this makes sense, as the more words you understand when you read a text, the easier that text will be to comprehend (and more enjoyable as well).

Nevertheless, effective vocabulary instruction has remained elusive in many class-rooms. Memorizing lists of words or looking words up in a dictionary is not conducive to vocabulary learning. However, there are evidence-based instructional strategies that we can implement to increase children's word knowledge. Michael Graves (2006) created four principles that guide effective vocabulary instruction:

1   Create a classroom environment that provides a variety of rich language experiences for students and opportunities for wide reading.
2   Provide explicit instruction in individual words that are used in texts.
3   Teach strategies for figuring out what an unknown word means.
4   Promote a sense of linguistic awareness, or word consciousness, in classrooms.

This chapter will provide a brief review of the research surrounding vocabulary instruction and provide several effective instructional practices that align with Graves's suggestions.

Complexity of Vocabulary Learning

Ascertaining what words children know, as well as the depth of their word knowledge, is complex; this can make lesson planning difficult. Moreover, vocabulary knowledge can be incremental, meaning we often progress through various phases of understanding until we can state with certainty that we *know* a word. Dale (1965) created an incremental scale to describe this process:

1   I never saw the word before.
2   I've heard the word before but don't know what it means.
3   I can recognize the word in context and understand it.
4   I know the word well and I can use it in speaking and writing.

Adding to this complexity is the multidimensional properties of word learning. These dimensions include how well we can apply a word within a spoken sentence, our ability to correctly use a word in writing, and our ability to recognize the grammatical properties of a word (e.g., parts of speech). Additionally, the polysemous nature of words (words with multiple meanings) can cause additional confusion.

Three-Tiered Model of Words

One way to conceptualize the complexity of word meanings is to apply a taxonomy like Beck, McKeown, and Kucan (2002) did when they established "tiers" for categorizing vocabulary words. This framework can be useful when assessing word knowledge and selecting words for instruction. See Table 6.1.

*   *Tier one* words are commonly used in everyday language by students. These words typically do not present a challenge to students and are frequently used in writing. Unless children are learning English as a second language, these words require the least amount of instruction. For example, happy, said, love, chair, and pretty are all examples of tier one words.

Table 6.1 Examples of Tiered Words

Tier One Words	Tier Two Words	Tier Three Words (Biology)
chair	ambiguous	antigen
school	prevalent	biome
run	irrational	biosynthesis
mom	fastidious	cell wall
dog	incredulous	cerebellum
tired	adhere	cytoplasm
sad	detract	phenotype

- *Tier two* words are words that are likely to appear in a wide variety of texts and could be considered part of a mature learner's lexicon. Children may have a conceptual understanding of some of these words, but they lack the specificity to provide a definition and need instruction on how to apply them flexibly in speaking and writing. The bulk of our vocabulary instruction should be done at the tier two level. Examples of tier two words include abhor, redundant, irrational, interrogate, benevolent, and mundane.
- *Tier three* words are discipline-specific words that are unique but less frequently used in day-to-day speech and writing. Tier three words are only required when reading, writing, and speaking in specific disciplines. For example, words like adjacent, parallel, and perpendicular are needed to understand mathematical concepts. These words should be taught within discipline-specific contexts to support comprehension of the topic under study.

How Is It Assessed?

Thoroughly assessing vocabulary knowledge is complex; it involves measuring an individual's oral and written communication, as well as expressive and receptive language. Moreover, complete knowledge of a word requires depth of understanding. For example, we may understand a word's meaning in context but be unable to produce it independently on our own when speaking (we are not fully sure how to use it). For classroom teachers, vocabulary assessment should focus upon pragmatic measures that improve and deepen vocabulary knowledge. Beck, McKeown, and Kucan (2002) provide several useful ways teachers can assess students' word knowledge through instructional activities. For example, instruction/assessment can include asking students to compare target words to other words, having students distinguish between examples and nonexamples of taught words, and providing context interpretation tasks that ask readers to make inferences about a targeted word used in context.

Of course, students who may exhibit oral language needs (expressive or receptive) should be thoroughly assessed by a speech and language therapist, who can provide a battery of diagnostic assessments (see Chapter 3).

Aligned Instructional Practices

- **Purposefully teach necessary words from the text:** Research suggests that reading can be improved if certain words—those that are needed for comprehending the text—are introduced and briefly taught while reading the text (Wright & Cervetti, 2017). There is some research to suggest that preteaching words can aid in comprehension, yet this approach must be used with caution, as too many word definitions will not be retained (Beck, McKeown, & Kucan, 2002). The key is that instruction is brief (less than one minute per word) and students are familiarized with the word. Additionally, if students can figure the word out through context or morphology, there is no reason to teach the word.
- **Repeated exposure/use:** A key aspect of word learning is repeated encounters with a word in different contexts. Once words have been introduced, it is important to revisit them and support children's repeated use of the words. Research suggests that approximately eight to ten exposures to a word are required before it is fully learned (Schmitt, 2008).
- **Teach words in a storybook read-aloud:** This practice can be used in the elementary grades and be incorporated into an interactive read-aloud or content area study. Since children can learn and understand words that are above their decoding ability, read-alouds are a useful device for bolstering vocabulary knowledge. A routine that effectively promotes word learning is as follows:
  1 Before the read-aloud, select two or three words that are important in the story.
  2 As you plan the lesson, write out a child-friendly definition of the words. You might consider using visuals or props that will support student understanding.
  3 When you come across the word in the text, provide the child-friendly definition. Use a vocabulary word wall to write the definition; provide a picture if you can.
  4 Now, ask children to say the word.
  5 After the read-aloud, revisit the words introduced and discuss them. Use movement, pictures, props, and examples to support understanding. Ask children to turn and talk and use the word in a sentence.
  6 Use the word several times over the days and weeks. Use it in writing and speaking. At least eight to ten exposures to the word are needed for children to process (Beck, McKeown, & Kucan, 2002).
  7 Throughout the next days and weeks, continue to reference the vocabulary words and ask students to use them in their speaking and writing.
- **Focus on active processing instead of dictionaries:** When instructing a target word in a text, research suggests (Wright & Cervetti, 2017) that we should teach children to actively process the meaning by connecting the word to one they know and having them use it in sentence (like the suggestions earlier). This supports vocabulary acquisition better than merely providing a definition or asking students to look the word up in the dictionary.

- **Independent/wide reading:** A robust strategy for developing vocabulary knowledge is through wide reading. Many of the words we know are acquired incidentally, through our interactions with text (Nagy, Herman, & Anderson, 1985). Thus, a strong reading program will provide opportunities for independent reading, read-alouds, and audiobook enjoyment (see Chapter 8 for additional information about independent reading).
- **Code switching:** Code switching is the ability to use alternative languages or dialects during speech or writing. The use of code switching for vocabulary acquisition is a research-aligned practice that teaches active processing of words and provides repeated exposure to newly taught vocabulary words. Educators can help students code-switch, or navigate between different discourses, by leveraging their learners' word knowledge use within informal contexts (such as slang) and bridging this knowledge to learning new academic vocabulary words (Emdin, 2013).

  Table 6.2 is adapted from Emdin (2013) and illustrates how educators can utilize their students' background knowledge to build deeper academic knowledge. In this approach (Brown & Spang, 2007), educators teach students to imagine that they are placed in contexts where only certain vocabulary words are used and valued. For example, when learning new terms in physics class, students are prompted to articulate how they would explain a concept or word to their friends; they express understanding of the term in everyday conversational language. After several minutes of discussion and learning, they are prompted to switch contexts and state how they would explain the same concept to a group of physicists in a university setting. Not only does this practice develop vocabulary acquisition but it is culturally responsive, as it recognizes, embraces, and values students' background knowledge and cultural identity.
- **Bilingual learners:** Educators working with learners who are bilingual need to emphasize vocabulary development. Instructional approaches for teaching vocabulary are no different for bilingual learners than they are for monolingual students. Beck, McKeown, and Kucan (2002) recommend teaching tier two words and ensuring that students are provided extended opportunities to discuss and use words in a meaningful context. Spanish-speaking learners can also be taught about the cognate relationships between Spanish and English. Repeated exposure is essential to bilingual students' word learning.
- **Create word awareness:** Teachers can develop word awareness by attending to the unique aspects of written and spoken language, including sound, rhythm, and form. We can also try to use tier two words in everyday

Table 6.2 Code-Switching Vocabulary

English Word (Tier Two Word)	Discipline-Specific Word/Definition	Slang Word/Authentic Definition
electricity	alternating current	lit (create definition in own words)
fancy	ornate	pimped

Note: Adopted from Emdin, C. (2016). *For white folks who teach in the hood… and the rest of y'all too.* Boston: Beacon Press.

contexts. For example, instead of asking students to return to their seats, we might say "Kindly elevate your bodies and navigate back to your desks." When we come across an interesting word in text, we should make a point of repeating it over the next several days. We should also encourage students to apply the word in their academic writing or speech.

• **Morphology or structural analysis:** Morphemes are units of meaning within a word; morphemic awareness provides insight into what a word means. Additionally, morphemic knowledge is generative, meaning morphemes are often found in multiple words. Research suggests that more than half of the words encountered by middle and high school readers are morphologically complex (Nagy & Anderson, 1984).

Morphemes can be described as either *bound* or *unbound*. For example, the word "cat" is a singular, unbound morpheme. However, the "s" in the word cats is a bound morpheme that means more than one. Bound morphemes cannot stand alone as a word. Other types of bound morphemes include suffixes and prefixes such as "-ing" or "pre-." Most of the words within the English language are derived from Greek and Latin morphological roots.

Thus, vocabulary instruction should help children learn to spell and structurally analyze morphemes. For example, if a child reads the word "unimaginable," he or she can analyze the word, break it into meaningful parts, and discern its meaning. Morphological awareness not only positively shapes reading comprehension (Carlisle, 2003) but it can also develop decoding and spelling ability (Henbest & Apel, 2017) as children learn to "chunk" the syllable morphemes in a multisyllable word.

• **Pictures and words—Dual coding:** Dual coding theory (Clark & Paivio, 1991) suggests that linguistic information is better retained when it is paired with visual information. Thus, middle and high school learners who take notes or keep discipline-specific notebooks with vocabulary terms should not only synthesize information in writing but can also be prompted to create sketches to help retain understanding of what was learned.

Dictionaries: Best Practices for Classroom Use

Dictionaries serve a valuable purpose but should be used with the right instructional goal in mind. For example, asking students to look up a list of words in the dictionary and learn their meaning is not an effective approach to word learning. However, dictionaries can be a meaningful tool: They can help writers apply a word correctly (especially if they are unsure of the word's meaning) or help clarify a word meaning. Thus, teaching specific dictionary skills is important. Here are practices that support dictionary use:

• Incorporate periodic lessons for children on how to use a dictionary (both print and online versions).
• Instruct how to alphabetically locate a word.
• Embed part-of-speech instruction and teach how this provides an indication to word meaning.
• Model how to look up a word with multiple definitions and how to and select the correct definition of the word by using context.

• **Words with multiple meanings:** Approximately 75 percent of commonly used words have more than one meaning (Lederer, 1991). Readers who

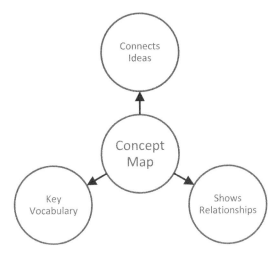

Figure 6.1 Concept map.

struggle and emerging bilinguals will need support for understanding polysemous words. During read-alouds, educators can explicitly demonstrate how they use context to understand a multiple-meaning word and provide students with several opportunities to read, speak, and write the word.

- **Graphic organizers:** Certain graphic organizers can be used to support vocabulary acquisition:
  - **Concept maps:** Although we typically think of vocabulary as individual words, concepts are also part of word learning. For example, the word *fascism* is a concept that is best understood by integrating prior knowledge and historical content. One way to develop students' conceptual understanding is by using concept maps. These are visual displays that help students understand how ideas are connected (Figure 6.1).
  - **Semantic feature analysis (SFA):** This is a great tool for helping students process how concepts or words are similar or different. SFA can be used in the content area classrooms to help students illustrate how a topic, such as polygons, are related. To create one for your students, select a category or theme. On the left-hand side, list the key vocabulary words related to the category. Then, on the top row list the features of the category. Students then place a Yes or No or a + or – to indicate the relationship between the word and its features. An example is provided here.

	Seed Eater	Bug Eater	Carnivore	Nocturnal	Migrates
Red Wing Blackbird					
Bald Eagle					
Bluebird					
Great Horned Owl					
Pileated Woodpecker					

Definition	Characteristics/Description/Facts
Examples	Non-Examples

Vocabulary Word

Figure 6.2 Graphic organizer.

- **Frayer model graphic organizers:** This type of graphic organizer assists students in learning how to fully and flexibly learn a word or concept. There are slightly different variations of this model but typically, the model resembles Figure 6.2.

Guiding Questions for Discussion

- How is vocabulary knowledge assessed?
- Is word learning a focus on K–6 instruction? K–12 instruction?
- Is repeated exposure to vocabulary words provided to students? How does this look at various grade levels?
- How is linguistic awareness approached throughout the grades?
- Are bilingual learners provided explicit vocabulary instruction?
- Is word learning explicitly taught?
- Do teachers have a framework for how to teach vocabulary?
- At what grade level are dictionary skills taught? Is this noted in a curriculum document, or do teachers instruct on an as-needed basis?
- What grade levels teach morphology?
- Are students provided regular opportunities to build their vocabulary knowledge through wide reading? At what grade levels?

Further reading

To extend your knowledge of the ideas presented in this section, read the following:

→ Beck, I.L., McKeown, M.G., & Kucan, L. (2002). *Bringing words to life: Robust vocabulary instruction*. New York, NY: Guilford Press.

→ Wright, T.S. & Cervetti, G.N. (2017). A systematic review of the research on vocabulary instruction that impacts text comprehension. *Reading Research Quarterly*, 52(2), 203–226.

 ⚠ STOP AND EVALUATE VOCABULARY

Evaluating Writing Grades K–12

Chapter Preview

The chapter begins with the importance of writing. Then, the main constructs for effective writing programs are explained and evaluated. Research, instructional practices, and aligned assessments are provided for each of the following constructs:

- The Writing Framework
- Narrative Writing
- Argumentative/Opinion Writing
- Informational Writing
- Digital Composition
- Handwriting
- Writing Conventions

Evaluation: A three-part rubric is used to evaluate all constructs:

Phase One Rubric:	Phase Two Rubric:	Phase Three Rubric:
Evaluates alignment of current instructional practices	Rates the quality of the current writing program provided to teachers	Rates the quality of the program up for adoption

Anchor Standards: The following Common Core Anchor Standards are addressed by this chapter:

Writing

Text Types and Purposes (K–12)
Production and Distribution of Writing (K–12)
Research to Build and Present Knowledge (K–12)
Range of Writing (3–12)

Introduction

Like reading, writing is an indispensable tool. Writing allows us to communicate needs, express feelings, and make sense of our lives. As a learner, we understand a topic or text better when we write about it. And, of course, writing makes us a better reader just as reading makes us a better writer. Indeed, there is a great phrase that goes something like this: *Read like a writer and write like a reader!* Put simply, writing and reading have a bond that is mutually beneficial, and as educators we need to nurture that bond.

Nevertheless, writing is complex and multifaceted. To write effectively, you must possess a comprehensive toolbox:

- You need to have deep background knowledge on the topic you are writing about and synthesize key ideas together in a comprehensible manner, so your writing is clear.
- You must have a well-defined plan and know how to convey ideas formally—in a manner quite different from oral speech.
- You must be engaged and motivated by the content you are writing about.
- You must be metacognitive: You need to execute the correct word choice, choose meaningful punctuation, and utilize appropriate sentence structure to convey the intended meaning to your reader.
- You must be able to clearly transition ideas and sentences.
- You must know how to discern credible from noncredible sources, so the information presented is trustworthy.
- You must know how to use digital tools and social media and write for various digital audiences (e.g., Twitter, Facebook, blogs, etc.).
- You must know your audience and be able to provide needed background information on the topic you are writing about. The ideas presented must be readable and coherent.
- Above all, you need to practice. A lot. Effective writing is a skill, and like all other skills, it is developed through repeated practice.

As educators, there is a great deal of nuance that goes into writing instruction beyond spelling and grammar. Unfortunately, writing instruction, despite its emphasis in the Common Core State Standards (CCSS), remains elusive for many teachers today (Graham & Harris, 2019). Recent research suggests that after third grade, very little instructional time is devoted to writing. Moreover, expectations for academic writing, both in and out of the classroom, remain scant. Given writing's pragmatic purposes and cognitive super-power, this is an unfortunate reality.

In the following sections, I describe the key constructs that are necessary for schools to foster an effective writing program throughout all classrooms. Following are the topics that are covered and evaluated in this chapter:

1 The Writing Framework
2 Narrative Writing
3 Argumentative/Opinion Writing
4 Informational Writing
5 Digital Composition
6 Handwriting
7 Writing Conventions

The Writing Framework

What Is It?

Put simply, a writing framework is how educators will approach daily writing instruction and plan that instruction throughout the year. A clear writing framework is a non-negotiable that districts should have in place for all educators to teach writing. A framework provides the ingredients (beyond curriculum) that are needed to propel effective writing. Such considerations include daily allotment for writing, a year-long calendar of genres to be covered, and tools for instructional design.

Why Does It Matter?

Writing instruction cannot be conducted haphazardly. Teachers must have a well-thought-out plan for how they are approaching instruction. Research suggests that writing achievement is possible when school time is dedicated to daily writing (approximately 45 minutes per day) that includes direct teaching on genre and process.

How Is It Assessed?

To assess if your school has a writing framework, the following questions should be answered affirmatively:

- Is it the expectation that writing is taught daily?
- Do teachers have a scope and sequence at each grade level for the writing genres and units they are teaching?
- Is the writing process and strategy instruction emphasized (researching, planning, revising, editing)?
- Is there a framework for each lesson where there is direct instruction and time for active writing time?
- Are students provided choice in what they write about? For example, if the writing unit is about narrative writing, are they given a choice about the narrative they are composing?
- Is the study of mentor texts an integral component of the writing framework?
- Is writing assessed, as are how children are progressing, and are data collected?
- Is a writing community established in each English Language Arts (ELA) classroom?

Aligned Instructional Practices

- **Time allotment:** Research suggests that elementary teachers should instruct writing for 45 minutes to one hour each day (What Works Clearinghouse Practice Guide). Obviously, that amount of time might be too long for our youngest learners, but working up to a 45-minute time frame for kindergarten to second grade K–2 is possible. Middle school students should also be engaged in daily writing.
- **Disciplinary focus:** As grade levels increase and subjects are departmentalized, disciplinary writing should be emphasized. For example, high school students may not be enrolled in an ELA course each semester. However,

chances are they are in a science or history class. These content areas should include plenty of time devoted to discipline-specific writing, such as argumentative and expository types of writing.

- **Writing community:** Writing is a social process. Research suggests that a writing community provides students with both a purpose and desire to learn (Graham & Perin, 2007). In a writing community, teachers foster authentic writing practices where students are given choice in much of what they write. Additionally, a writing community includes practices where:
  - ○ Students have a purpose and write authentically
  - ○ Independence and self-regulation are fostered
  - ○ Conferring between teachers and students is commonplace
  - ○ Collaboration between peers is supported
  - ○ Writers share their drafts and final products with the community
  - ○ Explicit instruction on writing craft, conventions, and process is provided
- **Genre study focus:** School districts should have a set scope and sequence regarding the genres that will be taught. Materials supporting the teaching of specific genres, including lesson topics and mentor texts, should be provided to teachers. What are the expectations as children develop from kindergarten through twelfth grade? Each grade level may have slightly different genre foci depending upon how you answer this question. What do students need to be able to write in college? In technical fields? These questions, as well as the writing standards set forth by your state, should guide how you determine the genre foci across the grade levels.
- **Writing strategy lessons:** A strong writing framework not only has a scope and sequence, it has strategy lessons aligned to the genres/content being taught (Graham & Perin, 2007). Specific writing moves should be demonstrated to students. For example, multiple lessons could be derived from the teaching of:
  - ○ Planning
  - ○ Sentence structure
  - ○ Use of transition words
  - ○ Use of punctuation to convey meaning
  - ○ Embedded grammar instruction
  - ○ Word choice
  - ○ Synthesizing ideas into writing
  - ○ Coherence
  - ○ Revision
  - ○ Editing
  - ○ Academic versus conversational tone
- **Feedback:** A well-designed writing framework should include a focus on providing frequent feedback to students (Wilson, 2019). Research suggests that effective feedback is characterized by the following:
  1 Helps the writer understand how his or her work compares to the success criteria. This can be accomplished by comparing student writing to exemplars or mentor texts.
  2 Provides a clear explanation of what needs to be done for the writer to improve and close the gap.
  3 Provides suggestions for moving forward—a writing strategy.

4 Provides varied suggestion. For example, teachers might provide *facilitative feedback,* which helps a writer self-reflect and query their own writing. They might use *direct feedback,* which provides explicit information about what needs to be revised. They might use *informative feedback,* which tells the writer about specific qualities of strong writing (e.g., "Argumentative writing includes research to support a claim—not merely your opinion."). Lastly, they might use *praise* and give positive feedback about specific aspects of the writing (e.g., "I really like how you opened your argument with a strong quote. That drew me in as a reader and made me want to keep reading.").

5 Focuses on how writers effectively use the writing process.

6 Focuses upon both lower-level and higher-level skills. Research has suggested that teachers often overly focus on low-level skills like handwriting and conventions (Clare, Valdes, & Patthey-Chavez, 2000). Instead, higher-level writing skills, like the writer's voice, use of vivid language, and elaborative skills, should be emphasized.

- **Motivating contexts:** The key to productivity and success with almost anything we do is motivation. Research has explored the role of motivation in writing and found the concept of *value* to be a helpful way to educators to understand writing motivation. For example, is the task of writing intrinsically valuable to the writer—do they enjoy it? Does the writing task have purpose—is it authentic? Does writing have *attainment value*, meaning does it allow the writer to express themselves? With these ideas of value in mind, there are several instructional practices we can rely upon to foster writing motivation (Boscolo & Gelati, 2019):
  - ❍ Provide authentic writing tasks. Writing should be completed for a purpose, not for a prompt. For example, if argument is the genre you are teaching, allow children to write an argument that matters to their own life, such as why the school playground needs a better basketball court. If informational writing is the genre being learned, allow students choice to research and write about topics they are passionate about.
  - ❍ Provide meaningful, and shorter, opportunities to write. Not all writing needs to be essay length - Condensed writing tasks can help writers "exercise" their writing muscles in meaningful ways. For example, educators can utilize dialogue journals, exit slips, letters, or double entry journals. These quick writes can be used across the disciplines to support overall writing skill.
  - ❍ Promote self-reflection Help writers reflect on their own learning about writing, their goals for improving, and actionable steps they can take to get better. Depending upon the grade level, this will look different in each class. For younger writers, a simple sentence stem at the end of the writing period might go like this: "One thing I learned about myself today as a writer was _____."
  - ❍ Use frequent feedback. Ongoing feedback not only supports the writing process, it provides writers with a tangible goal to work towards which can be inherently motivating. On a larger scale, embedding a writing portfolio into your writing framework allows writers to view their progress throughout the year and serves as an overall assessment of a student's writing.

- **Bilingual learner development:** A writing framework will be designed to tap into the rich linguistic repertoire (García & Kleifgen, 2019) of bilingual learners. As educators, it is essential to leverage children's first-language skills and build from those existing strengths (Pasquarella, 2019). Additional considerations for teaching bilingual learners include:
  - ○ Know your learners: Develop a portrait of your learners (Espinosa, Ascenzi-Moreno & Vogel, 2016) to tap into their interests as writers. The portrait can identify their (1) interests, (2) home language, (3) country of origin, and (4) understanding of writing practices in the home language. This information provides you with knowledge of your learners and enables you to leverage their interests, strengths, and background knowledge.
  - ○ Teach the writing process. Ensure that *all* students are provided access to the same rich instruction within the writing framework; this includes opportunities for dialogue, authentic writing practice, and meaningful feedback.
  - ○ Support hybrid writing practices that allow bilingual learners to rely on both languages to communicate meaning. When students write in their home language, or in a combination of English and their native language, they deepen their knowledge of the English writing system; this practice should not be discouraged.
  - ○ Use sentence and paragraph frames as necessary to support different genres of writing.
  - ○ Demonstrate how to apply phonemic segmentation and blending skills (see Chapter 3) to foster word writing development.
  - ○ Develop learners' metalinguistic skills and awareness of the similarities and differences between their native and second language.
  - ○ Provide opportunities for collaboration with peer writing and revising.
  - ○ Employ dialogue journals and other quick writes that facilitate risk-free writing experiences.
  - ○ Rely upon flexible grouping patterns that allow students the opportunity to engage in meaningful discussions with peers.

Guiding Questions for Discussion

- In our school district, is writing its own class, like science and social studies?
- Are a well-defined scope and sequence of writing units provided to teachers?
- What are the grade-level expectations for writing?
- Is feedback a component of writing instruction?
- Is motivating writers prioritized in instruction?
- Is bilingual literacy supported and leveraged within the writing framework?
- Are students frequently provided actionable feedback about their writing?
- Is explicit instruction in specific writing strategies consistently provided to students, beginning in kindergarten and continuing through high school classes?

> **Further reading**
>
> *To extend your knowledge of the ideas presented in this section, read the following:*
>
> → *Framework for Success in Postsecondary Writing* (2011) by the Council of Writing Program Administrators (CWPA), the National Council of Teachers of English (NCTE), and the National Writing Project (NWP)
> → Anderson, C. (2019). A *teacher's guide to writing conferences*. Portsmouth, NH: Heineman.
> → Warner, J. (2018). *Why they can't write: Killing the five-paragraph essay and other necessities*. Baltimore, MD: John Hopkins University Press.

 STOP AND EVALUATE WRITING FRAMEWORK

Narrative Writing

What Is It?

Narrative writing is a genre that allows writers to share human experiences through storytelling, rich dialogue, description, and emotion (Olson & Godfrey, 2019). Narratives can be fiction or nonfiction. They allow children to be self-reflective and explore their perceptions and feelings about the world and their own intimate life.

Why Does It Matter?

Narrative writing provides both cognitive and emotional benefits to students. For one, it allows children the opportunity to consider the perspective of others. When a child narrates a story about their life (or a story about someone else's life), they must also consider the viewpoint, feelings, and voice of individuals who might be quite different than they are. The writer must step inside the mind of someone else and describe those details to the reader. Additionally, narrative writing promotes cognitive strength (Olson & Godfrey, 2019), as it requires writers to choose precise vocabulary, employ meaningful sentence structure, map out the plot, use descriptive language, and consider the appropriate point of view. Moreover, narrative writing empowers children to express their own feelings and voice their own story. Through narrative writing students can leverage their own experiences and share relevant life events. For many, this is powerful work that is motivating in and of itself. Lastly, narrative writing is one of the main text types that students are expected to write in the CCSS.

How Is It Assessed?

Various literary elements associated with narrative writing, and these can be included as part of a narrative writing assessment. Assessments can also evaluate the qualities of writing. For example, a narrative rubric might assess how well the writer used descriptive language to develop the setting and context of the narrative. Additionally, teachers might choose to assess students' use of the writing process. The CCSS also narrative writing standards that can guide teachers to know the grade level expectations for the students they teach.

Aligned Instructional Practices

Narrative writing requires that educators explicitly teach the elements that comprise the genre; these include:

- **Narrative text qualities:** For emergent writers, narrative writing can develop in kindergarten, as students learn the basic elements of a story (setting, characters, plot, conflict resolution) through picture book read alouds. For example, students might use a story map to sequence the events of a story. Lessons might also explore writing craft in a mentor text by analyzing how an author developed a character within the mentor text. Lessons can teach children to apply those strategies to their own writing.
- **Plot structure:** As writers progress in their sophistication, they will advance in their understanding of literary devices, such as plot, that are essential to writing the genre. Thus, instruction will want to home in on the specific aspects of plot structure and provide explicit instruction on the following:
  - ○ **Exposition**. This refers to the setting of the story, the historical context, or the background knowledge that is needed for the reader to make sense of the narrative.
  - ○ **Inciting incident**. This is the part of the narrative where the main character becomes involved in the story's problem. It creates excitement for the reader and propels the story forward.
  - ○ **Rising action**. Writers should learn how to use a series of "rising action" events that build towards the climax of the story.
  - ○ **Climax**. This is the height of the drama in the story. A definitive moment where the story is the most intense.
  - ○ **Falling action**. Once the climax has happened, the falling action of the story shows the resulting outcomes.
  - ○ **Resolution**. The problem in the story is resolved.
  - ○ **Conclusion**. Any outstanding questions are answered, and the theme of the story is complete.
- **Showing, not telling:** Narrative writers must employ rich sensory language to help their reader understand the setting and characters in a story. Strong writers do this by showing how a character feels rather than by telling. Consider the difference in the following two sentences: (1) *She was scared getting into her car.* (2) *Despite the noise of the freeway behind her, she could hear her own heart pounding in her chest; her hands trembling as she fumbled for the car keys in her purse.* The second example shows the reader the woman is nervous without explicitly saying it. A unit on narrative writing should provide several lessons that help young writers develop this technique in their writing.
- **Use of internal and external dialogue:** To write an effective narrative, students should learn how to use dialogue effectively. Beginning writers might only rely upon external dialogue within their writing. However, to develop the use of internal dialogue, teachers can read aloud books that show the internal feelings of characters; students can analyze, and discuss these texts and be prompted to notice how authors incorporated internal dialogue strategically. Additionally, a key aspect of writing dialogue is learning the

punctuation rules that correspond to it. For example, instruction should include how to use paragraphing, how to use quotation marks, how to use commas and periods within dialogue, and how to identify who is speaking when multiple voices are conversing.

- **Theme:** Theme is the essence of the narrative. It concerns the deeper message that an author is trying to convey. It is important that educators teach the difference between theme and topic in a narrative. Olson and Godfrey (2019) describe the difference like this: "Think of the topic as the *What* of the story and the theme as the *So what?*" (p. 97). Thus, topics are general (e.g., friendship, bravery, family), whereas themes are specific to a message in the topic (e.g., Sometimes loving a child requires sacrifice).
- **Point of view:** Point of view refers to the perspective through which you write the story: first person (I), second person (you), or third person (he, she, or it). Point of view also refers to the perspective of the main character and other characters in the narrative. How do they feel, respond to events, and demonstrate a unique identity in the text? A writing curriculum that teaches narrative structure should provide lessons that instruct point of view (which will become increasingly more complex as children advance grade levels).
- **Mentor texts:** Narrative writing units should have dedicated mentor texts that grade-level teachers use for instruction. Lessons can be provided with mentor texts to teach the typical plot structure of a narrative. Teachers can deconstruct and closely study the mentor text with a story map or anchor chart. As students plan for their own narrative, they can use story maps to generate the plot structure in the piece they are writing.

Guiding Questions

- At what grade levels is narrative writing explicitly taught?
- What is the scope and sequence of narrative writing? For instance, at what grade level is internal dialogue taught? Theme? Point of view? How are we ensuring students are using these elements in their writing?
- What are the expectations for student understanding of plot structure in their writing?
- Are teachers provided with mentor texts at each grade level to support narrative writing?

> **Further reading**
> *To extend your knowledge of the ideas presented in this section, read the following:*
>
> → Hillocks, G. (2006). *Narrative writing: Learning a new model for teaching.* Portsmouth, NH: Heineman.

 **STOP AND EVALUATE NARRATIVE WRITING**

Argumentative/Opinion Writing

What Is It?

In argumentative writing the author takes a position on a topic that has varying opinions, provides logical evidence to support the position, and presents evidence using writing moves that resonate and persuade (Ferretti & Lewis, 2019). A strong writing program will have an emphasis on argumentative writing beginning in the early grades. For example, kindergarten writers can argue for their favorite restaurant or why chocolate ice cream is better than vanilla. By high school, students should be writing argumentative essays across the disciplines.

Why Does It Matter?

The ability to argue a position is essential to living in a democratic system. Our rights as American citizens are rooted in free speech (and free elections). Moreover, from a literacy standpoint, argumentative writing shares a bidirectional relationship with critical reading. The skill of argumentative writing supports a skill of critical reading and vice versa. For example, a reader who can critically evaluate an argument, the sources of evidence that support the argument, and accept (or decline) the merits of an argument is able to set out on writing their own argument using the techniques they have analyzed as a reader. Additionally, teaching argumentative writing, by nature, allows students to become critical consumers of what they read. For example, if a political candidate argues a position, a student who is well versed in the techniques of argumentative writing can discern legitimate sources from non-legitimate ones and is better apt to accept or not accept the political candidate's message. Lastly, argumentative writing is a main text type that students are expected to write in the CCSS.

How Is It Assessed?

Argumentative writing can be assessed by looking at how students apply the elements that comprise it. For emerging writers, this will be (1) claim, (2), reasons, and (3) evidence. As writers progress in their sophistication, they can be taught Toulmin's Model of Argument (1958). In it are the following six elements:

1   Claim: The main proposition of the argument.
2   Evidence: Data to support the claim.
3   Warrant: Bridges the evidence to the claim.
4   Qualifiers: Tools the writer relies upon to "qualify" the claim. For example, words like "often" and "most of the time" are qualifiers that make the argument more factually accurate and strong.
5   Backing: Statements that provide additional support to the warrant.
6   Rebuttal: Counter-arguments that the writer includes to show that there are times when the argument doesn't hold.

Assessment of argumentative writing can evaluate how writers applied these elements to craft their argument. Of course, the depth of application will depend upon the grade level and the instruction provided to students. The writing standards in the CCSS or standards from your specific state can guide you to the appropriate grade-level expectations for argumentative writing.

Aligned Instructional Practices

- **Structure of an Argument:** Although the elements listed earlier provide a thorough representation of an argument, a less complex way to begin teaching argumentation is through the TREE strategy (Graham & Harris, 1989). In this scaffold, writers think about the (T) Topic; (R) Reasons—at least three; (E) Explanations—elaboration on the reasons; and (E) Ending—the argument is concluded. This can be modified, depending upon the age of the learner. As students enter middle school and high school, they should learn more elements of argumentative writing, including warrants and rebuttal.

- **Argument vs. Persuasion:** Students should also learn that there is a difference between argument and persuasion. Persuasion concerns an opinion, whereas argument concerns facts. As such, persuasive writing can include personal anecdotes to support a claim. In argumentative writing, the author must use research-based facts, historical data, and logic to support the claim. Persuasive writing can also be more emotional, whereas argumentative writing is unemotional and logical.

- **Mentor Texts:** An effective way to teach argumentative writing is to read arguments. Each grade level should have a set of mentor texts that can be used to analyze and deconstruct an argument. Instruction can explore op-eds and other opinion pieces in the news media. Teachers of younger writers will want to craft their own argumentative piece that children can relate to and study.

- **Academic Language of Argument:** Effective teaching of argument will help students understand how to use academic terms specific to argument, such as:
  - ◌ Furthermore,
  - ◌ On the other hand
  - ◌ Some might disagree, however,…
  - ◌ To begin with,
  - ◌ For example,
  - ◌ Alternatively,
  - ◌ Therefore,
  - ◌ In conclusion,

- **Dialogic Discussions/Debates:** Discussion is an excellent way to prime the pump for argumentative writing (Ferretti & Lewis, 2019). Through talk, writers practice responding to alternative viewpoints and engage with an authentic audience. Moreover, research has suggested that dialogic debates result in more thorough written arguments (Kuhn & Crowell, 2011). An argumentative discussion that is dialogic will ensure that students make claims and provide evidence to support their views; they ask critical questions of their peers; they build on one other's thinking and defend their views with evidence. If you have set up your classroom with ground rules of talk (see the comprehension chapters), then transitioning to an argumentative discussion in writing class should be smooth.

- **Develop Content Knowledge Through the Argument:** Embedding argumentative writing in history or science is a purposeful way to develop content knowledge while also teaching writing. For example, if students are studying the Civil War, they can learn to create an argument, research information about the topic, and write about it. Almost every discipline can include instruction in argumentative writing. In English, students write literary essays; in history, students craft historical arguments; in science, students use scientific data from research or lab reports to support a claim. As such, content area teachers will want to infuse argumentative writing within instruction; scaffolds like the TREE acronym can be used to support this teaching. Most importantly, instruction will focus on the specialized knowledge and discourses unique to the discipline and how to use that knowledge when writing.

Guiding Questions

- What are grade-level expectations for argumentative writing?
- How is argumentative writing assessed?
- Does each grade level have suggested mentor texts to use to support argumentative writing?
- What is the role of academic debate in the writing classroom?

Further reading

To extend your knowledge of the ideas presented in this section, read the following:

→ Hillocks, G. (2011) *Teaching argument writing, grades 6-12: Supporting claims with relevant evidence and clear reasoning*. Portsmouth, NH: Heineman.

 STOP AND EVALUATE ARGUMENTATIVE WRITING

Informational Writing

What Is It?

Informational writing is nonfiction writing that provides detailed information about a topic. Informational writing is composed across the disciplines. Beginning in kindergarten, young children may craft short texts all about a favorite animal or insect. They can learn to write a fact or two to describe the animal. As writers advance, they will write across the disciplines in history, science, and art to craft informational pieces about a topic. The crux of this type of writing involves synthesizing information from sources.

Why Does It Matter?

Informational composition is an in-depth writing-to-learn activity. It requires several cognitive skills, such as reading and analyzing important details from a text, synthesizing the details together, and describing them in a logical fashion. It also requires readers to discern credible information from noncredible sources. Informational writing is also an important way for students to build background knowledge.

How Is It Assessed?

Informational writing can be assessed formatively through peer feedback and individual and small group conferences. To assess final written products, teachers will want to establish criteria before the writing unit begins and share that criteria with students. The criteria for evaluation should include how students summarized information, paraphrased sources, and provided a coherent report on the topic that was written about. The CCSS also provides grade level standards that can assist teachers with knowing what students need to accomplish as writers at each grade level.

Aligned Instructional Practices

- **Wide reading (and viewing) on a topic:** If a student is to write an informational piece, he or she must develop background knowledge about the topic. When teaching informational writing, teachers should provide students access to a wide variety of texts that are written at a variety of levels. Pairing an informational writing unit with a unit on nonfiction reading is also a wise choice. Through reading, students can build background knowledge about the topic, but at the same time, they can be taught to closely analyze the specific craft moves made by informational text authors. Additionally, students can build background knowledge on a topic through video and digital resources.
- **Locating sources:** Writers need to know how to navigate a library and locate credible sources. Instruction should focus upon the investigation of secondary sources, including print, visual, and digital sources. Additionally, writers need to know where to go locate primary sources and how to read them. Not all schools have a full-time librarian, so teachers might be tasked with this work.
- **Understanding Wikipedia:** A go-to website for many people searching about a topic is Wikipedia, a nonprofit, online, collaborative encyclopedia composed by anonymous volunteers. Given its popularity, students need to understand how a Wikipedia page is created and both its limitations and affordances. For example, Wikipedia can be edited and revised by anyone at any time. Thus, if inaccurate information is inputted into a page, it may go unnoticed for a short while and misinformation could spread. Additionally, a Wikipedia page is not recommended for use as a research citation. Educators should help middle school and high school students understand how to navigate Wikipedia, including how to evaluate the veracity of the content and critique the references.
- **Discerning credible sources:** Given the multitude of websites and sources that students will encounter when they research information, it is imperative that they are able to discern credible from noncredible sources. These lessons must begin early and be repeated often. One helpful tool is called the CRAPP test. In this heuristic, students use the acronym to evaluate their source (see Chapter 5 for additional information on the CRAPP test).
- **Summarizing:** The ability to summarize is both a powerful comprehension strategy and writing tool. Complex in nature, it requires a careful, close analysis of a text, as well as skills for selecting the key important details in

the text. Summarizing is a skill that must be taught as part of an informational writing unit. Various scaffolds, such as the one from Brown and Day (1983), can be used to support students in this process:

1 Read through the text.
2 Delete unimportant information.
3 Delete information that is repeated.
4 Create a category name when a list or series of events is used by an author (e.g., spiders and scorpions would be called "arachnids").
5 Select or create a topic sentence about what was summarized.

● **Note taking:** Note taking is a specific form of summary. It is not a skill that comes to easy to students, and thus explicit instruction is necessary (Boyle, 2013; Rahmani & Sadeghi, 2011). Several strategies support effective note taking, including:

    ○ **Cornell Notes:** This note-taking graphic organizer is a useful scaffold to help students take notes. On the left side of the paper, a key point is written; on the right, the student writes details. At the end of the note-taking period, the student summarizes the information together.

Key Points	Details
Summary	

    ○ **Using visuals:** Dual coding theory (Clark & Paivio, 1991) suggests that the use of imagery when learning something promotes better retention of the concept. As such, teaching students how to create "sketch notes" and use visuals as they are taking notes can promote better understanding and result in more complete writing.

- **Reading and summarizing across multiple sources:** Writers need strategies for how to compare multiple sources and synthesize the information found within them. An informational unit pairs well with reading strategies that focus on nonfiction reading. For example, students should review how to read multiple text structures and how to identify the purpose of the author (to inform, persuade, describe, etc.).
- **Paraphrasing and referencing:** Learning to paraphrase is essential. If students do not know how to paraphrase a direct quote and provide a reference, they might resort to plagiarism or craft a paper that is filled with direct quotes. Thus, helping students understand how to take a direct quote and paraphrase is a key component of teaching informational writing. Additionally, students must understand both the how and why of citations. Disciplinary teachers should not assume that students are well versed in writing citations. All teachers must assume responsibility for teaching and periodically reviewing this essential skill.
- **Discipline-specific vocabulary:** Through writing, students can learn to apply discipline-specific or tier III vocabulary words. For example, a student who is writing all about spiders might learn how to use discipline-specific vocabulary words such as "arachnid," "omnivore," "carnivore," and so on. This not only teaches students how to define words within an informational text but also supports vocabulary acquisition.

Further reading

To extend your knowledge of the ideas presented in this section, read the following:

→ Donovan, C.A. & Smolkin, L.B. (2011). Supporting informational writing in the elementary grades. *The Reading Teacher, 64*(6), 406–416.

Guiding Questions for Discussion

- What are the grade-level expectations for informational writing?
- Is there a continuum of writing development that helps teachers understand what specific writing moves students should be applying?
- When and how often are students taught how to discern credible sources?
- How is informational writing assessed?
- Is the use of discipline-specific vocabulary emphasized in lessons?

 **STOP AND EVALUATE INFORMATIONAL WRITING**

Digital Composition

What Is It?

Digital writing is using digital tools to create various forms of digital texts. Digital texts are multimodal, nonlinear (think hyperlinks on a web page), malleable (can be continuously edited), and shareable (Karchmer-Klein & Shinas, 2019). For example, blogs, Twitter, Facebook, and digital apps are all considered digital texts. Although they function quite differently than traditional texts, they are also consumed quite frequently, especially among adolescents.

Why Does It Matter?

Given how ubiquitous social media and digital tools are, it is essential that students know to how to create and consume the information that is on them. The use of digital tools provides purpose and authenticity to the writing process.

How Is It Assessed?

Assessment of digital composition is dependent upon the purpose. For example, if a student is writing a blog post as part of a unit on informational writing, then the key descriptors of the informational writing assessment would be used. However, this would be coupled with criteria for evaluating a quality blog post.

Aligned Instructional Practices

- **Blogging:** Blogging is an authentic writing activity that allows young authors to communicate content, use digital tools (such as images and hyperlinks), and get audience feedback. Since blogs are public, educators should seek out blogging platforms that are dedicated to student use. For example, Kidblog and Edublog are dedicated to student use. Parents and community members can provide comments to student writing, and the blog can also serve as a writing portfolio (showcasing student growth and demonstrating achievement).
- **Digital presentations:** A salient part of academic life, both in high school and college, is giving presentations. Indeed, many instructors require that students present their learning on a Google Slide, PowerPoint, or Prezi. Therefore, beginning in elementary school, students can learn to create digital presentations and learn essential practices that align to quality production, such as:
  - ❍ How to infuse images with text
  - ❍ How much text is too much on a slide
  - ❍ How to cite references within a slide
  - ❍ How to embed media into a slide show
  - ❍ How to summarize information into a slide
- **Social media:** All students need to learn responsible social media use. However, students can also use social media as a learning tool. In older grades, Twitter can be utilized to discuss specific topics, both in and out of school. Using a personal hashtag (#), teachers can pose questions and ask students to respond and discuss ideas; these discussions can be synchronous or asynchronous (e.g., a live Twitter chat versus a slow Twitter chat). Twitter can also be used for research on a specific topic. For example, an American Government course might ask students to look up the Twitter account of local and national politicians and analyze the content.
- **Digital tools:** Students should learn how to use digital tools to enhance their composition. Digital storytelling, moviemaking, podcasting, and digital

art can all be used to provide meaning to a written text and/or used as a rehearsal for writing, or as an end product. A writing program will leverage current digital tools used for enhancing writing.

Guiding Questions for Discussion

- How are digital tools used to support student writing?
- Do all students have access to technology?
- Are teachers provided adequate training and resources on how to effectively implement digital tools in the writing classroom?

Further reading

To extend your knowledge of the ideas presented in this section, read the following:

→ Hicks, T. (2015). *Assessing students' digital writing: Protocols for looking closely.* New York, NY: Teachers College Press.

⚠ STOP AND EVALUATE DIGITAL TOOLS

Handwriting

What Is It?
In this context, handwriting is referred to as manuscript and cursive writing. Keyboarding is not handwriting.

Why Does It Matter?
Research suggests that handwriting provides a unique contribution to literacy acquisition, as it facilitates children's ability to recognize letters, spell correctly, and write fluently. For example, research has indicated that when children write by hand, they produce a greater quantity of words and express more ideas than when they use a keyboard (Berninger et al., 2009). Moreover, when children write by hand instead of through keyboarding, there is greater neural activity occurring in the child's brain. Additional research has suggested that children who are explicitly taught handwriting are able to recognize the letters of the alphabet more fluently and produce more quality compositions (Limpo & Alves, 2013; Limpo, Alves, & Connelly, 2017). Although handwriting is often viewed as an elementary school activity, handwriting instruction benefits older students up through ninth grade (Alves & Limpo, 2015).

How Is It Assessed?
Handwriting can be assessed by evaluating (1) legibility and (2) fluency (Graham, Weintraub, & Berninger, 1998). For example, the Test of Legible Handwriting (TOLH) (Larsen & Hammill, 1989) is a field-tested measurement that can provide a legibility score that can be used to guide further instruction. Measuring handwriting fluency can be done by looking at how many legible letters and words are correctly written

in a certain amount of time. In this type of standardized assessment, students copy a short sentence or write as many letters as they can in a specified amount of time.

Effective Practices

- **Pencil grasp:** When children begin formal handwriting instruction, they should learn the correct way to grasp a pencil. Thus, children should learn that the thumb and index fingers hold the pencil in place as it lies on the first joint of the middle finger. Incorrect pencil grasps should be avoided.
- **Alphabet letter formation:** When children are learning proper letter formation, it's also a useful time to reinforce letter names and sounds. Preschool children might begin with capital letters first, as these do not have as many curved lines. As kindergarten children advance into alphabetic instruction with phonemic awareness, teachers can spend time on letter formation. Lined paper is a helpful scaffold to assist with letter formation.
- **Legibility:** To encourage greater legibility in young children's writing, teachers should spend time instructing children on how to apply proper spacing between words.
- **Authentic writing:** Sustained engagement in authentic writing tasks will promote writing fluency. Having a well-designed writing framework that provides for authentic daily writing exercise (not on a keyboard) is an essential aspect for developing handwriting.

Guiding Questions for Discussion

- Is handwriting explicitly taught in grades K–6?
- How are teachers trained on handwriting instruction? What resources are available?
- Is handwriting assessed?

> **Further reading**
> *To extend your knowledge of the ideas presented in this section, read the following:*
>
> → Santangelo, T. & Graham, S. (2015). A comprehensive meta-analysis of handwriting instruction. *Educational Psychology Review 28*(2), 225-265.

 **STOP AND EVALUATE HANDWRITING**

Writing Conventions

What Is It?

Writing conventions refers to the structure of written language, including form and function, parts of speech, syntax, spelling, mechanics, and the various rules that govern written language.

Why Does It Matter?

Grammar provides meaning and gives fluidity to written language. To communicate effectively, writers need to understand the function of grammar and apply grammatical conventions in a meaningful and purposeful manner. Research suggests that embedded grammar instruction is more advantageous than grammar instruction taught in isolation (e.g., worksheets and drills) (Graham & Perin, 2007). Grammar taught in isolation was suggested to have no impact on writing quality.

Aligned Instructional Practices

- **Embedded instruction:** The most effective grammar instruction is taught within the context of students' authentic writing. Thus, during writing conferences or in mini-lessons, teachers can provide explicit instruction on revising a sentence to make it grammatically correct with proper conventions. For example, a child who lists a series of nouns in their writing can be taught in a writing conference to use a comma to separate the nouns from one another. Likewise, a teacher might compose a story with the whole class and demonstrate how to use commas in a list. In summary, the command of the conventions of writing such as punctuation, capitalization, and parts of speech can be effectively taught within embedded writing instruction.
- **Sentence combining:** This practice has been consistently shown to have positive effects on student composition. In sentence combining instruction, students are taught how to take simple sentences and combine them together to create more complex sentences. For example, at the emergent level, a first grader might write. "My cat is soft. My cat is orange". During a writing conference, the student would be taught how to use a conjunctive (and) to combine the sentences together. During a whole-group writing activity, a third-grade class could collaborate on strategies to combine sentences to make more complex ones. Sentence combining also works in reverse to help students break down run-on sentences or sentences that are overly wordy. Moreover, sentence combining provides writers with an awareness of syntax and style—how the writing sounds. Practice with combining sentences supports metacognition and fosters revision.
- **Writing as revision:** One of the more difficult aspects of writing, for both children and adults, is understanding that writing is a process of revision. As educators, we should continually stress how our first sentence(s) or drafts are incomplete. Rather, we must show how we are constantly going back into our writing, reading and rereading, and revising along the way. For elementary teachers, this might mean having a collective class piece that you work on throughout a unit and revise together each day. This provides a living example of the "writing as revision" process.

Further reading

To extend educators' knowledge of the ideas presented in this section, the following resources are suggested:

- ➤ Killgallon, D. & Killgallon, J. (2019). *Getting started with middle school sentence composing: A student workbook.* Portsmouth, NH: Heineman.

Guiding Questions

➢ How are writing conventions taught?
➢ Is sentence combining taught within our current writing program?
➢ What are the expectations for grammar and writing conventions at each grade level?
➢ How are writing conventions assessed?

⚠ STOP AND EVALUATE WRITING CONVENTIONS

Frequently Asked Questions About Writing Programs and Practices

How often should writing occur? Writing is a subject like math or history and should be taught and practiced daily.

What is the role of writing prompts? Writers should be provided freedom to write what they want. Thus, when you are teaching narrative writing, writers choose the narrative. When writing argumentative writing, writers choose the argument. Prompts can be used to assess writing, but educators should ensure that the prompt is culturally relevant and aligned to the background experiences of *all* the students in your classroom.

What are mentor texts and how are they used? Mentor texts are books, short articles, or student- or teacher-crafted pieces that provide a solid example of the writing genre being taught. For example, if you are teaching a unit on argumentative writing, it is helpful to teach with examples showing specific craft moves by an author. You might use an opinion piece from the newspaper, deconstruct how the author wrote it, and use it during mini-lessons and conferences.

Should all writing be graded? No, the bulk of writing is drafting. Final pieces can be submitted and evaluated using the guidelines set forth by the teacher.

Is peer feedback a useful practice? It can be effective, but only when students are given the right instruction on how to give appropriate feedback. A useful type of peer review involves having one student serve as an editor for another student's writing. For example, student A will read student B's piece. When the writing is unclear, student A will discuss it with student B, and they will collaborate and find a mutually agreeable way to make the writing more comprehensible. Research has suggested that serving as a peer editor facilitates critical reading and strengthens the writing quality of both the reviewer and the writer.

What is the role of writer's notebooks? A writer's notebook is an essential tool for learning. As young children gain greater command over their handwriting and no longer rely heavily upon pictures to give meaning to their writing, a writer's notebook becomes necessary. Typically, in grades 3 and up, students will use their writer's notebook to generate ideas, experiment with ideas, compose drafts, and document the world around them. Ultimately, a writer's notebook emphasizes the authentic life of writers and develops the "habits of mind" employed by authors. In a writing classroom, students might go through several writing notebooks a year.

What about poetry and creative writing? Although many state standards, including the CCSS, preclude poetry and other forms of creative writing, this doesn't mean it isn't a valuable practice. Teaching poetry and creative writing can teach children to write metaphorically, use literary techniques, and employ literary devices. Moreover, creative writing provides students with the opportunity to express their feelings and share their unique perspectives of the world. Creative writing is a meaningful practice that has educative as well as socioemotional value.

8

Evaluating Classroom Libraries and Independent Reading

Chapter Preview

This brief chapter provides an overview of literacy elements that are necessary for all K–12 classrooms. Research, instructional practices, and aligned assessments are also provided. The following constructs are explored and evaluated:

Independent Reading
Inclusive, Engaging, and Culturally Relevant Classroom Libraries

Evaluation: A three-part rubric is used to evaluate all constructs:

Phase One Rubric:
Evaluates alignment of current instructional practices

Phase Two Rubric:
Rates the quality of the current reading program provided to teachers

Phase Three Rubric:
Rates the quality of the program up for adoption

Introduction

Certain elements of literacy programming and instruction are integral to reading achievement and cut across all areas and grade levels. For example, classroom libraries are not only important for developing comprehension—they also promote fluency, phonics, vocabulary, and engagement, and they should be a key consideration in all literacy classrooms. However, classroom libraries are useless if students are not given daily opportunities to read independently. A strong curriculum audit will attend to the constructs discussed in this chapter.

Independent Reading

What Is It?

Independent reading is defined as an approach where students silently read self-selected book—*with teacher support* in the form of conferences and discussion. Independent reading is often confused with sustained salient reading (SSR), which does not include teacher support. In SSR, the books students read are typically not monitored by the teacher, nor do students respond to the book in writing or discuss it with peers. When the National Reading Panel (2000) made recommendations about the key ingredients of reading instruction, SSR was not one of them. Given its de-emphasis upon teacher support, it is no wonder it was not a recommended practice.

However, research exploring independent reading contexts have found that effective teachers institute the following practices as part of their instruction (Sanden, 2012):

- Establish a comprehensive, well-organized classroom library that all students have access to.
- Establish a quiet reading community. During independent reading time, the classroom is quiet so students can focus; teacher and student interactions (conferring) are conducted unobtrusively.
- Encourage students to read and interact with their peers before, during, and after independent reading.
- Hold readers accountable for what they read through either written response or conferring/discussion.
- Facilitate before, during, and after reading activities that engage readers and help them dig deeper into the text.

Why Does It Matter?

Independent reading is derived from correlational research that suggests reading volume, or the amount children read, has a positive effect on reading achievement (Allington, 2014; Anderson, Wilson, & Fielding, 1988; Cunningham & Stanovich, 1998). Specific research has demonstrated that independent and wide reading promotes fluency (Armbruster, Lehr, & Osborn, 2001), develops vocabulary acquisition (Nagy & Anderson, 1992), and supports knowledge building, which is key to reading comprehension (Squires, 2004). Additional research has noted the following:

- Kim (2006) explored summer reading decline and its relationship to home language. His research suggested that students who did not read voluntarily at home had a greater decline of literacy skills than students who read more often.
- Ivey and Johnston (2013) explored students' perceptions as well as the outcomes of engaged reading within classrooms that focused on choice of independent reading text. Findings in this study suggested that students in engaged reading classrooms (1) frequently and voluntarily read books in and out of school, (2) developed a positive reading identity, (3) expanded their knowledge base, and (4) spontaneously discussed what they were reading with peers and other individuals. Additional increases in the state standardized test scores were also observed for students in the engaged reading curriculum.

- The effects of voluntary reading are even more robust when students are supported by teachers with scaffolded instruction (Kim & White, 2008). Thus, voluntary reading is important, but has a greater impact when it is coupled with expert teaching.

How Is It Assessed?

Assessment will be unique to the grade level. Moreover, the purpose of assessment is important. In kindergarten and first grade as readers are learning to crack the code, independent reading might include practice with grade-level texts, as well opportunities to self-select books with various complexity levels. In these contexts, children might study pictures and photographs, explore a familiar story, and listen to audiobooks. As readers progress to fully automatic readers, independent reading can be assessed by reader-response notebooks, teacher conferences, and monitoring the quantity of texts read.

Aligned Instructional Approaches

- **Student surveys:** In her book, *The Book Whisperer* (2010), Donalyn Miller makes an impassioned argument for embedding independent reading into the literacy classroom. She notes that her sixth-grade students are required to read 40 books a year (and many go above and beyond that). However, to foster this success, she spends time surveying students about their interests in and out of school and uses those responses make book recommendations for students. Please see Appendix B for an example of a survey you could use for gauging your students' interests.
- **Text selection:** Since independent reading is contingent on students reading (no fake reading allowed!), they will need support selecting texts that sustain their attention for a fair amount of time. As educators, we can support student engagement by implementing the following:
  ○ **Avoid leveled classroom libraries:** Once students are reading fluently (by third grade), instructional-level texts are unnecessary. There is little research to support the efficacy of reading levels. Although some teachers level their library and only allow student access to certain levels for independent reading, this practice is not rooted in research. Students do not have "one" reading level. Depending upon their background knowledge, a student may be able to read a book that is much higher than a reading level may indicate. Instructionally, levels may be useful for specific lessons; however, all children should be given access to a variety of texts across levels and topics. Consider placing texts in categories about topics and genres and then supporting children as they choose the right book to read. In the next section, I detail how to create an inclusive and engaging classroom library.
  ○ **Maintain an awareness of popular children's books:** Your school librarian and the local children's librarian, as well as websites like the American Library Association or the Children's Cooperative Book Center, provide resources for teachers.

    ○ **Conduct frequent book talks:** Read books and pitch them to your students. Book talks don't need to be lengthy (a couple of minutes at most). The book talk should include the cover, the genre, and what you liked about it. As your classroom community gets stronger, have your students give the book talks. Keep a list, either on an anchor chart or digitally, to help students remember which books were pitched.

    ○ **Provide lessons on how to select a great book:** Some students might only select a book because of the cover or because it "looks easy." Spend time helping students think about what their interests are and how to read the first page or so of a book to see if the words are decodable and understandable.

- **Reading outside of the classroom:** Although educators might believe that at-home reading is a challenge, some research has suggested that a comprehensively designed out-of-school reading framework—one that emphasizes access, choice, discussion, and book talks—can increase out-of-school reading volume (Fisher & Frey, 2018).

- **Depth of understanding:** Independent reading, by its nature, facilitates students' knowledge development, which is a critical aspect of reading comprehension. However, specific practices (not busy work) can be attached to independent reading so background knowledge is developed. For instance, students should be responding to what they read through book club discussion and through writing in reader response notebooks. Teachers can also provide guiding questions that ask students to reflect on what they are reading. However, it is important that any of these responses (discussion or written response) should not be overly time consuming Thus, avoid "inferencing" or "main idea" worksheets, packets, and excessive use of sticky notes. Writing about reading or dialogic discussions should be an enrichment for comprehension and not an exercise in "stuff" kids must do.

- **Monitored by teachers:** For independent reading to be effective, teachers need to monitor student reading volume to ensure reading is taking place. If students are not reading, then the teacher must consider alternative ways to support reading development (e.g., small-group instruction). Teachers should have a well-designed method of assessing in-class independent reading volume.

- **Reading logs: Yes or no?** Some teachers use these as an accountability mechanism with the idea that if students are required to document their school and at-home reading, they will read more. Rewards or prizes are often attached to completing the reading log. However, there is no research to suggest that the use of reading logs improves reading volume. Indeed, some research has suggested just the opposite: The use of mandatory reading logs reduces motivation and promotes a negative attitude towards independent reading (Pak & Weseley, 2012). Given the paucity of research on the practice, reading logs are *not* suggested as effective.

- **Inclusive/engaging classroom library:** For students to read a lot, they must be interested in what they read. Providing classroom libraries that offer a variety of texts can foster engagement and reading volume (see later for additional information on classroom libraries).

- **Audiobooks: Yes or no?** Audiobooks can be a support that some readers use during independent reading. Research has suggested that audiobooks can positively affect reading experiences and provide exposure to new vocabulary and develop background knowledge on a topic (Whittingham, Huffman, Christensen, & McAllister, 2013). However, the purpose of using the audiobook should be considered. If a middle school child wants to read a book that is written with difficult words above his decoding ability, then providing an audiobook can be a great way to engage him and develop background knowledge. However, this practice must be paired with decoding and fluency instruction that targets the student's needs. In sum, audiobooks should be carefully aligned to the word-level reading needs of the students, and their purpose should be carefully reflected upon. Following are some suggestions for how to appropriately use audiobooks:

○ Teachers should scaffold audiobook reading the same way they would for students traditionally reading a text (e.g., use surveys, give book talks, etc.).

○ Students should be discussing and responding to the audiobooks in a reader-response journal.

○ Students who are not yet automatic word readers should concurrently be getting phonics instruction and practice applying skills within connected texts to develop accuracy and fluency.

Inclusive, Engaging, and Culturally Relevant Classroom Libraries

What Is It?

A classroom library houses multiple texts, trade books, and other reading materials and includes a range of reading levels and genres. The classroom library is accessible to all children.

Why Does It Matter?

For independent reading to be successful, teachers need a library filled with engaging books that children will want to read. A well-stocked classroom library supports students' reading volume (Allington, 2014; Krashen, 1998) and positively affects reading achievement (Guthrie, Schafer, Von Secker & Alban, 2000).

Moreover, classroom libraries can promote a culturally relevant pedagogy. When libraries are diverse and intentionally curated to represent the diversity of the world that surrounds us, they open the world for children by allowing them to view people, places, and cultures, as well as the natural world that might be unfamiliar (Bishop, 1990). This access to knowledge through books is critical, as it supports empathy of others and builds background knowledge—which underpins successful reading comprehension. Unfortunately, most of the books that are published for children privilege the inclusion of only white characters.

How Is It Assessed?

The content of the classroom library is essential, and school districts should be auditing classroom libraries to ensure they represent all children within the classroom walls, as well as children and people who live in other communities, cities, states, and countries. Scholastic Publishing, the largest publisher of children's books, recommends that there are at least 20 books for every student in a classroom.

One way to assess a classroom library both for quantity and quality is to have teachers collect data about the books that are housed in their classroom library. A tally table, like the ones shown next, can be used for this purpose.

How many genres are represented in your classroom library?					
Realistic Fiction	Graphic Novels	Fantasy/ Science Fiction	Mystery/ Adventure	Nonfiction	Other (magazines, poetry)

How many of the following themes or communities are represented in books in your classroom library?	
African Culture	
Arab Heritage	
Asian and Asian American	
Bullying	
Christianity	
Judaism	
Muslim	
Buddhism	
LGBTQIA	
Hispanic/LatinX	
Immigration	
Native North Americans	
People with Physical Disabilities	
Race/Racism	

What levels* are represented in your classroom library?			
Emergent	Early	Early/Fluent	Advanced Fluent

*Guided reading levels, Lexile levels, or another system can be used.

Aligned Instructional Practices

- **Inclusive classroom libraries:** Rudine Sims Bishop (1990) used the metaphor "windows, mirrors, and doors" to explain the role of children's literature in children's lives.

  Books are sometimes windows, offering views of worlds that may be real or imagined, familiar or strange. These windows are also sliding glass doors, and readers have only to walk through in imagination to become part of whatever world has been created or recreated by the author. When lighting conditions are just right, however, a window can also be a mirror. Literature transforms human experience and reflects it back to us, and in that reflection we can see our own lives and experiences as part of the larger human experience. Reading, then, becomes a means of self-affirmation, and readers often seek their mirrors in books. (p. ix)

One way to apply this metaphor is to examine how the books in your classroom library support inclusion (Moller, 2016) and attend to issues of race, gender, disability, mental health, and so on. For example, *The Snowy Day* (Keats, 1962) is a book that features people of color as the central character. The story, however, does not address how the family copes with racism or discrimination. Thus, the book serves as a "people are people" model for children's literature (see later). As an educator, it would be important to have several other books in your classroom library where people of color are the central characters but the story might focus upon their distinctive cultural experiences or how they cope with discrimination.

Lastly, it is important for educators to not just think of inclusive libraries as those that have a variety of cultures but also include topics of gender, sexual identification, disability, and so on. Following is an example of a model (Moller, 2016) based on Bishop's (1990) work that can be used to evaluate the inclusivity of a classroom library. The model includes four categories based on themes and topics in the books.

	Consciously interracial (or intercultural)	People are people	Distinctive experience of being within a cultural group	Coping with discrimination such as racism and homophobia
Text Characteristics	Diverse characters in the text illustrate a multicultural society.	Underrepresented groups are important to the text, but the culture represented is no different from the dominant one.	Focus is upon highlighting a cultural group. The language, experiences, and values of the culture.	Focus of the text is to demonstrate the difficulties of living as a racial minority or dealing with LGBTQIA discrimination.
Examples	*The Day You Begin* by Jacqueline Woodson	*Peekaboo Morning* by Rachel Isadora	*Under My Hijab* by Hena Khan	*The Harvey Milk Story* by Kari Krakow

- **Select engaging nonfiction texts:** In many classrooms, fiction dominates the library (Doiron, 2003) and instruction (Duke, 2000), yet research has found that students often note a preference for nonfiction reading (Worthy, Moorman, & Turner, 1999). Thus, building a collection of nonfiction books is essential for advancing your students' wide reading. To ensure a rich nonfiction library, researchers have suggested that educators apply the five A's when selecting books:
  1 **Authority:** Who wrote the book, and what is their background to provide authority on the topic?

2 **Accuracy:** How accurate is the information provided?

3 **Appropriateness:** How does the author relay information to the reader, and is it appropriate for the classroom audience?

4 **Artistry:** How does the author's writing shape the artistry of the text? Is it crafted for engagement?

5 **Appearance:** Is the text visually appealing and one that students will want to read?

- **Multiple text levels:** Children should be provided access to books written below, at, and above their reading level. Thus, a strong classroom library will provide books with multiple reading levels. There is no research to suggest that a classroom library should be leveled. Rather, housing books by topic or genre is an effective approach. Reading levels should be used by the teacher only for specific instructional purposes, and students should be reading or listening to a wide variety of books each day.

Guiding Questions for Discussion

- Are libraries inclusive in most classrooms?
- Do all teachers have a rich classroom library?
- Are classroom libraries audited for inclusion?
- Are all children in our school represented in books within classroom libraries?
- Is independent reading a focus at all grade levels?
- Is reading volume monitored?
- Are students given choice over what they read?

Further reading

To extend your knowledge of the ideas presented in this section, read the following:

→ Bishop, R.S. (1990). Mirrors, windows, and sliding glass doors. *Perspectives*, 6(3), ix–xi.

⚠ **STOP AND EVALUATE CLASSROOM LIBRARIES AND INDEPENDENT READING**

9

Literacy Leadership Team Meeting #2: Concluding the Evaluation and Making Recommendations

Chapter Preview

In this chapter, the literacy leadership team (LLT) will conclude the evaluation and provide a recommendation. The following actions will comprise this meeting:

- Finish Evaluation
- Discuss Results
- Make Recommendation
- Plan Next Steps

Concluding the Evaluation and Making Recommendations

Welcome to our second literacy leadership meeting. This full-day meeting continues where the first meeting left off: evaluation of current materials and instructional practices. By the end of today's meeting, we will understand the curriculum and instruction that our district needs. There are various possibilities for this. To begin, the present materials might be satisfactory but certain aspects of instruction might need more support. Or the current materials might be satisfactory in some areas, but some areas have holes. Thus, new materials will need to be reviewed to fill those curricula holes. Another possibility is that our present literacy materials are problematic or outdated and a new literacy program needs to be ordered. Collectively, the group will make recommendations to the literacy leadership team leader. The meeting next month will review new materials for adoption, and then a final recommendation will be made.

Opening the Meeting Today: A Community Builder

You and your colleagues have been working at reviewing the district's current instructional materials and practices. Invariably, ideas, questions, and/or worries were triggered throughout this process. Given the intensity of evaluating a literacy curriculum, respond to the following statement using the compass points activity provided next. The facilitator of the LLT will post a chart paper in a visible location in the room for participants to place their sticky notes on.

When we finish evaluating the current literacy materials and practices, then we will have meaningful recommendations for making our school's literacy programming stronger.

E = Excited: What excites about this statement? What is positive about it?
W = Worrisome: What worries you about this statement?
N = Need to Know: What else do you need to know about this statement? What would help you?
S = Suggestion for Moving Forward: What is a suggestion you have regarding this statement?

Review Group Norms

The leader of the LLT will read the group norms out loud. In your small groups, discuss areas that are working well and areas that could be strengthened. The leader of the LLT can go around to each table and ask how the groups are doing. Any group that is struggling to collaborate positively should work together with the facilitator of the LLT to resolve conflicts.

Continue Evaluation

For the next one to two hours, continue to work on the materials and instruction evaluation process. Following is a reminder of the steps for completing this process:

1   Using the "Individual Score Sheet," each member of the expert team provides an individual score about the construct. Individual comments can also be written down.
2   The chair collects the scores, average the ratings, and inputs them on the "Composite Score Sheet."
3   The chair of the group will also curate the qualitative comments and provide them below the average score of the group.
4   Once the expert group has evaluated each construct provided in the chapter, the chair gives all forms to the facilitator of the LLT.
5   The facilitator of the LLT should record these scores on a digital spreadsheet for future reference.

Lunch Break

After lunch is over (and assuming the evaluation process is complete), collaborate on the following tasks:

Small-Group Documentation: Each small group in the LLT group should create an anchor chart with the main findings of the group. This can include the average rating of each construct evaluated, as well as a synthesis of the main qualitative responses (comments) that evaluators noted. When the anchor chart is complete, hang it on the wall.

Large-Group Gallery Walk: The entire LLT should engage in a gallery walk of the findings. Members of the LLT can post comments on any of the anchor charts. These can be affirmations of the scores, surprises noted, or questions.

Large-Group Discussion: Each chair of the team should lead the entire LLT in a question-and-answer session of the main findings within their section. This is an opportunity for everyone to understand what was uncovered in the evaluation, pose questions, and offer input.

Reconvene Small Groups: Once the large group discussion is over, small groups should work together to identify what needs to be done. The following four options are possible:

Option A: The review of the current curriculum showed all materials are aligned to research. Instruction is sound and no additional steps need to occur.

Option B: The review of the current materials and instructional practices discovered that materials are satisfactory, but instruction needs to be strengthened. Thus, recommendations for professional development will be made by the group.

Option C: The review of the current materials and instruction found that some or all of the materials are unsatisfactory. Instruction also needs to be strengthened in certain areas. New materials will need to be evaluated. Recommendations for new review of material and instructional support will made.

Option D: The review found that some or all the materials are unsatisfactory, but instruction is sound. Recommendations for new review of materials will be provided by the group.

Literacy review of new materials: If the LLT has decided that new materials for the literacy program need to be considered, they will need to investigate publishers of materials and provide a recommendation to the curriculum director of what programs they would like to review. The process might look like this:

Data Needed (Task)	Person(s) Responsible	Due Date
Order the following reading programs for review: ABC Reading Company XYZ Reading Company 123 Reading College	Curriculum director (facilitator of the LLT)	11/15 (next leadership meeting)

If you are only considering one area of your reading program for revision, the tasks might look like this:

Data Needed (Task)	Person(s) Responsible	Due Date
Phonics Programs for Review	Tanya Ashley	11/15 (next leadership meeting)
Scope and Sequence for Phonics	Sam	11/15 (next leadership meeting)
Decodable Texts for Review	Jose Katherine	11/15 (next leadership meeting)
Three Professional Development Books About Phonics	Jade	11/15 (next leadership meeting)

Instructional practice needs: After documenting material needs, the LLT must consider instructional practices. What did the review reveal about professional development needs? What type of professional learning would best support educators as they work to improve their instruction—professional development days, ongoing coaching, or both? These will be considered for both the pilot and the eventual rollout of a new program or materials. (Appendix D provides a blank template of this document.)

Professional Learning Needs	Grade Level	Rationale	Professional Development? Coaching? Both?
Phonics	K–3	Surveys revealed teachers wanted more resources for systematic instruction.	Both. A new phonics program along with ongoing professional learning and coaching would help improve instruction across the board.

10

Literacy Leadership Team Meeting #3: Evaluating the New Literacy Program or Materials

---

Chapter Preview

In this chapter, the literacy leadership team (LLT) will review new reading materials for potential adoption. They will use the phase three rubrics provided in Appendix C. The following actions will comprise this meeting:

- Evaluate New Literacy Materials/Programs
- Share Findings
- Make Recommendations
- Order Materials for the Pilot

Evaluating a New Reading Program

The purpose of this meeting is to evaluate a new reading program. Using the phase three rubric, teams will evaluate how their designated construct (e.g., early literacy skills, vocabulary, etc.) is approached in a new reading program.

Agenda

    I   **Community builder**
   II **Guidance/directives:** The facilitator of the LLT provides a timeline to the teams for working and reporting back.
 III **Teams evaluate:** Using the phase three rubric, begin the evaluation of the new curricula.
       1 Evaluate the new reading materials that are being considered for adoption.
       2 Provide an average rating for each construct (e.g., oral language).

    3   The chair of the team records individual scores on a rating sheet.

    4   The chair of the team averages the scores of each individual rating and records them on a "Group Composite Score Sheet."

IV   **Share findings:** Each team should report their final recommendation to the large group. Build a consensus on a program for adoption. The team makes a final recommendation on a new reading or writing program. If more than one program was strongly recommended, the curriculum director (or facilitator of the LLT) may decide to pilot more than one program and make a final decision once the pilot is complete.

V   **Conclude meeting:** Report scores with final recommendations to the facilitator of the LLT, who will then order materials for the February pilot meeting. Chapter 11 provides detailed directions on preparing for the first pilot meeting.

11

Pilot-Testing Recommendations

Chapter Preview

In this chapter, the process of pilot-testing a new reading program is described. This process is extended over several months and is sequenced in the following order:

1. Materials ordered for the pilot
2. Pilot team assembled
3. Pilot meeting #1
4. Pilot testing begins
5. Monthly review meetings
6. Final recommendations made

The audit is complete, recommendations were made, and now the pilot begins. Conducting a pilot test is an important step, as it gives you the opportunity to roll out a small-scale implementation of new materials (and practices) while gathering important data about the positives and negatives of the program. More specifically, a pilot test provides the following benefits:

1. The pilot ensures that any potential problems in a new curriculum will be spotted and avoided.
2. The pilot allows you to compare two or more literacy programs in multiple classrooms and analyze which one more fully aligns to the needs of your school district.
3. The pilot allows educators to have another voice in selecting a new literacy program.

Table 11.1 Action Steps for Pilot Testing Materials

	Task	Person(s) Responsible
January	Literacy leadership team (LLT) and expert groups make official recommendations about programs to pilot Materials for pilot-testing are ordered	LLT
February–May	Materials are pilot-tested in select classrooms Data on materials and programs being piloted are captured and monitored.	Reading specialists/coaches Teacher leaders (pilot-testing program) Building administrators
June	Final recommendation made Create curriculum map Create assessment plan Order new literacy program/ curriculum	Pilot team Curriculum director (facilitator of literacy evaluation)

4 The pilot will ensure that reading specialists or instructional coaches can troubleshoot or plan for any potential issues that may arise during the full-scale rollout.

5 The pilot will help shape the professional learning needs of the teachers during the full-scale rollout.

Table 11.1 begins where the evaluation left off. It illustrates the action steps between the pilot test and complete program adoption. Each school district is different, so you may need to adjust these times to align to your specific school district needs.

Preparing for the First Pilot Meeting

Before the pilot can begin, the facilitator of the literacy evaluation (typically the curriculum director) will need to prepare for the pilot. Table 11.2 provides a checklist for preparing for the pilot and the first meeting. They will need to decide upon the number of classrooms that will pilot-test materials, what materials will be pilot-tested, and order materials. Once that is complete, they will need to assemble a team who will lead the pilot initiative. This should be a smaller group that includes reading specialists and/or literacy coaches, teacher leaders, and administrators. This team will oversee how the pilot will proceed and provide data about how the program is working.

Who Should Be on the Pilot Team?

- Building reading specialists or literacy coaches: They will help plan the rollout, observe lessons, and reflect weekly with teachers on the program piloted.

Table 11.2 Preparing for the February Meeting

Preparing for the February Pilot Meeting		
Task	**Person Responsible**	**Check When Complete**
Prior to first pilot meeting, decide how many classrooms will pilot-test materials	Facilitator of the literacy evaluation with reading specialists or literacy coaches	
Order enough materials from each vendor if you are comparing programs	Facilitator of the literacy evaluation	
Assemble the pilot team (see earlier) and set a date for the first meeting	Facilitator of the literacy evaluation with reading specialists or literacy coaches	
Create agenda for first pilot meeting	Facilitator of the literacy evaluation team	

- Building administrators: They will help plan the rollout and reflect with teachers about the program pilot-tested during monthly meetings.
- Two or more teachers from each grade level (or elementary, middle, and high school depending upon the size of your district) who will pilot-test materials in their classroom. They will test out materials and evaluate the program being used.

February Meeting

At this meeting, reading specialists, literacy coaches, teacher leaders, and administrators meet to review materials and create an action plan for the pilot test. If you are pilot-testing more than one program, make sure that each program is tested by more than one teacher so a fair recommendation can be provided. Table 11.2 indicates the steps needed to prepare for this meeting.

Monthly Meetings March–May

Once per month, the teacher pilot-testing the new program should complete the form in Table 11.3 and submit it to the building principal or reading specialist/literacy coach. A copy of this form can be found in Appendix D. These data will help anchor the discussion when final recommendations are made. As evaluation forms are being submitted, the core pilot group should meet and track and monitor the data on the strengths and weaknesses of each program.

June Final Recommendation Meeting

In June, the group will meet, review the data, and make a final recommendation about the best program/materials and needs for ongoing professional development.

Table 11.3 Literacy Program Evaluation Form

Literacy Program Pilot Evaluation Form (due at the end of the month)	
Program Name	
Grade Level	
Skill Focus	
Aligned to Standards?	
Engaging/Culturally Relevant Materials?	
Differentiates?	
Supports Strong Instructional Practice?	
Please rate the program: **Highly recommend** **Recommend** **Recommend with reservations** **Do not recommend**	
Strengths of the Program:	
Weaknesses of the Program:	

12

Implementing a New Literacy Program: Professional Learning and Coaching

Chapter Preview

In this chapter, the process for rolling out a new literacy program is described. This process is extended over several months and includes the following:

- Developing a curriculum map
- Creating an assessment plan
- Designing year-long professional learning
- Creating a coaching cycle
- Rolling out the new curriculum

Once you decide upon a new literacy program, you will need to think about creating a curriculum map, planning professional learning, and establishing coaching expectations. Following is a timeline to help you think about the critical steps involved in the next phase:

Summer Work Group Action Plan		
June	Create curriculum map Create assessment plan Order new literacy program/ curriculum	Curriculum director Reading specialists/literacy coaches Building administrator Teacher leaders
July	Create year-long professional learning plan Create coaching cycle/expectations	Reading specialists/literacy coaches Curriculum director Building administrators Teacher leaders
August–June	Implement new program Provide continuous K–12 professional learning Provide ongoing literacy coaching	Reading specialists/literacy coaches Teacher leaders

Before the summer work begins, the curriculum director (or the facilitator of the evaluation) will need to determine who will be on the summer workgroup. This group will collaborate to develop a year-long action plan for unrolling the curriculum and providing professional learning and coaching. Considerations for this work include:

- Areas of the curriculum that require new or shifting instructional practices.
- Grade-level focus areas.
- Instructional practices that were determined weaker in the survey. Use the completed instructional needs document to ascertain this.
- If you are adopting both a reading and writing curriculum, you may want year 1 to focus solely on the reading program and year 2 to focus on writing. This might ensure greater buy-in (and less stress) from teachers.

June

In this month, the curriculum director or school administrator will need to determine the number of days that will be provided for professional learning and the logistics therein (e.g., substitute teachers, onsite or offsite professional learning, paid days before the school year begins for professional learning). These administrative decisions will need to be made at the onset of this process, as this information will be needed by the literacy coaches for planning. To begin, I would establish two work groups: (1) curriculum sequence and (2) assessment.

➢ **Develop grade-level scope and sequence with curriculum map:** This work group will need to align the new curriculum to a month-by-month scope and sequence at each grade level. They should begin by breaking apart the curriculum and deciding upon the units and instructional time required for each unit. Additionally, they should deconstruct specific areas within the units (e.g., foundational skills, comprehension, vocabulary) and map when they are taught. Lastly, they will need to align the curriculum to the state standards and benchmark assessments. This map will be reviewed and revised as the curriculum is rolled out.

➢ **Develop/refine benchmark assessments:** This work group will need to refine existing benchmark assessments or develop new ones. What literacy assessments will teachers be required to administer, and when will they be administered?

July

In this month, the professional learning plan and coaching expectations will be established. Thus, the topics for professional learning days, their duration, and how they will be structured will be critical. Of course, it will be important to leave some professional learning days open so specific needs can be addressed as they arise.

➢ **Plan professional learning:** Once your professional learning days are set, create a list of topics that will need to be emphasized at each professional learning session. This list will be unique for each school district, but some areas will be common for all, as shown in the following table.

Suggested Months	Suggested Topics
August	Introduce curriculum map Introduce assessment plan Introduce new literacy program Grade-level breakout sessions for beginning the year with the new curriculum
September	Assessment Working with coaches, Continuing the rollout, unit by unit
October–December	Continuing the rollout, unit by unit
January	Troubleshooting, teacher choice of professional learning
February–May	Continuing the rollout, unit by unit.
June	Revising the curriculum map and/or assessment plan

➢ **Create the coaching plan:** An important aspect to a successful curriculum adoption is literacy coaching. Elena Aguilar (2013) created a ten-step work plan that literacy leaders can use to support teachers' professional learning goals. Following is a condensed version of that process and how it would be aligned to a new curriculum rollout. If you are in a district with many teachers and a limited number of coaches, you might need to have coaches work with grade-level teams to accomplish these steps.

1 Identify specific curriculum and instructional areas that teachers at each grade level will need coaching on. Since the new curriculum is the focus, coaches will want to look at survey results and ascertain which areas of the curriculum where teachers need support. For example, if your district is adopting a new reading program with a rich phonics component, this might be the area of focus in first grade. In kindergarten, phonemic awareness might be the focus.

2 Identify standards and assessments. Part of the coaching conversation will be to work with teachers on both the new curriculum and the assessments. Thus, consider how to bring the new or revised benchmark assessments into the work plan and discuss how they are aligned to the standards.

3 Teachers Set Goals. With the teacher or grade-level teams, the coach can help teachers establish professional learning goals that help support a successful implementation of new materials or a program. The coach can use teacher surveys and areas of need to help educators write this goal.

4 Coaches plot the learning. Independently, coaches will work to create actionable steps to help teachers meet their goals. As such, the coach will need to chunk the learning into manageable parts based on the knowledge base of teachers and the current practices that they routinely implement.

5   Determine indicators of progress. Coaches work with teachers (or an individual teacher) and establish what artifacts will be used to determine if the goal is being met. Beyond the benchmark assessments, what else will teachers use to indicate progress towards their goal. Coaches write-up a plan. Once teachers and the coach have discussed their goals and needs for the new curriculum rollout, the coach will need to write up a plan that will illustrate how coaching will proceed to support teacher's needs.

Further reading

To extend knowledge of the coaching ideas presented in this section, the following resource is suggested:

➢ Aguilar, E. (2013). *The art of coaching: Effective strategies for school transformation.* Hoboken, NJ: Jossey-Bass.

August: Roll Out New Literacy Initiatives

Congratulations! Your commitment to a comprehensive evaluation process has you ready for a successful rollout of your new literacy program and practices. As you begin this journey, remember that with all things new, there may be a few bumps in the road. However, through ongoing collaboration, your literacy program and refreshed instructional practices will have a positive impact on the students and stakeholders within your school district.

Afterword

Throughout this book, you have explored research behind the *why* of instruction. You have reflected on your own instructional practices, reflected on the practices of your colleagues, and considered how curricula materials can best align to develop successful readers and writers. Moreover, you have learned how the field of literacy has evolved as our understanding of literacy acquisition grows.

What this book has not touched upon is the passion and magic that you must bring with you into the classroom to do your best work as a literacy educator. That is what is referred to as the *art of teaching*; this text has focused a great deal on the science of literacy learning. Yet we know that effective teachers are more than stewards of science—they are also instructional artists who foster positive relationships with students. As such, a healthy classroom community and energized instruction must underpin the work we do as educators. Although this book has delved mainly into cognitive aspects of reading and writing, the affective aspects of learning—including motivation and engagement—are essential to keep at the forefront of literacy instruction.

A goal of this text was to help deconstruct the complexities involved in learning to read. We began the evaluation journey by discussing how a strong reading curriculum needs to be aligned with instruction that develops foundational skills, such as concepts about print, phonological awareness, alphabet knowledge, phonics, spelling, and fluency. We learned about the importance of providing children with instruction that meets their unique needs as readers and writers. Powerful, evidence-based instruction at the K–3 level can ensure that students will be able to crack the code of written language. This complex cognitive act is essential for literacy acquisition.

However, we also noted that cracking the code and learning the constrained skills described in Chapter 3 are not enough. For children to develop as fully literate adults, they need ongoing engagement in learning communities that engage in rich classroom talk, knowledge building, and vocabulary development. Invariably, these learning communities must build upon students' strengths and unique funds of knowledge. As such, we discussed how our instruction must leverage inclusive, engaging, and culturally relevant practices.

We also explored how comprehension instruction must work to build students' background knowledge, as this is elemental to proficient reading. We discussed how the teaching of cognitive strategies for comprehension is insufficient on its own. Rather, students need ongoing knowledge development where multiple texts on a topic are read, analyzed, and discussed. Moreover, our students need access to engaging, diverse, and culturally relevant texts. Our classroom libraries must reflect the students within our buildings and the world beyond.

We also learned that instruction in the writing process is a non-negotiable and that the writing community we establish is foundational for success. In these writing spaces, all students are afforded daily opportunities to learn the strategies of effective writing and are given frequent feedback on their development as writers. As we have learned, this instruction can be powerfully connected to the reading work students are completing within their English language arts (ELA) and content area classrooms.

No literacy program is adequate without a writing framework, scope and sequence, and rich curriculum materials.

Even though the evaluation and adoption are complete and new literacy materials are in place, there is always work to be done. Unfortunately, there is no silver bullet for literacy achievement—and this process is no exception. Invariably, there will be some limitations to a quality literacy program, and districts must remain mindful of those areas. Moreover, educators deserve ongoing opportunities for professional learning. No literacy curriculum can safeguard against poor instructional practice—I repeat—no literacy curriculum can safeguard against poor instructional practice.

As such, educators need instructional coaching that can help shift their teaching habits and develop stronger ones. However, we must also remember that changing teacher practices takes time. For example, Dylan Wiliam and Siobhan Leahy (2015) have written about the power of embedding formative assessment techniques into classroom instruction. Nevertheless, they noted that any tweak to instructional practices can be onerous and time consuming for teachers to adopt:

> …we have to accept that teacher learning is slow. In particular, for changes in practice—as opposed to knowledge—to be lasting, it must be integrated into a teacher's existing routines, and this takes time. Many people involved in professional development are familiar with the experience of encouraging teachers to try out new ideas and seeing them enacted [as] they visit teachers' classrooms only to learn shortly afterward that the teachers revert to their former practices. (p. 18)

Even though new literacy materials have been adopted, educators need and deserve ongoing quality professional development that honors their expertise and moves their learning forward. District administrators must dedicate resources for sustainable coaching cycles and engage in periodic curricula reviews to ensure that the highest levels of learning are taking place.

In closing, my hope is that this text has sparked spirited discussions and that the literacy evaluation, new materials, and rollout have shaped instructional practices for the better. Ultimately, it is my greatest hope that this process has helped the children in your classrooms embark on a successful journey towards literacy acquisition while positively transforming your work as literacy educators and administrators.

Appendix A: Pre-Evaluation Form

Community Builders

1   **Meeting #1: Compass Points**. On chart paper, write the following: "The Literacy Leadership Team is charged with evaluating the reading program and instructional practices in the district." Now, on the same chart paper, create a "compass" of:

E = Excited: What excites about this statement? What is positive about it?
W = Worrisome: What worries you about this statement?
N = Need to Know: What else do you need to know about this statement? What would help you?
S = Suggestion for Moving Forward: What is a suggestion you have regarding this statement?

Have each individual write their responses on a sticky note. When they are done, they can place their ideas on the chart paper. Once the entire group is finished, they can read the ideas presented and discuss at tables. As the facilitator of the process, you may want to look for themes in these statements and address any concerns that are revealed.

2   **Meeting #2:** Using a name fold, write your name in the middle of one of the folded signs. Then, in each corner, use words, pictures, or quotes that represents a major life moment/occurrence that has gotten you to this point. You can go back in time as long as you need to. Then, on the side that is not visible to the rest of us, write down one dream you have for this school year. Individuals can share at their tables or in small groups.

Additional community builders that are short and sweet:

- Find something on your person that both best represents you and least represents you. Explain to the group.
- What is something that you value about the educator on your left?
- What is a celebration for this past year?
- When have you been challenged? By whom? What did it feel like? When do you challenge others? Why do you challenge?

Hypothesis Generation

Group Name

What are you noticing about the assessment data?

What are you noticing about the instructional survey data?

Among group members, what are three to five hypothesis about the literacy component you are reviewing?

1
2
3
4
5

Literacy Achievement Data

LITERACY ACHIEVEMENT DATA						
ASSESSMENT USED:						
YEAR:						
SUBGROUP or DISTRICT-WIDE						
NAME OF SUBGROUP (if appropriate)						
Grade	**Number of Students**	**% Proficient**	**Number of Students**	**% Proficient**	**Number of Students**	**% Proficient**
Literacy Area:	Reading	Reading	Writing	Writing	Total ELA	Total ELA
Building Name						
3						
4						
5						
6						
7						
8						

Appendix B: Surveys and Tools

Administrator Survey

Please respond to the following open-ended questions:

1   What are the strengths of the current English language arts (ELA) program in your school or district?

2   What areas do you believe need strengthening? Be specific (e.g., phonics or vocabulary) and state why.

3   How are students who struggle with literacy provided support, and what improvements could be made to this structure?

4   How consistent is the ELA instruction from teacher to teacher?

5   What opportunities for professional learning or coaching are needed?

6   What is the most pressing ELA need in your district?

7   How would rate the current ELA program (favorably, neutral, or unfavorably)? Elaborate on your response.

Literacy Practices Survey

Foundational Skills

This purpose of this survey is to better understand how emergent reading instruction is being implemented within the district. Your responses are completely anonymous. Your honesty is appreciated.

Grade level:

How much time do you spend per week on the following aspects of reading instruction (within your core instruction):

	Daily	Frequently (2–4 times a week)	Sometimes (1 time a week)	Infrequently (once per month)	Never	I am unfamiliar with this practice
Teaching letter and sound identification						
Teaching phonological awareness in small groups						
Teaching phonemic awareness in small groups						
Using shared reading to teach print concepts						
Teaching children how to use invented spelling in their writing						
Providing time for children to apply invented spelling in their writing						
Teaching handwriting						
Providing explicit phonics instruction in small groups (outside of guided reading or other approaches)						
Providing opportunities for fluency development (e.g., choral reading, reader's theater, repeated readings)						

Rate your agreement with the following statements:

	Strongly Agree	Agree	Unsure	Disagree	Strongly Disagree	N/A
I use a variety of instructional strategies to teach the many aspects of phonological awareness.						
The district has provided me with a sequence (easy to hard) for teaching phonological awareness skills.						
I am provided adequate materials for teaching phonological awareness.						

I rely upon a sequence for teaching alphabetic knowledge (letters and sounds).					
I rely upon a method for teaching handwriting.					
I rely upon a scope and sequence for teaching phonics patterns.					
I know methods for teaching phonics and implement them daily.					
I am provided adequate materials for teaching phonics.					
I know how to explicitly teach phonics.					
I know how to differentiate instruction in foundational skills for bilingual learners or readers who struggle.					
I know strategies for developing reading fluency.					

On average, indicate how often you receive the following support

	Daily	Frequently (several times a week)	Sometimes (once a month)	Infrequently (2–3 times a school year)	Never	N/A
Literacy coaching						
Implementing reading interventions						
Analyzing assessments						
Exploring new instructional strategies						

Literacy Practices Survey

Reading Comprehension (K–3)

This purpose of this survey is to better understand how emergent reading instruction is being implemented within the district. Your responses are completely anonymous. Your honesty is appreciated.

Grade level:

How often do you spend on the following aspects of reading instruction (within your core instruction):

	Daily	Frequently (2–4 times a week)	Sometimes (1 time a week)	Infrequently (once per month)	Never	I am unfamiliar with this practice
Engage in the specific method called dialogic reading (PK–1).						
Provide interactive read-alouds with discussion where students do the bulk of responding to a text.						
Provide interactive read-alouds with nonfiction texts.						
Provide students the opportunity to choose what book they read.						
Teach children how to summarize and retell a story or nonfiction text.						
Provide opportunities for children to respond to text through pictures or writing.						
Provide project-based learning and content knowledge development.						
Use text sets and read about one topic across multiple texts.						
Teach nonfiction text structures and text features.						
Differentiate, through small groups, for reading comprehension instruction.						

Rate your agreement with the following statements:

	Strongly Agree	Agree	Unsure	Disagree	Strongly Disagree	N/A
I understand the role of oral language in reading comprehension development.						
I am confident in my ability to assess my students' reading comprehension and plan instruction based on assessment results.						

(Continued)

	Strongly Agree	Agree	Unsure	Disagree	Strongly Disagree	N/A
I am confident in my ability to provide reading comprehension instruction to bilingual learners or readers who struggle.						
All of my students engage in discussion during an interactive read-aloud.						
I have agreed-upon rules for discussion and provide lessons on how to engage in academic discussions.						
I am confident in my ability to engage in student-centered discussions during a read-aloud.						
The reading materials and texts provided to me are culturally relevant.						
I model for students how to write about their reading and summarize texts.						
I am confident in my ability to provide think-alouds during a read-aloud.						
I teach reading comprehension across the curriculum.						
I frequently use text sets to support reading comprehension and knowledge development.						
I have adequate and quality resources and texts to teach both fiction and nonfiction genres.						
The books in my classroom represent diverse cultures and communities.						
I have enough time in my reading block to differentiate comprehension instruction for all readers.						
What materials do you rely upon to teach reading comprehension?						
How do you assess reading comprehension?						
Additional comments:						

Literacy Practices Survey

Reading Comprehension (4–12)

This purpose of this survey is to better understand how emergent reading instruction is being implemented within the district. Your responses are completely anonymous. Your honesty is appreciated.

Grade level:

How often do you spend on the following aspects of reading instruction (within your core instruction):

	Daily	Frequently (2–4 times a week)	Sometimes (1 time a week)	Infrequently (once per month)	Never	I am unfamiliar with this practice
Read multiple texts aloud about one topic (text sets).						
Teach close reading in small groups.						
Utilize texts that represent diverse cultures and communities.						
Engage students in project-based learning.						
Teach reading strategies to support comprehension (e.g., summarizing).						
Teach informational text structure.						
Read aloud and model meta-cognitive thinking.						
Use scaffolds like anticipation guides or graphic organizers to support student comprehension.						
Teach disciplinary literacy (e.g., how to read and write like a historian).						
Engage readers in discussion where they lead and do the bulk of the talking.						
Engage readers in Socratic Seminar, book clubs, or critical literacy discussions.						
Use writing to learn activities to support comprehension.						
Teach strategies for online reading comprehension.						
Differentiate, through small groups, for reading comprehension instruction.						

Rate your agreement with the following statements:

	Strongly Agree	Agree	Unsure	Disagree	Strongly Disagree	N/A
I believe background knowledge is essential improving reading comprehension.						

I am confident in my ability to assess my students' reading comprehension and plan instruction based on assessment results.					
I am confident in my ability to provide reading comprehension instruction to bilingual learners or readers who struggle.					
All my students engage in discussion during an interactive read-aloud.					
I have agreed-upon rules for discussion and have given my readers lessons on how to engage in academic discussions.					
I am confident in my ability to engage in student-centered discussions during a read-aloud.					
I model for students how to write about their reading and summarize texts.					
I am confident in my ability to provide think-alouds during a read-aloud.					
I teach reading comprehension across the curriculum.					
I teach strategies for note taking.					
I use text sets to support reading comprehension and knowledge development.					
I know strategies to teach online reading comprehension.					
I have adequate resources and texts to teach both fiction and nonfiction genres.					
The reading materials and texts provided to me are culturally relevant.					
I have enough time in my reading block to differentiate comprehension instruction for all readers.					
What materials do you rely upon to teach reading comprehension?					
Additional comments:					

Literacy Practices Survey

Vocabulary

This purpose of this survey is to better understand how emergent reading instruction is being implemented within the district. Your responses are completely anonymous. Your honesty is appreciated.

Grade level:

How often do you instruct the following aspects of reading instruction (within your core instruction):

	Daily	Frequently (2–4 times a week)	Sometimes (1 time a week)	Infrequently (once per month)	Never	I am unfamiliar with this practice
Explicitly teaching vocabulary words.						
Repeating newly taught vocabulary words.						
Facilitating word awareness or excitement about interesting words.						
Teaching dictionary use.						
Providing time for independent reading.						
Teaching morphemes (prefixes, suffixes, Greek and Latin roots).						

Rate your agreement with the following statements:

	Strongly Agree	Agree	Unsure	Disagree	Strongly Disagree	N/A
I understand the differences between the tiers of vocabulary words.						
When planning for a read-aloud, I pre-select two to three words to teach.						
I am comfortable giving child-friendly definitions to help learners understand new vocabulary words.						
I use a variety of strategies to help readers learn vocabulary words.						
My students keep a vocabulary notebook and visit it often to learn discipline-specific words.						

Comments:

Literacy Practices Survey

Writing

This purpose of this survey is to better understand how writing instruction is being implemented within the district. Your responses are completely anonymous. Your honesty is appreciated.

Grade level:

How much time do you spend per week on the following aspects of reading instruction (within your core instruction):

	Daily	Frequently (2–4 times a week)	Sometimes (1 time a week)	Infrequently (once per month)	Never	I am unfamiliar with this practice
Teaching the writing process						
Meeting individually or in small groups with writers						
Providing feedback to writers.						
Genre-based writing (e.g., narrative, informational, argument, etc.)						
Explicitly teaching writing strategies						
Providing authentic opportunities for sustained writing practice						

Rate your agreement with the following statements:

	Strongly Agree	Agree	Unsure	Disagree	Strongly Disagree	N/A
I teach the genre of narrative writing.						
I have been provided with a list of mentor texts to teach narrative writing.						
There are grade-level expectations for teaching narrative writing.						
I have a sequence of lessons that I teach for narrative writing.						
I teach the genre of argument writing.						
I have been provided with a list of mentor texts to teach argument writing.						
There are grade-level expectations for teaching argument writing.						
I have a sequence of lessons that I teach for argument writing						

(Continued)

	Strongly Agree	Agree	Unsure	Disagree	Strongly Disagree	N/A
I am a content area teacher and teach argument writing in my discipline.						
I teach the genre of informational (research) writing.						
My students have adequate resources for researching a topic.						
I have been provided with a list of mentor texts to teach informational writing.						
There are grade-level expectations for teaching informational writing.						
I have a sequence of lessons that I teach for informational writing						
I am a content area teacher and teach informational writing in my discipline.						
I emphasize the use of digital tools in writing instruction.						
I explicitly teach handwriting.						
Our district has clear expectations for the teaching of handwriting.						
I teach writing conventions.						
I teach sentence combining as part of writing instruction.						
I have adequate resources and training to teach bilingual writers in my classroom.						

On average, indicate how often you receive the following support

	Daily	Frequently (several times a week)	Sometimes (once a month)	Infrequently (2–3 times a school year)	Never	N/A
Instructional coaching for writing						
Analyzing student writing						
Exploring new instructional strategies for the teaching of writing						

Literacy Practices Survey

Independent Reading and Classroom Skills

This purpose of this survey is to better understand how emergent reading instruction is being implemented within the district. Your responses are completely anonymous. Your honesty is appreciated.

Grade level:

How often do you instruct the following aspects of reading instruction (within your core instruction):

	Daily	Frequently (2–4 times a week)	Sometimes (1 time a week)	Infrequently (once per month)	Never	I am unfamiliar with this practice
Allowing readers to choose what they want to read						
Providing time for daily independent reading						
Reading books aloud that have diverse characters						
Discussing books that have diverse characters						
Reading and discussing nonfiction books						

Rate your agreement with the following statements:

	Strongly Agree	Agree	Unsure	Disagree	Strongly Disagree	N/A
My classroom library is representative of all the children in my classroom (e.g., culture, race, socioeconomic status, gender, etc.)						
My classroom library contains a variety of genres.						
My classroom library has books with multiple reading levels.						
I have at least 20 books in my library for each child in my classroom.						
I monitor students' independent reading progress.						
It is important to provide opportunities for daily, independent reading.						

Comments:

Parent Survey

Please answer the following questions. Your responses will be anonymous.

1   The reading program at my child's school is meeting their needs.
    a   Strongly Agree
    b   Agree
    c   Disagree
    d   Strongly Disagree

2   The writing program at my child's school is meeting their needs.
    a   Strongly Agree
    b   Agree
    c   Disagree
    d   Strongly Disagree

3   I am provided information about what my child should learn and be able to do in reading and writing.
    a   Strongly Agree
    b   Agree
    c   Disagree
    d   Strongly Disagree

4   My child's teacher(s) adjust their instruction to meet their literacy needs.
    a   Strongly Agree
    b   Agree
    c   Disagree
    d   Strongly Disagree

5   My child's teacher has high expectations for their learning.
    a   Strongly Agree
    b   Agree
    c   Disagree
    d   Strongly Disagree

6   My child receives adequate support in reading to meet their needs.
    a   Strongly Agree
    b   Agree
    c   Disagree
    d   Strongly Disagree

7   My child enjoys reading when they are not in school.
    a   Strongly Agree
    b   Agree
    c   Disagree
    d   Strongly Disagree

8 My child seems engaged by the reading and writing program at their school.
   a   Strongly Agree
   b   Agree
   c   Disagree
   d   Strongly Disagree

9 Please list any strengths within the current reading and writing program.
10 Please list any areas for growth within the current reading and writing program.
11 Additional comments:

K–5 Student Survey

The following survey asks questions about your experiences learning to read and write. Please answer each question honestly.

1   How often does your teacher read aloud a book to your class?
   a   Every day
   b   Two or three times a week
   c   Once or twice a month
   d   Almost never

2   Do you talk about the books that your teacher reads aloud to you?
   a   Yes
   b   No
   c   Sometimes

3   At school, how often do you get to choose the books you read?
   a   Every day
   b   Two or three times a week
   c   Once or twice a month
   d   Almost never

4   Do you have to read books that the teacher selects for you?
   a   Every day
   b   Two or three times a week
   c   Once or twice a month
   d   Almost never

5   Do you read books at home or when you are not in school?
   a   Every day
   b   Two or three times a week
   c   Once or twice a month
   d   Almost never

6   Do you learn strategies for reading and pronouncing words?
   a   Every day
   b   Two or three times a week
   c   Once or twice a month
   d   Almost never

7   Do you learn strategies for pronouncing words in a book that you do not know?
   a   Every day
   b   Two or three times a week
   c   Once or twice a month
   d   Almost never

8   Do you learn strategies for spelling words?
   a   Every day
   b   Two or three times a week
   c   Once or twice a month
   d   Almost never

9   How do you feel about reading during school?
  a   I always enjoy it
  b   I sometimes enjoy it
  c   I rarely enjoy it
  d   I never enjoy it

10   How often do you work with your teacher in a small group?
  a   Every day
  b   Two or three times week
  c   Once or twice a month
  d   Almost never

11   In school, how often do you write?
  a   Every day
  b   Two or three times a week
  c   Once or twice a month
  d   Almost never

12   How often do you learn strategies for writing?
  a   Every day
  b   Two or three times a week
  c   Once or twice a month
  d   Almost never

13   How often does your teacher talk with you about your writing?
  a   Every day
  b   Once or twice a week
  c   Once or twice a month
  d   Almost never

6–12 Student Survey

1 Are you in middle or high school?
   a Middle school
   b High school

2 How often does your teacher read aloud a book to your class?
   a Every day
   b Two or three times a week
   c Once or twice a month
   d Almost never

3 Do you talk about the books that your teacher reads aloud to you?
   a Yes
   b No
   c Sometimes

4 At school, how often do you get to choose the books you read?
   a Every day
   b Two or three times a week
   c Once or twice a month
   d Almost never

5 Do you have to read books that the teacher selects for you?
   a Every day
   b Two or three times a week
   c Once or twice a month
   d Almost never

6 Do you read books at home or when you are not in school?
   a Every day
   b Two or three times a week
   c Once or twice a month
   d Almost never

7 Do the books in the library or in your classroom have characters or people that you can relate to?
   a Yes
   b A little bit
   c No

8 Do you learn strategies for spelling words?
   a Every day
   b Two or three times a week
   c Once or twice a month
   d Almost never

9 How do you feel about reading during school?
   a I always enjoy it
   b I sometimes enjoy it
   c I rarely enjoy it
   d I never enjoy it

10   How often do you work with your teacher in a small group?
   a   Every day
   b   Two or three times week
   c   Once or twice a month
   d   Almost never

11   How often do you participate in a small-group discussion about a book you are reading?
   a   Every day
   b   Once or twice a week
   c   Once or twice a month
   d   Almost never

12   In school, how often do you write?
   a   Every day
   b   Two or three times a week
   c   Once or twice a month
   d   Almost never

13   How often do you learn strategies for writing?
   a   Every day
   b   Two or three times a week
   c   Once or twice a month
   d   Almost never

14   How often do you receive specific feedback on your writing?
   a   Every day
   b   Once or twice a week
   c   Once or twice a month
   d   Almost never

15   How often does your teacher talk with you one on one you about your writing?
   a   Every day
   b   Once or twice a week
   c   Once or twice a month
   d   Almost never

Student Reading Interest Survey

*To be given to students by their ELA teacher to support independent reading engagement. See chapter 8 for information about administering this survey.

I look forward to reading your responses to the following survey. I am interested in learning all about you and finding out what engages you, in and out of school!

1   What do you like to do when you are not in school?

2   What is your favorite TV show?

3   Do you play video games?

    a   If you answered yes, what is your favorite video game?

4   Where were you born?

5   Do you speak another language?

6   Do you play any games or sports? Which ones?

7   What do you like about playing these games or sports?

8   What is your favorite part of the school day?

9   What is the best book you ever...?

    a   Read by yourself...

    b   Listened to...

10   What was the last book you read?

11   Do you like to read at school?

12   Do you like to read at home?

13   What job do you want to have when you get older?

14   What do you wish for in life?

Evaluation Tool of Children's Handwriting

Evaluation Tool of Children's Handwriting	
Skill Observed	**Yes or No**
Pencil grip is correct	
Prints letters on the line	
Uses proper spacing between letters	
Uses proper spacing between words	
Lower letter case letters are formed correctly and in the right direction	
Upper case letters are formed correctly and in the right direction	
My classroom library contains a variety of genres.	
Capitalizes first word in a sentence	
Letters are sized correctly	
Letters with tails are written below the writing line	
Lower case letters that are "tall" are written to the top line	

Appendix C: Composite Score Sheet

Foundational Skills Instructional Practices Evaluation Form

PHASE ONE: EVALUTING INSTRUCTIONAL PRACTICES

Foundational Skills Instructional Practices Evaluation:

1. To the best of your ability, evaluate the instructional practices used by most teachers in the district. The survey data will help inform this rating. *Reading materials are assessed in Phases Two and Three.*
2. Provide an average rating for each construct (e.g., oral language).
3. The chair of the team will record individual scores on a rating sheet.
4. The chair of the team will average the scores of each individual rating and record on them on the group composite score sheet.

1 Never Evident	2 Sometimes Evident	3 Satisfactorily Evident	4 Often Evident	5 Always Evident

Concepts About Print

Instructional Practices	Shared reading with print referencing and concept of word development are explicitly taught	1	2	3	4	5
Are evidence-based instructional practices routinely implemented?	Instruction includes shared writing with focus on concept about print	1	2	3	4	5
	Concepts about print is assessed and results guide small-group instruction	1	2	3	4	5
Concepts About Print Average Rating:						

Alphabetic Knowledge

Instructional Practices	Scope and sequence for systematic alphabet knowledge is utilized	1	2	3	4	5
Are evidence-based instructional practices routinely implemented?	Explicit and differentiated instruction in letters and sounds is provided	1	2	3	4	5
	Instruction focuses upon correct pronunciation of letter sounds	1	2	3	4	5
	Alphabet charts or sound walls are purposefully used on classroom walls and within instruction	1	2	3	4	5
	Letters and sounds are taught together	1	2	3	4	5
	Quality alphabet books are accessible to children in the classroom library	1	2	3	4	5
	Handwriting is explicitly taught (see Chapter 7 for full evaluation of handwriting instruction)	1	2	3	4	5
Alphabetic Knowledge Average Rating:						

Phonological Awareness						
Instructional Practices Are evidence-based instructional practices routinely implemented?	Phonological awareness—importantly phonemic awareness is frequently assessed; results are used to guide instruction	1	2	3	4	5
	Scope and sequence for systematic phonological awareness instruction is utilized	1	2	3	4	5
	Differentiated (small group) explicit instruction in phonological and, importantly, phonemic awareness is provided	1	2	3	4	5
	Phonemic awareness instruction averages approximately 20 hours (yet differentiated for specific needs of children)	1	2	3	4	5
	Readers who struggle are provided phonemic awareness intervention with more intensive instruction	1	2	3	4	5
	Phonemic awareness instruction progresses from simple (e.g., hearing initial sounds) to more complex activities (e.g., manipulating sounds)	1	2	3	4	5
	Opportunities for writing through invented spelling and dictation are provided	1	2	3	4	5
	Shared writing is used to support phonemic awareness	1	2	3	4	5
	Phonological Awareness Average Rating:					
Phonics						
Instructional Practices Are evidence-based instructional practices routinely implemented?	Phonics knowledge is assessed, and results are used to guide small-group instruction	1	2	3	4	5
	Explicit, daily phonics instruction is provided in small-group lessons	1	2	3	4	5
	Scope and sequence for systematic phonics instruction is utilized; simple to more complex patterns are presented for instruction	1	2	3	4	5
	Phonics lessons include a focus on hearing sounds, segmenting, blending, and spelling words with taught pattern	1	2	3	4	5
	Phonics lessons include opportunities for recently learned patterns to be practiced in texts that contain taught pattern (decodable texts are used in early phonics lessons)	1	2	3	4	5
	Students are taught to use phonics patterns to read words in connected text; context is only suggested as a confirmation strategy (not taught as a decoding strategy)	1	2	3	4	5
	Strategies for multisyllable word analysis are provided to students as they advance in their phonics knowledge	1	2	3	4	5
	High-frequency words are assessed, taught, and practiced by students in both reading and writing	1	2	3	4	5
	Spelling is assessed and explicitly taught alongside phonics	1	2	3	4	5
	Spelling instruction includes an emphasis upon phonology, orthography, and morphology	1	2	3	4	5
	Assessments are consistently used to monitor phonics and spelling acquisition	1	2	3	4	5
	Phonics Average Rating:					

Fluency							
Instructional Practices Are evidence-based instructional practices routinely implemented?	Fluency is assessed for prosody as well as speed	1	2	3	4	5
	Practices such as echo reading, choral reading, partner reading, repeated reading, and readers theater are used to support oral reading fluency	1	2	3	4	5
	Wide reading: students have daily uninterrupted time to practice reading in a variety of connected texts (not just decodables)	1	2	3	4	5
	Prosody is a key focus of fluency instruction	1	2	3	4	5
	Fluency Average Rating:						
Additional Comments: Please provide any additional insights: Is instruction organized around a structured year-long plan? Are teachers given a framework to structure their reading block to teach foundational skills? Is coaching and quality professional development provided to teachers?							

PHASE TWO: EVALUTING CURRENT PROGRAM PROVIDED IN THE DISTRICT								

Foundational Skills Current Program Evaluation:

1. Evaluate the current reading materials provided by the school district. This only includes materials the school district has purchased for instructional use. This does not include materials teachers purchase on their own.
2. Provide an average rating for each construct (e.g., oral language).
3. The chair of the team will record individual scores on the rating sheet.
4. The chair of the team will average the scores of each individual rating and record on them on the group composite score sheet.

1 Never Evident	2 Sometimes Evident	3 Satisfactorily Evident	4 Often Evident	5 Always Evident

Concepts About Print						
Program/Materials Currently Available Do current district materials support foundational skills?	Lessons on shared reading with print referencing are provided in the program	1	2	3	4	5
	Lessons include concept of word development and opportunities for student practice	1	2	3	4	5
	Lessons for shared writing are provided	1	2	3	4	5
	Concepts about print is assessed and results guide small-group instruction	1	2	3	4	5
	Concepts About Print Average Rating:					

Alphabetic Knowledge						
Program/Materials Currently Available Do current district materials support foundational skills?	Scope and sequence for systematic alphabet knowledge are provided	1	2	3	4	5
	Lessons provide explicit instruction in letters and sounds	1	2	3	4	5
	Lessons focus upon correct pronunciation of letter sounds	1	2	3	4	5
	Guidance on using alphabet charts or sound walls is provided in the program	1	2	3	4	5
	Letters and sounds are taught together	1	2	3	4	5
	Quality alphabet books are accessible to children in the classroom library	1	2	3	4	5
	Handwriting is explicitly taught (see Chapter 7 for full evaluation on handwriting)	1	2	3	4	5
	Alphabetic Knowledge Average Rating:					

Phonological Awareness						
Program/Materials Currently Available Do current district materials support foundational skills?	Phonological awareness—importantly phonemic awareness—is frequently assessed; results are used to guide instruction	1	2	3	4	5
	Scope and sequence for systematic phonological awareness (including phonemic awareness) instruction are provided	1	2	3	4	5

	Lessons provide for differentiated (small group) explicit instruction in phonological and, importantly, phonemic awareness	1	2	3	4	5
	Program provides approximately 20 hours of phonemic awareness instruction (yet can be differentiated for specific needs of children)	1	2	3	4	5
	Program provides additional instruction for children who struggle with phonemic awareness	1	2	3	4	5
	Phonemic awareness instruction progresses from simple (e.g., hearing initial sounds) to more complex activities (e.g., manipulating sounds)	1	2	3	4	5
	Opportunities for writing through invented spelling and dictation are provided	1	2	3	4	5
	Lessons on shared writing are provided to support phonemic awareness	1	2	3	4	5
	Phonological Awareness Average Rating:					
Phonics						
Program/Materials Currently Available Do current district materials support foundational skills?	Phonics knowledge is assessed, and results are used to guide small-group instruction	1	2	3	4	5
	Explicit daily phonics instruction is provided through small group, differentiated lessons.	1	2	3	4	5
	Scope and sequence for systematic phonics instruction is provided in the program; simple to more complex patterns are presented for instruction	1	2	3	4	5
	Phonics lessons are straightforward and include a focus on hearing sounds, segmenting, blending, and spelling words with taught pattern	1	2	3	4	5
	Phonics lessons include opportunities for recently learned patterns to be practiced in texts that contain taught pattern (decodable texts are provided in the early stages of phonics instruction)	1	2	3	4	5
	Instructional materials prompt students to rely on phonics patterns to read words in connected text; context is only suggested as a confirmation strategy (not taught as a decoding strategy).	1	2	3	4	5
	Advanced phonics lessons for multisyllable word analysis are provided	1	2	3	4	5
	High-frequency words are assessed, taught, and practiced by students in both reading and writing	1	2	3	4	5
	Spelling is assessed and explicitly taught alongside phonics	1	2	3	4	5
	Spelling instruction includes an emphasis upon phonology, orthography, and morphology	1	2	3	4	5
	Assessments are consistently used to monitor phonics and spelling acquisition	1	2	3	4	5
	Phonics Average Rating:					

Fluency						
Program/Materials Currently Available Do current district materials support foundational skills?	Fluency is assessed for prosody as well as speed	1	2	3	4	5
	Fluency lessons such as echo reading, choral reading, partner reading, repeated reading, and readers theater are provided to support oral reading fluency	1	2	3	4	5
	Wide reading: students have daily uninterrupted time to practice reading in a variety of connected texts (not just decodables)	1	2	3	4	5
	Prosody is a key focus of fluency lessons in the program	1	2	3	4	5
	Fluency Average Rating:					
Additional Comments: Please provide insights about any of the scores pertaining to the current program: Are materials engaging? Culturally relevant? Teacher friendly? Is assessment dynamic? Other comments						

PHASE THREE: EVALUTING NEW PROGRAM FOR ADOPTION

Foundational Skills New Program Evaluation:

1. Evaluate the new reading materials that are being considered for adoption.
2. Provide an average rating for each construct (e.g., oral language).
3. The chair of the team will record individual scores on the rating sheet.
4. The chair of the team will average the scores of each individual rating and record them on the group composite score sheet.

1 Never Evident	2 Sometimes Evident	3 Satisfactorily Evident	4 Often Evident	5 Always Evident

Concepts About Print						
Program/Materials Under Review Does the program under review support comprehension development?	Lessons on shared reading with print referencing are provided in the program	1	2	3	4	5
	Lessons include concept of word development and opportunities for student practice	1	2	3	4	5
	Lessons for shared writing are provided	1	2	3	4	5
	Concepts about print is assessed and results guide small-group instruction	1	2	3	4	5
	Concepts About Print Average Rating:					

Alphabetic Knowledge						
Program/Materials Under Review Does the program under review support foundational skills?	Scope and sequence for systematic alphabet knowledge are provided	1	2	3	4	5
	Lessons provide explicit instruction in letters and sounds	1	2	3	4	5
	Lessons focus upon correct pronunciation of letter sounds	1	2	3	4	5
	Guidance on using alphabet charts or sound walls is provided in the program	1	2	3	4	5
	Letters and sounds are taught together	1	2	3	4	5
	Quality alphabet books are are accessible to children in the classroom library	1	2	3	4	5
	Handwriting is explicitly taught (see Chapter 7 for full evaluation on handwriting)	1	2	3	4	5
	Alphabetic Knowledge Average Rating:					
Phonological Awareness						
Program/Materials Under Review Does the program under review support foundational skills?	Phonological awareness—importantly phonemic awareness—is frequently assessed; results are used to guide instruction	1	2	3	4	5
	Scope and sequence for systematic phonological awareness (including phonemic awareness) instruction are provided	1	2	3	4	5
	Lessons provide for differentiated (small group) explicit instruction in phonological and, importantly, phonemic awareness	1	2	3	4	5
	Program provides approximately 20 hours of phonemic awareness instruction; yet can be differentiated based on specific needs of children	1	2	3	4	5
	Program provides additional instruction for children who struggle with phonemic awareness	1	2	3	4	5
	Phonemic awareness instruction progresses from simple (e.g., hearing initial sounds) to more complex activities (e.g., manipulating sounds)	1	2	3	4	5
	Opportunities for writing through invented spelling and dictation are provided	1	2	3	4	5
	Lessons on shared writing are provided to support phonemic awareness	1	2	3	4	5
	Phonological Awareness Average Rating:					
Phonics						
Program/Materials Under Review Does the program under review support foundational skills?	Phonics knowledge is assessed, and results are used to guide small-group instruction	1	2	3	4	5
	Explicit daily phonics instruction is provided through small group, differentiated lessons.	1	2	3	4	5
	Scope and sequence for systematic phonics instruction are provided in the program; simple to more complex patterns are presented for instruction	1	2	3	4	5

	Phonics lessons are straightforward and include a focus on hearing sounds, segmenting, blending, and spelling words with taught pattern	1	2	3	4	5
	Phonics lessons include opportunities for recently learned patterns to be practiced in texts that contain taught pattern(decodable texts are provided in the early stages of phonics instruction)	1	2	3	4	5
	Instructional materials prompt students to rely on phonics patterns to read words in connected text; context is only suggested as a confirmation strategy (not taught as a decoding strategy).	1	2	3	4	5
	Advanced phonics lessons for multisyllable word analysis are provided	1	2	3	4	5
	High-frequency words are assessed, taught, and practiced by students in both reading and writing	1	2	3	4	5
	Spelling is assessed and explicitly taught alongside phonics	1	2	3	4	5
	Spelling instruction includes an emphasis upon phonology, orthography, and morphology	1	2	3	4	5
	Assessments are consistently used to monitor phonics and spelling acquisition	1	2	3	4	5
	Phonics Average Rating:					
Fluency						
Program/Materials Under Review	Fluency is assessed for prosody as well as speed	1	2	3	4	5
Does the program under review support foundational skills?	Fluency lessons such as echo reading, choral reading, partner reading, repeated reading and readers theater are provided to support oral reading fluency	1	2	3	4	5
	Wide reading: students have daily uninterrupted time to practice reading in a variety of connected texts (not just decodables)	1	2	3	4	5
	Prosody is a key focus of fluency lessons in the program	1	2	3	4	5
	Fluency Average Rating:					
Additional Comments: Please provide insights about any of the scores pertaining to materials under review: Are materials engaging? Culturally relevant? Teacher friendly? Is assessment dynamic? Other comments?						

K–3 Reading Comprehension Instructional Practices Evaluation Form

PHASE ONE: EVALUTING INSTRUCTIONAL PRACTICES				
K–3 Reading Comprehension Instructional Practices Evaluation:				
1 To the best of your ability, evaluate the instructional practices used by most teachers in the district. The survey data will help inform this rating. *Reading materials are assessed in Phases Two and Three.*				
2 Provide an average rating for each construct (e.g., oral language).				
3 The chair of the team will record individual scores on the rating sheet.				
4 The chair of the team will average the scores of each individual rating and record on group composite score sheet.				
1 Never Evident	2 Sometimes Evident	3 Satisfactorily Evident	4 Often Evident	5 Always Evident

Oral Language/Listening Comprehension		
Instructional Practices Are evidence-based instructional practices routinely implemented?	Oral language and listening comprehension are elements of instruction	1 2 3 4 5
	Native language and dialect are embraced	1 2 3 4 5
	Children are provided opportunities for listening, sharing, and oral language development	1 2 3 4 5
	Dialogic reading is used in grades K–1	1 2 3 4 5
	Oral language is assessed	1 2 3 4 5
	Retelling is assessed	1 2 3 4 5
	Bilingual learners are assessed and provided differentiated instruction as needed	1 2 3 4 5
	Listening and speaking activities are provided for bilingual learners and include culturally relevant mentor texts with discussions	1 2 3 4 5
	Bilingual learners are provided small-group learning that leverages strengths and background knowledge	1 2 3 4 5
	Oral Language Average Rating:	

Read-Alouds with Discussion		
Instructional Practices Are evidence-based instructional practices routinely implemented?	Students have ground rules for talk and have strategies for engaging in academic discussions	1 2 3 4 5
	Read-alouds with student-centered discussion are routinely implemented; teachers engage in dialogic classroom discussions; students add on, ask questions, and provide challenges to ideas to construct deeper understanding of a text or topic	1 2 3 4 5
	High-level questions are prioritized during read-alouds	1 2 3 4 5
	Teachers use think-alouds and model how to comprehend complex texts (e.g., point of view, author's craft, text structure).	1 2 3 4 5
	Range of text types (fiction, nonfiction, grade level, and complex) and several texts about a theme or topic are read aloud and discussed	1 2 3 4 5
	Read-Alouds With Discussion Average Rating:	

Informational Text and Content-Based Approaches						
Instructional Practices Are evidence-based instructional practices routinely implemented?	Nonfiction read-alouds with texts sets are used; knowledge developed across a topic	1	2	3	4	5
	Text features/graphical devices are explicitly taught	1	2	3	4	5
	Opportunities for authentic nonfiction text reading are provided	1	2	3	4	5
	Close reading and comparing/contrasting complex texts are routinely instructed	1	2	3	4	5
	High-quality project-based learning opportunities are provided	1	2	3	4	5
	Assessments help identify who needs support with nonfiction comprehension	1	2	3	4	5
	Informational Text Average Rating:					

Cognitive Strategies						
Instructional Practices Are evidence-based instructional practices routinely implemented?	Comprehension/cognitive strategies are taught for authentic purposes	1	2	3	4	5
	Cognitive strategy instruction is taught through a gradual release model	1	2	3	4	5
	Text structures (narrative and information) are taught and used to support comprehension	1	2	3	4	5
	Summarization is explicitly taught; students practice summarizing	1	2	3	4	5
	Text-based questioning is utilized during instruction and supports critical thinking about a text	1	2	3	4	5
	Self-monitoring strategies for comprehension are taught	1	2	3	4	5
	Readers are provided opportunities for answering and asking questions about a text	1	2	3	4	5
	Assessments are consistently used to monitor comprehension	1	2	3	4	5
	Cognitive Strategy Average Rating:					

Writing to Learn						
Instructional Practices Are evidence-based instructional practices routinely implemented?	Writing in response to reading is emphasized (e.g., reader's notebook)	1	2	3	4	5
	Content area summary writing is implemented	1	2	3	4	5
	Writing To Learn Average Rating:					

Additional Comments: Please provide any additional insights: Is instruction organized around a structured year-long plan? Are teachers given a framework to structure their reading block to teach comprehension? Is coaching and quality professional development provided to teachers?	

PHASE TWO: EVALUTING CURRENT PROGRAM PROVIDED IN THE DISTRICT
K-3 Reading Comprehension Current Program Evaluation:

1 Evaluate the current reading materials provided by the school district. This only includes materials the school district has purchased for instructional use. This does not include materials teachers purchase on their own.
2 Provide an average rating for each construct (e.g., oral language).
3 The chair of the team will record individual scores on the rating sheet.
4 The chair of the team will average the scores of each individual rating and record them on the group composite score sheet.

1 Never Evident	2 Sometimes Evident	3 Satisfactorily Evident	4 Often Evident	5 Always Evident

Oral Language and Listening Comprehension

Program/Materials Currently Available Do current district materials support comprehension development?	Oral language and listening comprehension are elements of instruction	1	2	3	4	5
	Native language and dialect are embraced	1	2	3	4	5
	Children are provided opportunities for sharing and oral language development	1	2	3	4	5
	Dialogic reading is used in grades K–1	1	2	3	4	5
	Oral language is assessed	1	2	3	4	5
	Retelling is assessed	1	2	3	4	5
	Bilingual learners are assessed and provided differentiated instruction as needed	1	2	3	4	5
	Listening and speaking activities are provided for bilingual learners and include an emphasis on discussion with culturally relevant texts	1	2	3	4	5

	Bilingual learners are provided small-group learning that leverages strengths and background knowledge	1	2	3	4	5
	Oral Language Average Rating:					

Read-Alouds with Discussion

Program/Materials Currently Available	Read-alouds with student-centered discussion are emphasized in the reading program	1	2	3	4	5
Do current district materials support comprehension development?	Lessons includes ground rules for talk and support engagement in student-led discussions about a book	1	2	3	4	5
	High-level questions are prioritized during read-alouds and include questions about character actions, traits, and other story elements	1	2	3	4	5
	Readers ask and answer questions throughout the read-aloud; by third grade, readers provide text evidence to support their responses	1	2	3	4	5
	Instruction provides opportunities for teacher to model or use a think-aloud to demonstrate specific reading skills (point of view, author's craft, characterization, and text structure)	1	2	3	4	5
	Range of text types, including fiction and nonfiction, as well as complex texts, are provided in the reading program and used for teacher read-alouds	1	2	3	4	5
	Literature and other texts are of high quality and culturally relevant	1	2	3	4	5
	Multiple texts on a topic and theme are provided in the reading program and used to build knowledge through teacher read-alouds	1	2	3	4	5
	Read-Alouds With Discussion Average Rating:					

Informational Text and Content-Based Approaches

Materials Currently Available	Nonfiction read-alouds with texts sets are provided; materials provide the opportunity for students to learn about a topic in depth	1	2	3	4	5
Do current district materials support comprehension development?	Opportunities for learning and demonstrating understanding of text features/graphical devices are provided	1	2	3	4	5
	Instruction provides opportunities for learners to analyze texts and determine the validity of an argument	1	2	3	4	5
	Nonfiction magazines and articles (online or traditional print) are routinely read and discussed	1	2	3	4	5
	Project-based learning opportunities are provided	1	2	3	4	5
	A wide range of high-quality nonfiction texts, including both complex and grade-level texts, for independent practice are provided	1	2	3	4	5
	High-quality assessments are provided and used to monitor who needs support with nonfiction comprehension	1	2	3	4	5
	Informational Text Average Rating:					

Cognitive Strategies		
Program/Materials Currently Available Do current district materials support comprehension development?	Comprehension/cognitive strategies are taught and practiced for authentic purposes; materials provide the opportunity for students to read grade-level texts independently	1 2 3 4 5
	Cognitive strategy instruction is taught through a gradual release model; lessons emphasize how strategies can support comprehension	1 2 3 4 5
	Story element lessons are provided and used to support students' ability to retell	1 2 3 4 5
	Informational text structures are explicitly taught	1 2 3 4 5
	Lessons on summarization are provided; students practice summarizing for meaningful purposes	1 2 3 4 5
	Graphic organizers are provided to help readers track their comprehension while reading	1 2 3 4 5
	Text-based questioning and responding are emphasized within the reading program	1 2 3 4 5
	Lessons about self-monitoring for comprehension are provided	1 2 3 4 5
	High-quality assessments are provided and used to formatively monitor comprehension	1 2 3 4 5
	Differentiated instruction is provided for readers who need more or less support with cognitive strategy use	1 2 3 4 5
	Cognitive Strategy Average Rating:	
Writing to Learn		
Program/Materials Currently Available Do current district materials support comprehension development?	Writing in response to reading is emphasized	1 2 3 4 5
	Content area summary writing is done through quick writes that allow readers to summarize what was learned	1 2 3 4 5
	Writing to Learn Average Rating:	
Additional Comments: Please provide insights about any of the scores pertaining to current materials/program. Is pacing appropriate? Are materials engaging? Culturally relevant? Teacher friendly? Is comprehension assessment dynamic? Other comments?		

PHASE THREE: EVALUTING NEW PROGRAM FOR ADOPTION

K-3 Reading Comprehension New Program Evaluation:

1. Evaluate the new reading materials that are being considered for adoption.
2. Provide an average rating for each construct (e.g., oral language).
3. The chair of the team will record individual scores on the rating sheet.
4. The chair of the team will average the scores of each individual rating and record them on the group composite score sheet.

1 Never Evident	2 Sometimes Evident	3 Satisfactorily Evident	4 Often Evident	5 Always Evident

Oral Language and Listening Comprehension

Program/ Materials Under Review Does the program under review support comprehension development?	Oral language and listening comprehension are elements of instruction	1 2 3 4 5
	Native language and dialect are embraced	1 2 3 4 5
	Children are provided opportunities for sharing and oral language development	1 2 3 4 5
	Dialogic reading is used in grades K–1	1 2 3 4 5
	Oral language is assessed	1 2 3 4 5
	Retelling is assessed	1 2 3 4 5
	Bilingual learners are assessed and provided differentiated instruction as needed	1 2 3 4 5
	Listening and speaking activities are provided for bilingual learners and include an emphasis on discussion with culturally relevant texts	1 2 3 4 5
	Bilingual learners are provided small-group learning that leverages strengths and background knowledge	1 2 3 4 5
	Oral Language Average Rating:	

Read-Alouds with Discussion

Program/ Materials Under Review Does the program under review support comprehension development?	Read-alouds with student-centered discussion are emphasized in the reading program	1 2 3 4 5
	Lessons includes ground rules for talk and support engagement in student-led discussions about a book	1 2 3 4 5
	High-level questions are prioritized during read-alouds and include questions about character actions, traits, and other story elements	1 2 3 4 5
	Readers ask and answer questions throughout the read-aloud; by third grade, readers provide text evidence to support their responses	1 2 3 4 5
	Instruction provides opportunities for teacher to model or use a think-aloud to demonstrate specific reading skills (point of view, author's craft, characterization, and text structure)	1 2 3 4 5
	Range of text types, including fiction and nonfiction, as well as complex texts, are provided in the reading program and used for teacher read-alouds	1 2 3 4 5

	Literature and other texts are of high quality and culturally relevant	1	2	3	4	5
	Multiple texts on a topic and theme are provided in the reading program and used to build knowledge through teacher read-alouds	1	2	3	4	5
	Read-Alouds with Discussion Average Rating:					
Informational Text/Content-Based Approaches						
Program/ Materials Under Review Does the program under review support comprehension development?	Nonfiction read-alouds with texts sets are provided; materials provide the opportunity for students to learn about a topic in depth	1	2	3	4	5
	Opportunities for learning and demonstrating understanding of text features/graphical devices are provided	1	2	3	4	5
	Instruction provides opportunities for learners to analyze texts and determine the validity of an argument	1	2	3	4	5
	Nonfiction magazines and articles (online or traditional print) are routinely read and discussed	1	2	3	4	5
	Project-based learning opportunities are provided	1	2	3	4	5
	A wide range of high-quality nonfiction texts, including both complex and grade-level texts, for independent practice are provided	1	2	3	4	5
	High-quality assessments are provided and used to monitor readers who need support with nonfiction comprehension	1	2	3	4	5
	Informational Text Average Rating:					
Cognitive Strategies						
Program/ Materials Under Review Does the program under review support comprehension development?	Comprehension/cognitive strategies are taught and practiced for authentic purposes; materials provide the opportunity for students to read grade-level texts independently	1	2	3	4	5
	Cognitive strategy instruction is taught through a gradual release model; lessons emphasize how strategies can support comprehension	1	2	3	4	5
	Story element lessons are provided and used to support students' ability to retell	1	2	3	4	5
	Informational text structures are explicitly taught	1	2	3	4	5
	Lessons on summarization are provided; students practice summarizing for meaningful purposes.	1	2	3	4	5
	Graphic organizers are provided to help readers track their comprehension while reading	1	2	3	4	5
	Text-based questioning and responding are emphasized within the reading program	1	2	3	4	5
	Lessons about self-monitoring for comprehension are provided	1	2	3	4	5

	High-quality assessments are provided and used to formatively monitor comprehension	1	2	3	4	5
	Differentiated instruction is provided for readers who need more or less support with cognitive strategy use	1	2	3	4	5
	Cognitive Strategy Average Rating:					
Writing to Learn						
Program/ Materials Under Review	Writing in response to reading is emphasized	1	2	3	4	5
Does the program under review support comprehension development?	Content area summary writing is done through quick writes that allow readers to summarize what was learned	1	2	3	4	5
	Writing to Learn Average Rating:					
Additional Comments: Please provide insights about any of the scores pertaining to materials under review: Is pacing appropriate? Are materials engaging? Culturally relevant? Teacher Friendly? Is comprehension assessment dynamic? Other comments?						

4–12 Reading Comprehension Instructional Practices Evaluation Form

PHASE ONE: EVALUTING INSTRUCTIONAL PRACTICES

4–12 Reading Comprehension Instructional Practices Evaluation:

1. To the best of your ability, evaluate the instructional practices used by most teachers in the district. The survey data will help inform this rating. *Reading materials are assessed in Phases Two and Three.*
2. Provide an average rating for each construct (e.g., oral language).
3. The chair of the team will record the individual scores on the rating sheet.
4. The chair of the team will average the scores of each individual rating and record them on the group composite score sheet.

1 Never Evident	2 Sometimes Evident	3 Satisfactorily Evident	4 Often Evident	5 Always Evident

Discussion-Based Approaches		
Instructional Practices Are evidence-based instructional practices routinely implemented?	Discussion-based approaches for text discussion such as Socratic Seminar or book club are utilized	1 2 3 4 5
	Opportunities for critical literacy discussions are provided	1 2 3 4 5
	Students are taught strategies for engaging in student-led discussions	1 2 3 4 5
	Student-centered discussion are routinely implemented; teachers engage in dialogic classroom discussions; students add on, ask questions, and provide challenges to ideas to construct deeper understanding of a text or topic	1 2 3 4 5
	Instructional supports for bilingual learners are utilized	1 2 3 4 5
	Student participation in discussions is assessed and formatively monitored	1 2 3 4 5
	Discussion-Based Approaches Average Rating:	

Content-Based Approach		
	Close reading with complex texts is taught; students practice reading complex texts and get practice asking and answering text-dependent questions	1 2 3 4 5
	Culturally relevant texts are used for instruction and practice	1 2 3 4 5
	Readers are taught to compare/contrast texts on a similar topic	1 2 3 4 5
	Project-based learning is utilized to deepen content knowledge	1 2 3 4 5
	Bilingual learners provided opportunity to learn content in native language as well as English (e.g., through audio and video supports)	1 2 3 4 5
	Content strategies like Questioning the Author are used to build knowledge	1 2 3 4 5
	Formative and summative assessments are used to monitor comprehension	1 2 3 4 5
	Content-Based Approaches Average Rating:	

Cognitive Strategy Instruction							
Instructional Practices Are evidence-based instructional practices routinely implemented?	Cognitive strategy instruction is taught through a gradual release model	1	2	3	4	5	
	Cognitive strategies are purposefully instructed (not overdone)	1	2	3	4	5	
	Instruction in text structure is provided to help readers navigate expository texts	1	2	3	4	5	
	Cognitive strategies are taught through meaningful activities such as Reciprocal Teaching or DRTA	1	2	3	4	5	
	Graphic organizers are utilized to support active engagement during reading	1	2	3	4	5	
	Cognitive Strategy Instruction Average Rating:						
Disciplinary Literacy							
Instructional Practices Are evidence-based instructional practices routinely implemented?	Opportunities for reading a variety of discipline-specific texts are provided. Includes analysis of primary and secondary sources in history; technical and scientific reports in science	1	2	3	4	5	
	Digital tools or multimodal texts are used to support knowledge building	1	2	3	4	5	
	Discipline specific writing skills are taught such as DBQs or science writing heuristic	1	2	3	4	5	
	Disciplinary reading comprehension is assessed	1	2	3	4	5	
	Disciplinary Literacy Average Rating:						
Writing to Learn							
Instructional Practices Are evidence-based instructional practices routinely implemented?	Students are taught strategies for note taking	1	2	3	4	5	
	Graphic organizers are frequently used to develop comprehension on a topic	1	2	3	4	5	
	Exit slips and admit slips or other quick writes are used to develop comprehension and formatively assess student learning	1	2	3	4	5	
	Writing About Reading Average Rating:						
Online Reading Comprehension							
Instructional Practices Are evidence-based instructional practices routinely implemented?	Students are taught strategies for locating credible sources	1	2	3	4	5	
	Students are taught strategies for evaluating sources	1	2	3	4	5	
	Online reading comprehension is monitored	1	2	3	4	5	
	Online Reading Comprehension Average Rating:						

Additional Comments: Please provide any additional insights: Is instruction organized around a structured year-long plan? Are teachers given a framework to structure their reading block to teach comprehension? Is coaching and quality professional development provided to teachers?	

PHASE TWO: EVALUTING CURRENT PROGRAM PROVIDED in the DISTRICT

4–12 Reading Comprehension Current Program Evaluation:

1. Evaluate the current reading materials provided by the school district. This only includes materials the school district has purchased for instructional use. This does not include materials teachers purchase on their own.
2. Provide an average rating for each construct (e.g., oral language).
3. The chair of the team will record the individual scores on the rating sheet.
4. The chair of the team will average the scores of each individual rating and record them on the group composite score sheet.

1 Never Evident	2 Sometimes Evident	3 Satisfactorily Evident	4 Often Evident	5 Always Evident

Discussion-Based Approaches						
Program/ Materials Currently Available Do current district materials support comprehension development?	Discussion-based approaches for text discussion such as Socratic Seminar or book club are emphasized	1	2	3	4	5
	Lessons on critical literacy discussions are provided/ emphasized	1	2	3	4	5
	Lessons on strategies for engaging in student-led discussions are provided	1	2	3	4	5
	Frequent opportunities for speaking and listening are provided. Materials emphasize classroom discussions where students add on, ask questions, and provide challenges to ideas to construct deeper understanding of a text or topic.	1	2	3	4	5
	Strategies for teaching bilingual learners are provided	1	2	3	4	5
	Student participation in discussions is assessed and formatively monitored	1	2	3	4	5
	Discussion-Based Approaches Average Rating:					

Content-Based Approach							
	Culturally relevant texts are provided for instruction	1	2	3	4	5	
	Differentiated lessons on close reading with complex texts are provided; with scaffolding, students read and reread complex texts and ask and answer text-based questions	1	2	3	4	5	
	Lessons on how to compare and contrast two topics within a text or two or more texts on a similar topic are provided	1	2	3	4	5	
	Project-based learning is used in concert with content instruction	1	2	3	4	5	
	Bilingual learners are provided opportunity to learn content in native language as well as English (e.g., through audio and video supports)	1	2	3	4	5	
	Content strategies like Questioning the Author are used to build knowledge	1	2	3	4	5	
	Formative and summative assessments are provided and used to monitor comprehension and differentiate instruction	1	2	3	4	5	
	Content-Based Approaches Average Rating:						
Cognitive Strategy Instruction							
Program/ Materials Currently Available Do current district materials support comprehension development?	Cognitive strategy instruction is included through a gradual release model	1	2	3	4	5	
	Expository text structure lessons are provided	1	2	3	4	5	
	Cognitive strategies are purposefully instructed (not overdone) and used to support depth of content knowledge	1	2	3	4	5	
	Various types of graphic organizers are included and used to support reading comprehension	1	2	3	4	5	
	Cognitive strategies are taught through meaningful activities such as Reciprocal Teaching or DRTA	1	2	3	4	5	
	Cognitive Strategy Instruction Average Rating:						
Disciplinary Literacy							
Program/ Materials Currently Available Do current district materials support comprehension development?	Lessons on how to read a variety of discipline-specific texts are provided.	1	2	3	4	5	
	Discipline-specific comprehension lessons for analyzing primary and secondary sources in history in grades 6–12 are provided.	1	2	3	4	5	
	Discipline-specific comprehension lessons for analyzing science and technical texts in STEM fields in grades 6–12 are provided.	1	2	3	4	5	
	Digital tools or multimodal texts are used to support knowledge building	1	2	3	4	5	
	Discipline-specific writing skills are emphasized such as DBQs or science writing heuristic	1	2	3	4	5	
	Disciplinary reading comprehension is assessed	1	2	3	4	5	
	Disciplinary Literacy Average Rating:						

Writing to Learn							
Program/ Materials Currently Available Do current district materials support comprehension development?	Lessons on note taking are provided	1	2	3	4	5
	Graphic organizers are included and used to support comprehension	1	2	3	4	5
	Exit slips and admit slips or other quick writes are used to develop comprehension and formatively assess student learning	1	2	3	4	5
	Writing About Reading Average Rating:					
Online Reading Comprehension							
Program/ Materials Currently Available Do current district materials support comprehension development?	Lessons for locating credible sources are provided	1	2	3	4	5
	Lessons for evaluating sources are included	1	2	3	4	5
	Online reading comprehension is monitored/assessed	1	2	3	4	5
	Online Reading Comprehension Average Rating:					
Additional Comments: Please provide any additional insights: Are materials engaging? Culturally relevant? Teacher friendly? Is comprehension assessment dynamic? Other comments?							

| | **PHASE THREE: EVALUTING NEW PROGRAM FOR ADOPTION** |

4–12 Reading Comprehension New Program Evaluation:

1 Evaluate the new reading materials that are being considered for adoption.
2 Provide an average rating for each construct (e.g., oral language).
3 The chair of the team will record the individual scores on the rating sheet.
4 The chair of the team will average the scores of each individual rating and record them on the group composite score sheet.

1 Never Evident	2 Sometimes Evident	3 Satisfactorily Evident	4 Often Evident	5 Always Evident

Discussion-Based Approaches

Program/ Materials Under Review Does the program under review support comprehension development?	Discussion-based approaches for text discussion such as Socratic Seminar or nook club are emphasized	1	2	3	4	5
	Opportunities for critical literacy discussions are provided/emphasized	1	2	3	4	5
	Lessons on strategies for engaging in student-led discussions are provided	1	2	3	4	5
	Frequent opportunities for speaking and listening are provided. Materials emphasize classroom discussions where students add on, ask questions, and provide challenges to ideas to construct deeper understanding of a text or topic.	1	2	3	4	5
	Strategies for teaching bilingual learners are provided	1	2	3	4	5
	Student participation in discussions is assessed and formatively monitored	1	2	3	4	5
	Discussion-Based Approaches Average Rating:					

Content-Based Approach

Program/ Materials Under Review Does the program under review support comprehension development?	Culturally relevant texts are provided for instruction.	1	2	3	4	5
	Lessons on close reading with complex texts is are provided; with scaffolding, students read and reread complex texts and ask and answer text-based questions.	1	2	3	4	5
	Lessons on how to compare and contrast two topics within a text or two or more texts on a similar topic are provided	1	2	3	4	5
	Project-based learning is used in concert with content instruction	1	2	3	4	5
	Bilingual learners are provided opportunity to learn content in native language as well as English (e.g., through audio and video supports).	1	2	3	4	5
	Content strategies like Questioning the Author are used to build knowledge	1	2	3	4	5
	Formative and summative assessments are provided and used to monitor comprehension	1	2	3	4	5
	Content-Based Approaches Average Rating:					

Cognitive Strategy Instruction						
Program/ Materials Under Review Does the program under review support comprehension development?	Cognitive strategy instruction is included through a gradual release model	1	2	3	4	5
	Expository text structure lessons are provided	1	2	3	4	5
	Cognitive strategies are purposefully instructed (not overdone) and used to support depth of content knowledge	1	2	3	4	5
	Various types of graphic organizers are included and used to support reading comprehension	1	2	3	4	5
	Cognitive strategies are taught through meaningful activities such as Reciprocal Teaching or DRTA	1	2	3	4	5
	Cognitive Strategy Instruction Average Rating:					
Disciplinary Literacy						
Program/ Materials Under Review Does the program under review support comprehension development?	Lessons on how to read a variety of discipline-specific texts are provided.	1	2	3	4	5
	Discipline-specific comprehension lessons for analyzing primary and secondary sources in history in grades 6–12 are provided.	1	2	3	4	5
	Discipline-specific comprehension lessons for analyzing science and technical texts in STEM fields in grades 6–12 are provided.	1	2	3	4	5
	Digital tools or multimodal texts are used to support knowledge building	1	2	3	4	5
	Discipline-specific writing skills are emphasized such as DBQs or science writing heuristic	1	2	3	4	5
	Disciplinary reading comprehension is assessed	1	2	3	4	5
	Disciplinary Literacy Average Rating:					
Writing to Learn						
Program/ Materials Under Review Does the program under review support comprehension development?	Lessons on note taking are provided	1	2	3	4	5
	Graphic organizers are included and used to support comprehension	1	2	3	4	5
	Exit slips and admit slips or other quick writes are used to develop comprehension and formatively assess student learning	1	2	3	4	5
	Writing About Reading Average Rating:					
Online Reading Comprehension						
Program/ Materials Under Review Does the program under review support comprehension development?	Lessons for locating credible sources are provided	1	2	3	4	5
	Lessons for evaluating sources are included	1	2	3	4	5
	Online reading comprehension is monitored/assessed	1	2	3	4	5
	Online Reading Comprehension Average Rating:					

Additional Comments: Please provide any additional insights: Are materials engaging? Culturally relevant? Teacher friendly? Is comprehension assessment dynamic? Other comments?	

Vocabulary Instructional Practices Evaluation Form

PHASE ONE: EVALUTING INSTRUCTIONAL PRACTICES				

Vocabulary Instructional Practices Evaluation:

1. To the best of your ability, evaluate the instructional practices used by most teachers in the district. The survey data will help inform this rating. *Reading materials are assessed in Phases Two and Three.*
2. Provide an average rating for each construct (e.g., oral language)
3. The chair of the team will record the individual scores on the rating sheet.
4. The chair of the team will average the scores of each individual rating and record them on the group composite score sheet.

1 Never Evident	2 Sometimes Evident	3 Satisfactorily Evident	4 Often Evident	5 Always Evident				
Vocabulary								
	Tier two words are primarily selected for instruction unless specific words in the disciplines (tier three words) are necessary for comprehending a text		1	2	3	4	5	
	Instruction provides student-friendly definitions of target vocabulary words		1	2	3	4	5	
	Storybook read-alouds are used to teach vocabulary words		1	2	3	4	5	
	Modeling of how to process and understand a new vocabulary word through repeated exposure and discussion is utilized		1	2	3	4	5	
	Code switching is emphasized as a useful instructional practice		1	2	3	4	5	
	Word awareness is cultivated in classroom instruction		1	2	3	4	5	
	Students spend time each day reading independently		1	2	3	4	5	
	Morphology/structural analysis is explicitly taught		1	2	3	4	5	
	Graphic organizers are routinely used to support word learning		1	2	3	4	5	
	Vocabulary Instructional Practices Average Rating:							
Additional Comments: Please provide any additional insights: Is coaching and quality professional development provided to teachers?								

PHASE TWO: EVALUTING CURRENT PROGRAM PROVIDED in the DISTRICT

Vocabulary Current Program Evaluation:

1. Evaluate the current reading materials provided by the school district. This only includes materials the school district has purchased for instructional use. This does not include materials teachers purchase on their own.
2. Provide an average rating for each construct (e.g., oral language).
3. The chair of the team will record the individual scores on the rating sheet.
4. The chair of the team will average the scores of each individual rating and record them on the group composite score sheet.

1 Never Evident	2 Sometimes Evident	3 Satisfactorily Evident	4 Often Evident	5 Always Evident

Vocabulary

Program/Materials Currently Available Do current district materials support vocabulary development?						
	New vocabulary words that will be encountered in a text are front-loaded and emphasized during instruction	1	2	3	4	5
	Lessons on learning tier two vocabulary words are provided through storybook read-alouds	1	2	3	4	5
	Lessons include modeling of how to process and understand new vocabulary words each week	1	2	3	4	5
	Lessons emphasize repeated exposure and use of newly taught vocabulary words	1	2	3	4	5
	Code switching is emphasized as a useful instructional practice	1	2	3	4	5
	Word awareness is emphasized in the vocabulary program	1	2	3	4	5
	Independent reading is purposefully used to support vocabulary development	1	2	3	4	5
	Lessons on morphology and structural analysis are included in the program	1	2	3	4	5
	Lessons on how to teach multiple meaning words are provided	1	2	3	4	5
	Graphic organizers are used to support vocabulary learning	1	2	3	4	5
	Vocabulary Current Program Average Rating:					
Additional Comments: Please provide insights about any of the scores pertaining to materials under review: Are materials engaging? Culturally relevant? Teacher friendly? Other comments?						

PHASE THREE: EVALUTING NEW PROGRAM FOR ADOPTION						
Vocabulary New Program Evaluation:						

1. Evaluate the new reading materials that are being considered for adoption.
2. Provide an average rating for each construct (e.g., oral language).
3. The chair of the team will record the individual scores on the rating sheet.
4. The chair of the team will average the scores of each individual rating and record them on the group composite score sheet.

1 Never Evident	2 Sometimes Evident	3 Satisfactorily Evident	4 Often Evident	5 Always Evident		
Vocabulary						
Program/ Materials Under Review Does the program under review support vocabulary development?	New vocabulary words that will be encountered in a text are front-loaded and emphasized during instruction	1	2	3	4	5
	Lessons on learning tier two vocabulary words are provided through storybook read-alouds	1	2	3	4	5
	Lessons include modeling of how to process and understand new vocabulary words each week	1	2	3	4	5
	Lessons emphasize repeated exposure and use of newly taught vocabulary words	1	2	3	4	5
	Code switching is emphasized as a useful instructional practice	1	2	3	4	5
	Word awareness is emphasized in the vocabulary program	1	2	3	4	5
	Independent reading is purposefully used to support vocabulary development	1	2	3	4	5
	Lessons on morphology and structural analysis are included in the program	1	2	3	4	5
	Lessons on how to teach multiple meaning words are provided	1	2	3	4	5
	Graphic organizers are used to support vocabulary learning	1	2	3	4	5
	Vocabulary Program Under Review Average Score:					
Additional Comments: Please provide insights about any of the scores pertaining to materials under review: Are materials engaging? Culturally relevant? Teacher friendly? Other comments?						

Writing Instructional Practices Evaluation Form

PHASE ONE: EVALUTING INSTRUCTIONAL PRACTICES

Writing Instructional Practices Evaluation:

1. To the best of your ability, evaluate the **instructional practices** used by most teachers in the district. The survey data will help inform this rating. *Writing materials are assessed in Phases Two and Three.*
2. Provide an average rating for each construct (e.g., oral language)
3. The chair of the team will record the individual scores on the rating sheet.
4. The chair of the team will average the scores of each individual rating and record them on the group composite score sheet.

1 Never Evident	2 Sometimes Evident	3 Satisfactorily Evident	4 Often Evident	5 Always Evident				

Writing Framework							
Instructional Practices Are evidence-based instructional practices routinely implemented?	Writing is instructed for approximately 45 minutes per day (depending upon grade level)	1	2	3	4	5
	A writing community is cultivated in the approach to instruction	1	2	3	4	5
	A genre study focus with a scope and sequence is provided	1	2	3	4	5
	Writing strategies are explicitly taught	1	2	3	4	5
	Writers are provided time to practice authentic writing each day (not worksheets)	1	2	3	4	5
	Writers are assessed and given frequent feedback on their progress	1	2	3	4	5
	Motivation is a key consideration for instruction; students are encouraged to write about meaningful topics through choice and authentic writing opportunities	1	2	3	4	5
	Instructional support for bilingual writers is provided	1	2	3	4	5
	Writing Framework Average Rating:					
Narrative Writing							
Instructional Practices Are evidence-based instructional practices routinely implemented?	Narrative writing instruction focuses on plot structure	1	2	3	4	5
	Narrative writing instruction teaches writers to show and not tell	1	2	3	4	5
	Narrative writing teaches the use of internal and external dialogue (develops in sophistication as grade levels increase)	1	2	3	4	5
	Narrative writing teaches theme as part of a narrated event	1	2	3	4	5
	Narrative writing teaches point of view	1	2	3	4	5

	Mentor texts are used to teach narrative writing	1	2	3	4	5
	Students are provided ample time to practice narrative writing skills (in authentic writing tasks) specific to their grade level	1	2	3	4	5
	Cognitive Strategy Instruction Average Rating:					
Argument Writing						
Instructional Practices Are evidence-based instructional practices routinely implemented?	The structure of an argument is taught and practiced in authentic argument writing	1	2	3	4	5
	As writers develop, they are taught the difference between persuasive and argument writing	1	2	3	4	5
	Academic language and transition words of writing are explicitly taught and practiced	1	2	3	4	5
	Content knowledge is developed through argument writing (when appropriate)	1	2	3	4	5
	Mentor texts are used to teach argument writing	1	2	3	4	5
	Argument Writing Average Rating:					
Informational Writing						
Instructional Practices Are evidence-based instructional practices routinely implemented?	Wide reading on a topic is used to support informational writing	1	2	3	4	5
	Students are taught and practice strategies for locating sources for informational writing	1	2	3	4	5
	Students are taught and practice how to discern credible sources	1	2	3	4	5
	Students are taught and practice summarizing summarize information in a text	1	2	3	4	5
	Students are taught to synthesize information across multiple text types	1	2	3	4	5
	Students are taught and practice strategies for note taking to use in their informational writing	1	2	3	4	5
	Students are taught strategies for paraphrasing	1	2	3	4	5
	Students are taught strategies for using discipline-specific vocabulary words in writing	1	2	3	4	5
	Students write and create informational texts on topics of their choice	1	2	3	4	5
	Informational Writing Average Rating:					
Digital Composition						
Instructional Practices Are evidence-based instructional practices routinely implemented?	Opportunities for presenting writing in digital formats, like blogging, are provided	1	2	3	4	5
	Digital tools are used to support writing	1	2	3	4	5
	Students are provided opportunities to present their writing through digital presentations	1	2	3	4	5
	Online search engines and social media are used to teach information gathering	1	2	3	4	5
	Digital Writing Average Rating:					

Handwriting						
Instructional Practices Are evidence-based instructional practices routinely implemented?	Handwriting is explicitly taught in K–5 and practiced daily	1	2	3	4	5
	Pencil grasp is explicitly taught and practiced	1	2	3	4	5
	Correct letter formation is instructed and practiced	1	2	3	4	5
	Handwriting legibility is instructed and practiced	1	2	3	4	5
	Handwriting is practiced regularly in authentic contexts and is not subordinate to keyboarding	1	2	3	4	5
	Handwriting Average Rating:					
Writing Conventions						
Instructional Practices Are evidence-based instructional practices routinely implemented?	Grammar instruction is mainly embedded in the context of authentic writing	1	2	3	4	5
	Sentence combining exercises are explicitly taught	1	2	3	4	5
	Lessons focus upon writing as a process of revision	1	2	3	4	5
	Writing Conventions Average Rating:					

PHASE TWO: EVELUTING CURRENT PROGRAM PROVIDED IN THE DISTRICT

Writing Instructional Practices Evaluation:

1 Evaluate the current reading materials provided by the school district. This only includes materials the school district has purchased for instructional use. This does not include materials teachers purchase on their own.
2 Provide an average rating for each construct (e.g., oral language).
3 The chair of the team will record the individual scores on the rating sheet.
4 The chair of the team will average the scores of each individual rating and record them on the group composite score sheet.

1 Never Evident	2 Sometimes Evident	3 Satisfactorily Evident	4 Often Evident	5 Always Evident

Writing Framework						
Program/ Materials Currently Available Do current district materials support writing?	Writing is instructed for approximately 45 minutes per day (depending upon grade level)	1	2	3	4	5
	A writing community is cultivated in the approach to instruction	1	2	3	4	5
	A genre study focus with a scope and sequence is provided	1	2	3	4	5
	Writing strategies are explicitly taught	1	2	3	4	5
	Writers are assessed and given frequent feedback on their progress	1	2	3	4	5

	Motivation is a key consideration for instruction; students are encouraged to write about meaningful topics through choice and authentic writing opportunities	1	2	3	4	5
	Considerations for bilingual writers are provided	1	2	3	4	5
	Writing Framework Average Rating:					
Narrative Writing						
Program/ Materials Currently Available Do current district materials support the teaching and learning of writing?	Narrative writing lessons focuses on plot structure	1	2	3	4	5
	Narrative writing lessons teach writers to show and not tell	1	2	3	4	5
	Narrative writing lessons focus upon the use of internal and external dialogue (develops in sophistication as grade levels increase)	1	2	3	4	5
	Narrative writing lessons focus on theme as part of a narrated event	1	2	3	4	5
	Narrative writing lessons teach point of view	1	2	3	4	5
	Mentor texts are provided to support narrative writing instruction	1	2	3	4	5
	Narrative Writing Instruction Average Rating:					
Argument Writing						
Program/ Materials Currently Available Do current district materials support the teaching and learning of writing?	Lessons on the structure of an argument are provided	1	2	3	4	5
	As writers develop, lessons teach between persuasive and argument writing	1	2	3	4	5
	Lessons include academic language use and use of transition words	1	2	3	4	5
	Content knowledge is developed through argument writing (when appropriate)	1	2	3	4	5
	Mentor texts are provided to support argument writing	1	2	3	4	5
	Argument Writing Average Rating:					
Informational Writing						
Program/ Materials Currently Available Do current district materials support the teaching and learning of writing?	Wide reading on a topic is used to support informational writing	1	2	3	4	5
	Lessons on locating sources for informational writing are provided	1	2	3	4	5
	Lessons provided on how to discern credible sources	1	2	3	4	5
	Lessons provided on how to teach summarization for informational writing	1	2	3	4	5
	Lessons provided on how to teach writers to synthesize information across multiple text types	1	2	3	4	5
	Lessons for note taking are provided	1	2	3	4	5
	Lessons for paraphrasing are provided	1	2	3	4	5
	Lessons for writing with discipline-specific vocabulary words are provided	1	2	3	4	5
	Informational Writing Average Rating:					

Digital Composition						
Program/ Materials Currently Available	Writing program includes opportunities for presenting writing in digital formats, like blogging	1	2	3	4	5
	Digital tools are emphasized to support writing and presentation of writing	1	2	3	4	5
Do current district materials support the teaching and learning of writing?	Lessons on Internet searching are used to teach information gathering	1	2	3	4	5
	Digital Writing Average Rating:					
Handwriting						
Program/ Materials Currently Available	Handwriting is explicitly taught in K–5 and practiced daily	1	2	3	4	5
	Lessons on pencil grasp are provided in handwriting program	1	2	3	4	5
Do current district materials support the teaching and learning of writing?	Lessons on correct letter formation are provided	1	2	3	4	5
	Handwriting legibility lessons are included	1	2	3	4	5
	Handwriting is practiced regularly in authentic contexts and is not subordinate to keyboarding	1	2	3	4	5
	Handwriting assessments are included	1	2	3	4	5
	Handwriting Average Rating:					
Writing Conventions						
Program/ Materials Currently Available	Grammar instruction is mainly embedded in the context of authentic writing	1	2	3	4	5
	Lessons on sentence combining exercises are provided	1	2	3	4	5
Do current district materials support the teaching and learning of writing?	Lessons focus on writing as a process of revision	1	2	3	4	5
	Writing Conventions Average Rating:					

PHASE THREE: EVALUTING NEW PROGRAM FOR ADOPTION							
Writing Instructional Practices Evaluation:							

1   Evaluate the new reading materials that are being considered for adoption.
2   Provide an average rating for each construct (e.g., oral language).
3   The chair of the team will record the individual scores on the rating sheet.
4   The chair of the team will average the scores of each individual rating and record them on the group composite score sheet.

1 Never Evident	2 Sometimes Evident	3 Satisfactorily Evident	4 Often Evident	5 Always Evident

Writing Framework

Program/ Materials Under Review Does the program under support the teaching and learning of writing?	Writing is instructed for approximately 45 minutes per day (depending upon grade level)	1	2	3	4	5
	A writing community is cultivated in the approach to instruction	1	2	3	4	5
	A genre study focus with a scope and sequence is provided	1	2	3	4	5
	Writing strategies are explicitly taught	1	2	3	4	5
	Writers are assessed and given frequent feedback on their progress	1	2	3	4	5
	Motivation is a key consideration for instruction; students are encouraged to write about meaningful topics through choice and authentic writing opportunities	1	2	3	4	5
	Considerations for bilingual writers are provided	1	2	3	4	5
	Writing Framework Average Rating:					

Narrative Writing

Program/ Materials Under Review Does the program under support the teaching and learning of writing?	Narrative writing lessons focuses on plot structure	1	2	3	4	5
	Narrative writing lessons teaches writers to show and not tell	1	2	3	4	5
	Narrative writing lessons teaches the use of internal and external dialogue (develops in sophistication as grade levels increase)	1	2	3	4	5
	Narrative writing lessons focus on theme as part of a narrated event	1	2	3	4	5
	Narrative writing lessons teach point of view	1	2	3	4	5
	Mentor texts are provided to support narrative writing instruction	1	2	3	4	5
	Narrative Writing Instruction Average Rating:					

Argument Writing							
Program/ Materials Under Review Does the program under support the teaching and learning of writing?	Lessons on the structure of an argument are provided	1	2	3	4	5
	As writers develop, lessons teach between persuasive and argument writing	1	2	3	4	5
	Lessons include academic language use and use of transition words	1	2	3	4	5
	Content knowledge is developed through argument writing (when appropriate)	1	2	3	4	5
	Mentor texts are provided to support argument writing	1	2	3	4	5
	Argument Writing Average Rating:					
Informational Writing							
Program/ Materials Under Review Does the program under support the teaching and learning of writing?	Wide reading on a topic is used to support informational writing	1	2	3	4	5
	Lessons on locating sources for informational writing are provided	1	2	3	4	5
	Lessons provided on how to discern credible sources	1	2	3	4	5
	Lessons provided on how to teach summarization for informational writing	1	2	3	4	5
	Lessons provided on how to teach writers to synthesize information across multiple text types	1	2	3	4	5
	Lessons for note taking are provided	1	2	3	4	5
	Lessons for paraphrasing are provided	1	2	3	4	5
	Lessons for writing with discipline-specific vocabulary words are provided	1	2	3	4	5
	Informational Writing Average Rating:					
Digital Composition							
Program/ Materials Under Review Does the program under support the teaching and learning of writing?	Writing program includes opportunities for presenting writing in digital formats, like blogging	1	2	3	4	5
	Digital tools are emphasized to support writing and presentation of writing	1	2	3	4	5
	Lessons on Internet searching are used to teach information gathering	1	2	3	4	5
	Digital Writing Average Rating:					
Handwriting							
Program/ Materials Under Review Does the program under support the teaching and learning of writing?	Handwriting is explicitly taught in K–5 and practiced daily	1	2	3	4	5
	Lessons on pencil grasp are provided in handwriting program	1	2	3	4	5
	Lessons on correct letter formation are provided	1	2	3	4	5
	Handwriting legibility lessons are included	1	2	3	4	5
	Handwriting is practiced regularly in authentic contexts and is not subordinate to keyboarding	1	2	3	4	5
	Handwriting assessments are included	1	2	3	4	5
	Handwriting Average Rating:					

Writing Conventions						
Program/ Materials Under Review	Grammar instruction is mainly embedded in the context of authentic writing	1	2	3	4	5
	Lessons on sentence combining exercises are provided	1	2	3	4	5
Does the program under support the teaching and learning of writing?	Lessons focus upon writing as a process of revision	1	2	3	4	5
	Writing Conventions Average Rating:					

Independent Reading and Classroom Libraries Evaluation Form

PHASE ONE: EVALUTING INSTRUCTIONAL PRACTICES						
(This evaluation form is streamlined so it looks different from the others in this text.) Independent Reading and Classroom Libraries Instructional Practices Evaluation: 1　To the best of your ability, evaluate the instructional practices used by most teachers in the district. The survey data will help inform this rating. *Reading materials are assessed in Phases Two and Three.* 2　Provide an average rating for each construct (e.g., oral language). 3　The chair of the team will record the individual scores on the rating sheet. 4　The chair of the team will average the scores of each individual rating and record them on the group composite score sheet.						
1 Never Evident	2 Sometimes Evident	3 Satisfactorily Evident	4 Often Evident	5 Always Evident		
Independent Reading/Classroom Libraries						
Instructional Practices Are evidence-based instructional practices routinely implemented?	Students are surveyed about their interests as readers	1	2	3	4	5
	Independent reading is used with the intention to support reading achievement	1	2	3	4	5
	Instruction emphasizes opportunities for student choice of text	1	2	3	4	5
	Students are scaffolded towards longer durations of independent reading	1	2	3	4	5
	Teachers monitor student reading volume (no reading logs)	1	2	3	4	5
	Teachers audit their libraries for inclusive literature and engaging texts	1	2	3	4	5
	Instruction emphasizes reading nonfiction texts	1	2	3	4	5
	Independent Reading/Classroom Libraries Current Instructional Practices Average Rating:					
Additional Comments: Please provide any additional insights: Is coaching and quality professional development provided to teachers?						

PHASE TWO: EVALUTING CURRENT PROGRAM PROVIDED IN THE DISTRICT							
Independent Reading/Classroom Libraries Current Program Evaluation: 1 Evaluate the current reading materials provided by the school district. This only includes materials the school district has purchased for instructional use. This does not include materials teachers purchase on their own. 2 Provide an average rating for each construct (e.g., oral language). 3 The chair of the team will record the individual scores on the rating sheet. 4 The chair of the team will average the scores of each individual rating and record them on the group composite score sheet.							

1 Never Evident	2 Sometimes Evident	3 Satisfactorily Evident	4 Often Evident	5 Always Evident			
Independent Reading Materials							
Program/Materials Currently Available Do current district materials support independent reading?	Classroom libraries provide inclusive, culturally relevant texts that represent diverse cultures and communities	1	2	3	4	5	
	Reading materials include surveys to query students about their interests as readers	1	2	3	4	5	
	Independent reading is monitored and used to intentionally support reading achievement	1	2	3	4	5	
	Opportunities for students to engage in independent reading with books of their choice as well as texts for specific instructional purposes are provided	1	2	3	4	5	
	Materials are engaging and leverage student interests	1	2	3	4	5	
	Lessons for scaffolding independent reading are provided	1	2	3	4	5	
	Instructional strategies for how to monitor student reading volume (not through reading logs) are provided	1	2	3	4	5	
	At least 20 books per student in each K–12 ELA classroom library are provided	1	2	3	4	5	
	Nonfiction texts are a substantial part of all classroom libraries	1	2	3	4	5	
	Books for the classroom library that are written at multiple levels of readability are provided	1	2	3	4	5	
	Independent Reading/Classroom Libraries Current Program Average Rating:						

Additional Comments: Please provide insights about any of the scores pertaining to materials under review: Are materials engaging? Culturally relevant? Do teachers have funds for purchasing books each year? Other comments?						

PHASE THREE: EVALUTING NEW PROGRAM FOR ADOPTION

Independent Reading and Classroom Libraries New Program Evaluation:

1. Evaluate the new reading materials that are being considered for adoption.
2. Provide an average rating for each construct (e.g., oral language).
3. The chair of the team will record the individual scores on the rating sheet.
4. The chair of the team will average the scores of each individual rating and record them on the group composite score sheet.

1 Never Evident	2 Sometimes Evident	3 Satisfactorily Evident	4 Often Evident	5 Always Evident

Independent Reading Materials

Program/ Materials Under Review	Classroom libraries provide inclusive, culturally relevant texts that represent diverse cultures and communities	1	2	3	4	5
Does program under review support independent reading?	Reading materials include surveys to query students about their interests as readers	1	2	3	4	5
	Independent reading is monitored and used to intentionally support reading achievement	1	2	3	4	5
	Opportunities for students to engage in independent reading with books of their choice as well as texts for specific instructional purposes are provided	1	2	3	4	5
	Materials are engaging and leverage student interests	1	2	3	4	5
	Lessons for scaffolding independent reading are provided	1	2	3	4	5
	Instructional strategies for how to monitor student reading volume (not through reading logs) are provided	1	2	3	4	5
	At least 20 books per student in each K–12 ELA classroom library are provided	1	2	3	4	5
	Nonfiction texts are a substantial part of all classroom libraries	1	2	3	4	5

eRESOURCES

	Books for the classroom library that are written at multiple levels of readability are provided	1	2	3	4	5
	Independent Reading/Classroom Libraries Program Under Review Average Rating:					
Additional Comments: Please provide insights about any of the scores pertaining to materials under review: Are materials engaging? Culturally relevant? Do teachers have funds for purchasing books each year? Other comments?						

Reading Evaluation Document: Group Composite Scores

Directions: This page is for documenting the average score of the group. The chair of the committee will average all individual scores and input in the following table.

FOUNDATIONAL SKILLS	Instructional Practices	Present Materials/ Program	Materials/Program Under Review
Concepts About Print			
Alphabet Knowledge			
Phonological Awareness			
Phonics and Spelling			
Fluency			
THEMES IN COMMENTS:			
	***Scores of 3 or less suggest a need for sustained professional development	***Scores of 3 or less necessitate a review of new materials	***Scores of 3 or less suggest material under review does not promote quality instruction

K–3 COMPREHENSION	Instructional Practices	Present Materials/ Program	Materials/Program Under Review
Oral Language			
Read-Alouds with Discussion			
Informational Text and Content-Based Approaches			
Cognitive Strategy Lessons			
Writing to Learn			
THEMES IN COMMENTS:			
	***Scores of 3 or less suggest a need for sustained professional development	***Scores of 3 or less necessitate a review of new materials	***Scores of 3 or less suggest material under review does not promote quality instruction

4–12 COMPREHENSION	Instructional Practices	Present Materials/ Program	Materials/Program Under Review
Discussion-Based Approaches			
Content-Based Instruction			
Cognitive Strategy Instruction			
Disciplinary Literacy			
Writing to Learn			
Online Reading Comprehension			
THEMES IN COMMENTS:			
	***Scores of 3 or less suggest a need for sustained professional development	***Scores of 3 or less necessitate a review of new materials	***Scores of 3 or less suggest material under review does not promote quality instruction

VOCABULARY	Instructional Practices	Present Materials/ Program	Materials/Program Under Review
Overall Rating:			
THEMES IN COMMENTS:			
	***Scores of 3 or less suggest a need for sustained professional development	***Scores of 3 or less necessitate a review of new materials	***Scores of 3 or less suggest material under review does not promote quality instruction

WRITING	Instructional Practices	Present Materials/ Program	Materials/Program Under Review
Writing Framework			
Narrative Writing			
Argument Writing			
Informational Writing			
Digital Composition			
Handwriting			
Writing Conventions			
THEMES IN COMMENTS:			
	***Scores of 3 or less suggest a need for sustained professional development	***Scores of 3 or less necessitate a review of new materials	***Scores of 3 or less suggest material under review does not promote quality instruction

INDEPENDENT READING AND CLASSROOM LIBRARIES	Instructional Practices	Present Materials/Program	Materials/Program Under Review
Independent Reading and Classroom Libraries			
THEMES IN COMMENTS:			
	***Scores of 3 or less suggest a need for sustained professional development	***Scores of 3 or less necessitate a review of new materials	***Scores of 3 or less suggest material under review does not promote quality instruction

Appendix D: Post-Evaluation Form

Instructional Needs Template

Use this chart after the audit has been completed to document instructional needs of staff.

Professional Learning Needs	Grade Level	Rationale	Professional Development? Coaching? Both?
Example: Phonics	K–3	*Surveys revealed teachers wanted more resources for systematic instruction.*	*Both. A new phonics program along with ongoing professional development and coaching would help improve instruction across the board.*

Feedback Form for Pilot-Tested Program

Program Name	
Grade Level	
Skill Focus	
Aligned to Standards?	
Engaging/Culturally Relevant Materials?	
Differentiates?	
Supports Strong Instructional Practice?	
Please rate the program: **Highly recommend** **Recommend** **Recommend with reservations** **Do not recommend**	
Strengths of the Program:	
Weaknesses of the Program:	

References

Adams, M. J. (1990). *Beginning to read: Thinking and learning about print*. Cambridge, MA: MIT Press.

Afflerbach, P., Pearson, P. D., & Paris, S. (2017). Skills and strategies: Their differences, their relationships, and why they matter. In K. Mokhtari (Ed.), *Improving reading comprehension through metacognitive reading strategies instruction* (pp. 33–49). Lanham, MD: Rowman & Littlefield.

Aguilar, E. (2013). *The art of coaching: Effective strategies for school transformation*. Hoboken, NJ: Jossey-Bass.

Alexander, R. (2009). *Towards dialogic teaching: Rethinking classroom talk* (4th ed.). Thirsk: Dialogos.

Allington, R. L. (2002). What I've learned about effective reading instruction from a decade of studying exemplary elementary classroom teachers. *Phi Delta Kappan*, *83*(10), 740–747.

Allington, R. (2014). How reading volume affects both reading fluency and reading achievement. *International Electronic Journal of Elementary Education*, *7*(1), 13–26.

Almasi, J., O'Flahavan, J., & Arya, P. (2001). A comparative analysis of student and teacher development in more and less proficient discussions of literature. *Reading Research Quarterly*, *36*, 96–120. doi: 10.1598/RRQ.36.2.1.

Alves, R., & Limpo, T. (2015). Progress in written language bursts, pauses, transcription, and written composition across schooling. *Scientific Studies of Reading*, *19*(5), 374–391.

Anderson, R. C., & Nagy, W. E. (1992). The vocabulary conundrum. *American Educator*, *14*(18), 44–46.

Anderson, R. C., Hiebert, E., Scott, J. A., & Wilkinson, I. A. (1985). *Becoming a nation of readers: The report of the commission on reading*. Champaign, IL. Center for the Study of Reading.

Anderson, R. C., & Freebody, P. (1981). Vocabulary knowledge. In J. Guthrie (Ed.), *Comprehension and teaching: Research reviews* (pp. 77–117). Newark, DE: International Reading Association.

Anderson, R. C., & Pearson, P. D. (1984). A schema-theoretic view of basic processes in reading comprehension. In P. D. Pearson (Ed.), *Handbook of reading research* (pp. 255–291). New York, NY: Longman.

Anderson, R. C., Wilson, P. T., & Fielding, L. G. (1988). Growth in reading and how children spend their time outside of school. *Reading Research Quarterly*, *23*(3), 285–303.

Apel, K. (2009). The acquisition of mental orthographic representations for reading and spelling development. *Communication Disorders Quarterly*, *31*(1), 42–52. https://doi.org/10.1177/1525740108325553.

Applebee, A., Langer, J., Nystrand, M., & Gamoran, A. (2003). Discussion-based approaches to developing understanding: Classroom instruction and student performance in middle and high school English. *American Educational Research Journal*, *40*, 685–730.

Armbruster, B. B., Lehr, F., Osborn, J., & Adler, C. R. (2001). *Put reading first: The research building blocks of reading instruction: Kindergarten through grade 3* (3rd ed.). Washington, D.C.: National Institute for Literacy.

Bangert-Drowns, R. L., Hurley, M. M., & Wilkinson, B. (2004). The effects of school-based writing-to-learn interventions on academic achievement: A meta-analysis. *Review of Educational Research*, *74*(1), 29–58. doi: 10.3102/00346543074001029.

Barnes, D., Britten, J., & Rosen, H. (1969). *Language, the learner and the school*. Harmondsworth, UK: Penguin.

Barry, A. (2008) Reading the past: Historical antecedents to contemporary reading methods and materials. *Reading Horizons*, *49*(1), 31–52.

Bear, D., Invernizzi, M., Templeton, S., & Johnston, F. (2016). *Words their way: Word study for phonics, vocabulary, and spelling instruction* (6th ed.). Boston, MA: Allyn & Bacon.

Beck, I. L., McKeown, M. G., & Kucan, L. (2002). *Bringing words to life: Robust vocabulary instruction*. New York, NY: Guilford Press.

Beck, I. L., & McKeown, M. G. (2006). *Improving comprehension with Questioning the Author: A fresh and expanded view of a powerful approach.* New York, NY: Scholastic.

Beck, I., & Beck, M. (2013). *Making sense of phonics: The how's and why's* (2nd ed.). New York, NY: Guilford.

Bennett, S., Maton, K., & Kervin, L. (2008). The 'digital natives' debate: A critical review of the evidence. *British Journal of The New Literacies of Online Research and Comprehension, 39*(5), 775–786. doi: 10.1111/j.1467-8535.2007.00793.x.

Berninger, V. W., Abbott, R. D., Jones, J., Wolf, B. J., Gould, L., Anderson-Youngstrom, M., … Apel, K. (2006). Early development of language by hand: Composing, reading, listening, and speaking connections; three letter-writing modes; and fast mapping in spelling, *Developmental Neuropsychology, 29*(1), 61–92. doi: 10.1207/s15326942dn2901_5.

Berninger, V. W., Abbott, R. D., Augsburger, A., & Garcia, N. (2009). Comparison of pen and keyboard transcription modes in children with and without learning disabilities. *Learning Disability Quarterly, 32*(3), 123–141. https://doi.org/10.2307/27740364

Bezdicek, J., & García, E. G. (2012). Working with preschool English language learners: A sociocultural approach. In B. Yoon & H. K. Kim (Eds.), *Teachers' roles in second language learning: Classroom applications of sociocultural theory* (pp. 171–188). Charlotte, NC: Information Age Publishing.

Billings, L., & Fitzgerald, J. (2002). Dialogic discussion and the paideia seminar. *American Educational Research Journal, 39*(4), 907–941.

Bishop, R. S. (1990). Mirrors, windows, and sliding glass doors. *Perspectives, 6*(3), ix–xi.

Blevins, W. (2017). *Phonics from A-Z: A practical guide* (3rd ed.). New York, NY: Scholastic.

Boscolo, P., & Gelati, C. (2019). Motivating writers. In S. Graham, C. A. MacArthur, & M. Hebert (Eds.), *Best practices in writing instruction* (3rd ed., pp. 3–28). New York, NY: Guilford Press.

Boyle, J. R. (2013). Strategic note-taking for inclusive middle school science classrooms. *Remedial and Special Education, 34*(2), 78–90. https://doi.org/10.1177/0741932511410862.

Bowers, J., & Bowers P. N. (2017). Beyond phonics: The case for teaching children the logic of the English spelling system. *Educational Psychologist, 52*(2), 124–141.

Bowling, E. C., & Cabell, S. Q. (2018). Developing readers: Understanding concept of word in text development in emergent readers. *Early Childhood Education Journal, 47*(2), 143–151.

Brady, S., Gillis, M., Smith, T., Lavalette, M. E, Liss-Bronstein, L., Lowe, E., … Wilder, D. T. (2009). First grade teachers' knowledge of phonological awareness and code concepts: Examining gains from an intensive form of professional development and corresponding teacher attitudes. *Reading and Writing, 22*(4), 425–455.

Bressler, C. (2007). *Literacy criticism: An introduction to theory and practice.* Upper Saddle River, NJ: Prentice Hall.

Brown, A. L., & Day, J. D. (1983). Macrorules for summarizing texts: The development of expertise. *Journal of Verbal Learning & Verbal Behavior, 22*(1), 1–14. https://doi.org/10.1016/S0022-5371(83)80002-4.

Brown, B. A., & Spang, E. (2007). Double talk: Synthesizing everyday and science language in the classroom. *Science Education, 92*(4), 708–732.

Bruner, J. S. (1983). *Child's talk: Learning to use language.* Oxford, UK: Oxford University Press.

Byrnes, J. P., & Wasik, B. A. (2009). *Solving problems in the teaching of literacy. Language and literacy development: What educators need to know.* New York, NY: Guilford Press.

Cardenas-Hagan, E. (2016). Listening comprehension: Special considerations for English learners. *Perspectives on Language and Literacy: Auditory Processing and Comprehension, 42*(3), 31–35.

Cardoso-Martins, C., Mesquita, T. C., & Ehri, L. C. (2011). Letter names and phonological awareness help children to learn letter-sound relations. *Journal of Experimental Child Psychology, 109*(1), 25–38.

Carlisle, J. F. (2003). Morphology matters in learning to read: A commentary. *Reading Psychology, 24*(3-4), 291–322. doi: 10.1080/02702710390227369.

Castek, J., Zawilinski, L., McVerry, J. G., O'Byrne, W. I., & Leu, D. J. (2011). The new literacies of online reading comprehension: New opportunities and challenges for students with learning difficulties. In C. Wyatt-Smith, J. Elkins, & S. Gunn (Eds.), *Multiple perspectives on difficulties in learning literacy and numeracy* (pp. 91–110). New York, NY: Springer. doi: 10.1007/978-1-4020-8864-3_4.

Castles, A., Rastle, K., & Nation, K. (2018). Ending the reading wars: Reading acquisition from novice to expert. *Psychological Science in the Public Interest, 19*(1), 5–51. doi: 10.1177/1529100618772271.

Catts, H. W., Fey, M. E., Zhang, X., & Tomblin, J. B. (2001). Estimating the risk of future reading difficulties in kindergarten children: A research-based model and its clinical implementation. *Language, Speech, and Hearing Services in Schools, 32*, 38–50.

Cervetti, J. N., & Heibert, H. (2015). The sixth pillar of reading: Knowledge development. *The Reading Teacher, 68*(7), 548–551.

Chapman, J. W., & Tunmer, W. E. (2003). Reading difficulties, reading-related self-perceptions, and strategies for overcoming negative self-beliefs. *Reading & Writing Quarterly, 19*(1), 5–24, doi: 10.1080/10573560308205.

Chard, D. J., Vaughn, S., & Tyler, B. (2002). A synthesis of research on effective interventions for building fluency with elementary students with learning disabilities. *Journal of Learning Disabilities, 35*(5), 386–406.

Chenoweth, T. G., & Everhart, R. B. (2002). *Navigating comprehensive school change: A guide for the perplexed.* Larchmont, NY: Eye on Education.

Chinn, C., Anderson, R., & Waggoner, M. (2001). Patterns of discourse in two kinds of literature discussion. *Reading Research Quarterly, 36*(4), 378–410.

Clare, L., Valdes, R., & Patthey-Chavez, G. G. (2000). *Learning to write in urban elementary and middle schools: An investigation of teachers' written feedback on student compositions.* Technical Report. National Center for Research on Evaluation, Standards, and Student Testing (CRESST), University of California, Graduate School of Education & Information Studies. Los Angeles.

Clark, J. M., & Paivio, A. (1991). Dual coding theory and education. *Educational Psychology Review,* 3(3), 149–170.

Coleman, D. (2011, April 28th). *Bringing the common core to life speech presented at state education building.* Albany, NY.

Coleman, D., & Pimentel, S. (2012*). Revised publishers' criteria for the Common Core State Standards in English language arts and literacy, grades 3–12.* Retrieved from www.corestandards. org/assets/ Publishers_Criteria_for_3-12.pdf

Craig, S. A. (2003). The effects of an adapted interactive writing intervention on kindergarten children's phonological awareness, spelling, and early reading development. *Reading Research Quarterly, 38*, 438–440.

Cunningham, A. E., & Stanovich, K. E. (1998). The impact of print exposure on word recognition. In J. L. Metsala & L. C. Ehri (Eds.), *Word recognition in beginning literacy* (pp. 235–262). Mahwah, NJ: Lawrence Erlbaum Associates Publishers.

Daane, M. C., Campbell, J. R., Grigg, W. S., Goodman, M. J., and Oranje, A. (2005). Fourth-Grade Students Reading Aloud: NAEP 2002 Special Study of Oral Reading (NCES 2006-469). U.S. Department of Education. Institute of Education Sciences, National Center for Education Statistics. Washington, DC: Government Printing Office.

Dale, E. (1965). Vocabulary measurement: Techniques and major findings. *Elementary English, 42*(8), 895–901.

Dickson, S. V., Simmons, D. C., & Kame'enui, E. J. (1995). *Text organization and its relation to reading comprehension: A synthesis of the research (Tech. Rep. No. 17).* Eugene, OR: University of Oregon, National Center to Improve the Tools of Educators.

Doiron, R. (2003). *Boy books, girls, books: Should we re-organize our school library collections?* Teacher Librarian, 30, 14–17.

Donovan, C. A., & Smolkin, L. B. (2011). Supporting informational writing in the elementary grades. *The Reading Teacher, 64*(6), 406–416.

DuFour, R., & Marzano, R. (2011). *Leaders of learning: How district, school, and classroom leaders improve student achievement.* Bloomington, IN: Solution Tree.

Duke, N. K. (2000). 3.6 minutes per day: The scarcity of informational texts in first grade. *Reading Research Quarterly, 35,* 202–224.

Duke, N., & Mesmer, H. A. E. (2018–2019). Phonics faux pas. Avoiding instructional missteps in teaching letter-sound relationships. *American Educator.* Retrieved from https://www.aft.org/ae/winter2018-2019/duke_mesmer

Duke, N. K., Pearson, P. D., Strachan, S. L., & Billman, A. K. (2011). Essential elements of fostering and teaching reading comprehension. In S. J. Samuels & A. E. Farstrup (Eds.), *What research has to say about reading instruction* (4th ed., pp. 51–93). Newark, DE: International Reading Association.

Durkin, D. (1978). What classroom observations reveal about reading comprehension instruction. *Reading Research Quarterly, 14*(4), 481–533.

Edwards, O. W., & Taub, G. E., (2016) The influence of specific phonemic awareness processes on the reading comprehension of African American students. *Journal of Research in Childhood Education, 30*(1), 74–84, doi: 10.1080/02568543.2015.1105332.

Eeds, M., & Wells, D. (1989). Grand conversations: An exploration of meaning construction in literature study groups. *Research in the Teaching of English, 23*(1), 4–29.

Ehri, L. C. (2000). Learning to read and learning to spell: Two sides of a coin. *Topics in Language Disorders, 20*(3), 19–36. doi: 10.1097/00011363-200020030-00005.

Ehri, L. C., & Flugman, B. (2018). Mentoring teachers in systematic phonics instruction: Effectiveness of an intensive year long program for kindergarten through 3rd grade teachers and their students. *Reading and Writing, 31,* 425–456.

Ehri, L. C., & McCormick, S. (1998) Phases of word learning: Implications for instruction with delayed and disabled readers. *Reading and Writing Quarterly, 14*(2), 135–163.

Ehri, L.C. (1994). Development of the ability to read words: Update. In R. Ruddell, M. Ruddell, & H. Singer (Eds.), *Theoretical models and processes of reading.* (4th ed., pp. 323–358). Newark, Del: International Reading Association.

Ehri, L. C., Nunes, S. R., Stahl, S. A., & Willows, D. M. (2001). Systematic phonics instruction helps students learn to read: Evidence from the National Reading Panel's meta-analysis. *Review of Educational Research, 71*(3), 393–447.

Emdin, C. (2013). *For white folks who teach in the hood...and the rest of y'all too.* Boston, MA: Beacon Press.

Evans, M., Teasdale, R. M., Gannon-Slater, N., La Londe, P. G., Crenshaw, H. L., Greene, J. C., ... Schwandt, T. A. (2019). How did that happen? Teachers' explanations for low test scores. *Teachers College Record, 121*(2) 1–40.

Ferretti, R. P., & Lewis, W. E. (2019). Argumentative writing. In S. Graham, C. A. MacArthur, & M. Hebert (Eds.), *Best practices in writing instruction* (3rd ed., pp. 135–161). New York, NY: Guilford Press.

Fielding, L., Kerr, N., & Rosier, P. (2007). *Annual growth for all students, catch-up growth for those who are behind.* Kennewick, WA: The New Foundation Press.

Fisher, D. B., Frey, N., Anderson, H. L., & Thayre, M. (2015). *Text-dependent questions, grades 6-12: Pathways to close and critical reading.* Thousand Oaks, CA: Corwin.

Fisher, D., & Frey, N. (2018). Raise reading volume through access, choice, discussion, and book talks. *The Reading Teacher, 72*(1), 89–97. https://doi.org/10.1002/trtr.1691

Ford, K. L., Cabell, S. Q., Konold, T. R., Invernizzi, M., & Gartland, L. B. (2013). Diversity among Spanish-speaking English language learners: Profiles of early literacy skills in kindergarten. *Reading and Writing, 26*(6), 889–912.

Fountas, I., & Pinnell, G. S. (2016). *Guided reading: Responsive reaching across the grades* (2nd ed.). Portsmouth, MA: Heineman.

Freebody, P., & Luke, A. (1990). "Literacies" programs: Debates and demands in cultural context. *Prospect, 5,* 7–16.

Fuchs, L. S., Fuchs, D., Hosp, M. K., & Jenkins, J. R. (2001). Oral reading fluency as an indicator of reading competence: A theoretical, empirical, and historical analysis. *Scientific Studies of Reading, 5,* 239–256. http://dx.doi.org/10.1207/S1532799XSSR0503_3.

Gabriel, R. & Wenz, C. (2017). Three directions for disciplinary literacy. *Educational Leadership, 74*, 5.

Gallagher, A., Frith, U., & Snowling, M. J. (2000), Precursors of literacy delay among children at genetic risk of dyslexia. *Journal of Child Psychology and Psychiatry, 41*, 203–213. doi: 10.1111/1469-7610.00601.

García, O., & Li, Wei. (2014). *Translanguaging: Language, bilingualism and education.* New York, NY: Palgrave Macmillan.

García, O. & Kleifgen, J. A. (2019). Translanguaging and literacies. *Reading Research Quarterly, 55*(4). doi:10.1002/rrq.286.

Gaskins, I. W., Downer, M. A., Anderson, R. C., Cunningham, P. M., Gaskins, R. W., & Schommer, M. (1988). A metacognitive approach to phonics: Using what you know to decode what you don't know. *Remedial and Special Education, 9*, 36–41.

Gee, J. P. (1989). Literacy, discourse, and linguistics: Introduction. *Journal of Education, 171*(1), 5–17.

Goddard, R. D., Hoy, W. K., & Hoy, A. W. (2004). Collective efficacy beliefs: Theoretical developments, empirical evidence, and future directions. *Educational Researcher, 33*(3), 3–13. doi: 10.3102/0013189X033003003.

Goodman, K. S. (1967). Reading: A psycholinguistic guessing game. *Journal of the Reading Specialist, 6*(4), 126–135. https://doi.org/10.1080/19388076709556976.

Goswami, U. (2000), Phonological representations, reading development and dyslexia: Towards a cross-linguistic theoretical framework. *Dyslexia, 6*, 133–151. doi: 10.1002/(SICI)1099-0909(200004/06)6:2<133::AID-DYS160>3.0.CO;2-A.

Gough, P. B., & Tunmer, W. E. (1986). Decoding, Reading, and Reading Disability. Remedial and Special Education, 7, 6–10. http://dx.doi.org/10.1177/074193258600700104.

Graham, S., & Harris, K. R. (2019). Evidenced-based practices in writing. In S. Graham, C. A. MacArthur & M. Hebert (Eds.), *Best practices in writing instruction* (3rd ed., pp. 3–28). New York, NY: Guilford Press.

Graham, S., & Harris, K. R. (1989). Improving learning disabled students' skills at composing essays: Self-instructional strategy training. *Exceptional Children, 56*, 201–214.

Graham, S., & Hebert, M. A. (2010). *Writing to read: Evidence for how writing can improve reading. A Carnegie Corporation Time to Act Report.* Washington, D.C.: Alliance for Excellent Education.

Graham, S., & Perin, D. (2007). *Writing next: Effective strategies to improve writing of adolescents in middle and high schools – A report to Carnegie Corporation of New York.* Washington, D.C.: Alliance for Excellent Education.

Graham, S., Weintraub, N., & Berninger, V. W. (1998). The relationship between handwriting style and speed and legibility. *Journal of Educational Research, 91*(5), 290–296.

Graves, M. (2006). *The vocabulary book: Learning & instruction.* Newark, DE: International Reading Association.

Guthrie, J. T., & Klauda, S. L. (2014). Effects of classroom practices on reading comprehension, engagement, and motivations for adolescents. *Reading research quarterly, 49*(4), 387–416.

Guthrie, J., Schafer, W., Von Secker, C., & Alban, T. (2000). Contributions of instructional practices to reading achievement in a statewide improvement program. *Journal of Educational Research, 93*(4), 211–225.

Hall, A. H., Toland, M. D., Grisham-Brown, J., & Graham, S. (2014). Exploring interactive writing as an effective practice for increasing Head Start students' alphabet knowledge skills. *Early Childhood Education Journal, 42*, 423–430.

Halvorsen, A-L., Duke, N. K., Strachan, S. L., & Johnson, C. M. (2018). Engaging the community with a project-based approach. *Social Education, 82*(1), 24–29.

Hand, B., Wallace, C. W., & Yang, E. (2004). Using a science writing heuristic to enhance learning outcomes from laboratory activities in seventh-grade science: Quantitative and qualitative aspects. *International Journal of Science Education, 26*(2), 131–149, doi: 10.1080/0950069032000070252.

Harris, K. R., Graham, S., Friedlander, B., & Laud, L. (2013). Bring powerful writing strategies into your classroom! Why and how. *The Reading Teacher, 66*(7), 538–542. doi: 10.1002/TRTR.1156.

Hasbrouck, J., & Tindal, G. (2017). *An update to compiled ORF norms (Technical Report No. 1702). Behavioral research and teaching,* Eugene, OR: University of Oregon.

Hatcher, P. J., Hulme, C., & Snowling, M. J. (2004). Explicit phoneme training combined with phonic reading instruction helps young children at risk of reading failure. *Journal of Child Psychology and Psychiatry, and Allied Disciplines*, 45(2), 338–358.

Henbest, V. S., & Apel, K. (2017). Effective word reading instruction: What does the evidence tell us? *Communication Disorders Quarterly*, 39, 303–311.

Hindman, A. H., & Wasik, B. A. (2012). Morning Message time: An exploratory study in Head Start. *Early Childhood Education Journal*, 40(5), 275–283. doi: 10.1007/s10643-011-0459-8.

Hirsch, E. D. (2006). The case for bringing content into the language arts block and for a knowledge-rich curriculum core for all children. *American Educator*, Spring 2006. Retrieved from: https://www.aft.org/periodical/american-educator/spring-2006/building-knowledge

Hogan, T. P., Catts, H. W., & Little, T. D. (2005). The relationship between phonological awareness and reading: Implications for the assessment of phonological awareness. *Language, Speech, and Hearing Services in Schools*, 36(4), 285–293.

Hoover, W. A. and Gough, P. B. (1990) The simple view of reading. *Reading and Writing: An Interdisciplinary Journal*, 2, 127–160.

Ivey, G., & Johnston, P. H. (2013). Engagement with young adult literature: Outcomes and processes. *Reading Research Quarterly*, 48(3), 255–275.

Jones, C. D., Clark, S. K., & Reutzel, D. R. (2012). Enhancing alphabet knowledge instruction: Research implications and practical strategies for early childhood educators. *Early Childhood Education Journal*.

Justice, L. M., & Ezell, H. K. (2002). Use of storybook reading to increase print awareness in at-risk children. *American Journal of Speech-Language Pathology*, 11(1), 17–29.

Justice, L. M., Pence, K., Bowles, R. B., & Wiggins, A. (2006). An investigation of four hypotheses concerning the order by which 4-year-old children learn the alphabet letters. *Early Childhood Research Quarterly*, 21(3), 374–389. doi:10.1016/j.ecresq.2006.07.010.

Justice, L. M., McGinty, A. S., Piasta, S. B., Kaderavek, J. N., & Fan, X. (2010). Print-focused read-alouds in preschool classrooms: Intervention effectiveness and moderators of child outcomes. *Language, Speech, and Hearing Services in Schools*, 41(4), 504–520.

Kamil, M. L., Borman, G. D., Dole, J., Kral, C. C., Salinger, T., & Torgesen, J. (2008). *Improving adolescent literacy: Effective classroom and intervention practices: A practice guide (NCEE 2008-4027)*. Washington, D.C.: National Center for Education Evaluation and Regional Assistance, Institute of Education Sciences, U.S. Department of Education.

Karchmer-Klein, R., & Shinas, V. H. (2019) Adolescents' navigation of linguistic and nonlinguistic modes when reading a digital narrative. *Journal of Research in Reading*, 42, 469–484. https://doi.org/10.1111/1467-9817.12278.

Keats, E. J. (1962). *The snowy day*. New York: Viking Press.

Kendeou, P., van den Broek, P., White, M. J., & Lynch, J. (2009). Predicting reading comprehension in early elementary school: The independent contributions of oral language and decoding skills. *Journal of Educational Psychology*, 101(4), 765–778. doi: 10.1037/a0015956.

Kilpatrick, D. (2016). *Essentials of assessing, preventing, and overcoming reading difficulties*. Hoboken, NJ: Wiley.

Kim, J. (2006). Effects of a voluntary summer reading intervention on reading achievement: Results from a randomized field trial. *Educational Evaluation and Policy Analysis*, 28, 335.

Kim, J. S., & White, T. G. (2008). Scaffolding voluntary summer reading for children in grades 3 to 5: An experimental study. *Scientific Studies of Reading*, 12(1), 1–23.

Kintsch, W. (2004). The construction-integration model of text comprehension and its implications for instruction. In R. B. Ruddell & N. J. Unrau (Eds.), *Theoretical models and processes of reading* (pp. 1270–1328). Newark, DE: International Reading Association.

Krakow, K. (2002). *The Harvey Milk story* (D. Gardner, Illus.). Ridley Park, PA: Two Lives.

Krashen, S. (2001). More smoke and mirrors: A critique of the National Reading Panel report on fluency. *Phi Delta Kappan*, 83(2), 119–123. doi: org/10.1177/003172170108300208.

Kucan, L., & Beck, I. L. (2003). Inviting students to talk about expository texts: A comparison of two discourse environments and their effects on comprehension. *Reading Research and Instruction*, 42, 1–29.

Kuhn, D., & Crowell, A. (2011). Dialogic argumentation as a vehicle for developing young adolescents' thinking. *Psychological Science*, 22(4), 545–552. doi: 10.1177/095679761140251.

Kuhn, M. R. (2009). *The how's and why's of fluency instruction*. Boston, MA: Allyn & Bacon.

Kuhn, M. R., & Levy, L. (2015). *Developing fluent readers: Teaching fluency as a foundational skill*. New York, NY: Guilford Press.

Kuhn, M. R., Schwanenflugel, P. J., & Meisinger, E. B. (2010). Aligning theory and assessment of reading fluency: Automaticity, prosody, and definitions of fluency. *Reading Research Quarterly*, 45(2), 230–251. doi:10.1598/RRQ.45.2.4.

Kuhn, M. R., & Stahl, S. A. (2003). Fluency: A review of developmental and remedial practices. *Journal of Educational Psychology*, 95, 3–21.

Lederer, R. (1991). *The miracle of language*. New York, NY: Pocket Books.

Leslie, L., & Caldwell, J. (2017). *Qualitative reading inventory 6*. New York, NY: Pearson Education.

Leu, D. J., Forzani, E., Rhoads, C., Maykel, C., Kennedy, C., & Timbrell, N. (2015). The new literacies of online research and comprehension: Rethinking the reading achievement gap. *Reading Research Quarterly*, 50(1), 1–23. Newark, DE: International Reading Association. doi: 10.1002/rrq.85.

Limpo, T., & Alves, R. A. (2013). Modeling writing development: Contribution of transcription and self-regulation to Portuguese students' text generation quality. *Journal of Educational Psychology*, 105(2), 401–413.

Limpo, T., Alves, R. A., & Connelly, V. (2017). Examining the transcription-writing link: Effects of handwriting fluency and spelling accuracy on writing performance via planning and translating in middle grades. *Learning and Individual Differences*, 53, 26–36.

Lonigan, C. J., Anthony, J. L., Bloomfield, B. G., Dyer, S. M., & Samwel, C. S. (1999). Effects of two shared-reading interventions on emergent literacy skills of at-risk preschoolers. *Journal of Early Intervention*, 22(4), 306–322.

Lonigan, C. J., & Whitehurst, G. J. (1998). Relative efficacy of parent and teacher involvement in a shared-reading intervention for preschool children from low-income backgrounds. *Early Childhood Research Quarterly*, 13(2), 263–290.

LaBerge, D., & Samuels, S. J. (1974). Toward a theory of automatic information process in reading. *Cognitive Psychology*, 6, 293–323.

Marzano, R. J., Waters, T., & McNulty, B. A. (2005). *School leadership that works: From research to results*. Alexandria, VA: Association for Supervision and Curriculum Development.

McKeown, M., Beck, I., & Blake, R. G. K. (2011). Rethinking reading comprehension instruction: A comparison of instruction for strategies and content approaches. *Reading Research Quarterly*, 44(3), 218–253.

Mehan, H. (1979). *Learning lessons: Social organization in the classroom*. Cambridge, MA: Harvard University Press.

Mesmer, H. A. (2019). *Letter lessons and first words: Phonics foundations that work*. Portsmouth, MA: Heinemann.

Meyer, B. J. (1975). *The organization of prose and its effects on memory*. Amsterdam, Netherlands: North-Holland Publishing.

Michaels, S. (1981). Sharing time: Children's narrative styles and differential access to literacy. *Language in Society*, 10, 423–443.

Michaels, S., O'Connor, M. C., Hall, M. W., & Resnick, L. (2010). *Accountable talk sourcebook: For classroom conversation that works* (version 3.1). Pittsburgh, PA: University of Pittsburgh.

Miller, D. (2010). *The book whisperer*. Hoboken, NJ: Jossey-Bass.

Moller, K. (2016). Creating diverse classroom literature collections using Rudine Sims Bishop's conceptual metaphors and analytical frameworks as guides. *Journal of Children's Literature*, 42(2), 64–74.

Murris, K. S. (2008). Philosophy with children, the stingray and the educative value of disequilibrium. *Journal of Philosophy Education*, 42(3–4), 667–685.

Nagy, W., & Anderson, R. (1984). How many words are there in printed school English? *Reading Research Quarterly*, 19, 304–330.

Nagy, W. E., Herman, P. A., & Anderson, R. C. (1985). Learning words from context. *Reading Research Quarterly, 20*, 233–253.

Nagy, W., & Scott, J. (2000). Vocabulary processes. In M. L. Kamil, P. B. Mosenthal, P. D. Pearson, & R. Barr (Eds.), *Handbook of reading research* (Vol. 3, pp. 269–284). Mahwah, NJ: Erlbaum.

National Early Literacy Panel. (2008). *Developing early literacy: Report of the National Early Literacy Panel*. Washington, D.C.: National Institute for Literacy.

National Governors Association Center for Best Practices & Council of Chief State School Officers. (2010). *Common Core State Standards for English language arts and literacy in history/ social studies, science, and technical subjects*. Washington, D.C.: Authors.

National Reading Panel (U.S.), & National Institute of Child Health and Human Development (U.S.). (2000). *Report of the National Reading Panel: Teaching children to read: An evidence-based assessment of the scientific research literature on reading and its implications for reading instruction: Reports of the subgroups*. Washington, D.C.: National Institute of Child Health and Human Development, National Institutes of Health.

Nystrand, M. (2006). Research on the role of classroom discourse as it affects reading comprehension. *Research in the Teaching of English, 40*, 393–412.

Nystrand, M., & Gamoran, A. (1991). Instructional discourse, student engagement, and literature achievement. *Research in the Teaching of English, 25*, 261–289.

Olivia-Olson, C., Espinosa, L. M., Hayslip, W., & Magruder, E. S. (2019). Many languages, one classroom: Supporting children in superdiverse settings. *Teaching Young Children, 12*(2). Retrieved from https://www.naeyc.org/resources/pubs/tyc/dec2018/supporting-children-superdiverse-settings

Olson, C. B., & Godfrey, L. (2019). Narrative writing. In S. Graham, C. A. MacArthur, & M. Hebert (Eds), *Best practices in writing instruction* (3rd ed., pp. 81–107). New York, NY: Guilford Press.

Ouelette, G., & Sénéchal, M. (2017). Invented spelling in kindergarten as a predictor of reading and spelling in grade 1: A new pathway to literacy, or just the same road, less known? *Developmental Psychology, 53*(1), 77–88. http://dx.doi.org/10.1037/dev0000179.

Pak, S. S., & Weseley, A. J. (2012). The effect of mandatory reading logs on children's motivation to read. *Journal of Research in Education, 22*(1), 251–265.

Palincsar, A. S., & Brown, A. L. (1984). Reciprocal teaching of comprehension-fostering and comprehension-monitoring activities. *Cognition and Instruction, 1*(2), 117–175.

Paris, S. (2005). Reinterpreting the development of reading skills. *Reading Research Quarterly 40*(2), 184–202. doi: 10.1598/RRQ.40.2.3.

Pearson, P. D., & Cervetti, G. N. (2015). Fifty years of reading comprehension theory and practice. In P. D. Pearson & E. H. Hiebert (Eds.), *Research-based practices for teaching Common Core literacy* (pp. 1–24). New York, NY: Teachers College Press.

Pennell, C. (2014). In the age of analytic reading: Understanding readers' engagement with text. *The Reading Teacher, 68*(4), 251–260. doi: 10.1002/trtr.1292.

Pennell, C. (2018). Exploring classroom discourse in the Common Core era: A multiple case study. *Literacy Research and Instruction, 57*(4), 306–329.

Perfetti, C. A. (1985) *Reading ability*. New York, NY: Oxford University Press.

Perfetti, C., & Roth, S. (1981). Some of the interactive processes in reading and their role in reading skill. In A. M. Lesgold & C. A. Perfetti (Eds.), *Interactive processes in reading* (pp. 269–297). Hillsdale, NJ: Erlbaum.

Piasta, S. B., Purpura, D. J., & Wagner, R. K. (2010). Fostering alphabet knowledge development: A comparison of two instructional approaches. *Reading and Writing, 23*(6), 607–626.

Pikulski, J. J., & Chard, D. J. (2005). Fluency: Bridge between and reading comprehension. *The Reading Teacher, 58*(6), 510–519. doi: 10.1598/RT.58.6.2.

Pressley, M. (2002). Effective beginning reading instruction. *Journal of Literacy Research, 34*(2), 165–188. doi.org/10.1207/s15548430jlr3402_3.

Pressley, M. (1998). *Reading instruction that works: The case for balanced teaching*. New York, NY: Guilford Press.

Pressley, M. (2006). *Reading instruction that works: The case for balanced teaching* (3rd ed.). New York: Guilford.

Pressley, M., El-Dinary, P. B., Gaskins, I. W., Schuder, T., Bergman, J. L., Almasi, J., … Brown, R. (1992). Beyond direct explanation: Transactional instruction of reading comprehension strategies. *The Elementary School Journal*, 92(5), 513–555.

Rahmani, M., & Sadeghi, K. (2011). Effects of note-taking training on reading comprehension and recall. *Reading Matrix: An Online International Journal*, 11(2), 116–128.

Raphael, T. E., & McMahon, S. I. (1994). Book club: An alternative framework for reading instruction. *The Reading Teacher*, 48(2), 102–116.

Rasinski, T. V. (1989). Fluency for everyone: Incorporating fluency instruction in the classroom. *The Reading Teacher*, 42(9), 690–693.

Rasinski, T. V. (2006). A brief history of reading fluency. In S. J. Samuels & A. E. Farstrup (Eds.), *What research has to say about fluency instruction* (pp. 4–23). Newark, DE: International Reading Association.

Rasinski, T. V., Reutzel, C. R., Chard, D., & Linan-Thompson, S. (2011). Reading fluency. In M. L. Kamil, P. D. Pearson, E. B. Moje, & P. Afflerbach (Eds.), *Handbook of Reading Research* (Vol. 4, pp. 286–319). New York, NY: Routledge.

Recht, D., & Leslie, L. (1988). Effect of prior knowledge on good and poor readers' memory of text. *Journal of Educational Psychology*, 80(1), 16–20.

Resnick, L. B., Asterhan, C., & Clarke, S. (Eds.) (2015). *Socializing intelligence through academic talk and dialogue*. Washington: D.C. American Educational Research Association.

Richardson, J. (2016). *The next step forward in guided reading: An assess-decide-guide framework for supporting every reader*. New York, NY: Scholastic.

Roberts, K. L., Norman, R. R. Duke, N. K., Morsink, P., Martin, N. M., &, Knight, J. A. (2013). Diagrams, timelines, and tables—oh, my! Fostering graphical literacy. *The Reading Teacher*, 67(1), 12–23. doi: 10.1002/TRTR.1174.

Rosenblatt, L. M. (1978). *The reader, the text, the poem: The transactional theory of the literary work*. Carbondale, IL: Southern Illinois University.

Roth, K., & Guinee, K. (2011). Ten minutes a day: The impact of interactive writing instruction on first graders' independent writing. *Journal of Early Childhood Literacy*, 11, 331–361.

Reutzel, D. R., Smith, J. A., & Fawson, P. C. (2005). An evaluation of two approaches for teaching reading comprehension strategies in the primary years using science information texts. *Early Childhood Research Quarterly*, 20(3), 276–305.

Sanden, S. (2012). Independent reading: Perspectives and practices of highly effective teachers. *Reading Teacher*, 66, 222–231.

Sabatini, J., Wang, Z., & O'Reilly, T. (2019). Relating reading comprehension to oral reading performance in the NAEP fourth-grade special study of oral reading. *Reading Research Quarterly*, 54(2), 253–271. doi: 10.1002/rrq.226.

Saunders, W., & Goldenberg, C. (1999). Effects of instructional conversations and literature logs on limited- and fluent-English-proficient students' story comprehension and thematic understanding. *The Elementary School Journal*, 99(4), 277–301.

Scarborough H. S. (1998). Early identification of children at risk for reading disabilities. In: B. K. Shapiro, P. J. Accardo, & A. J. Capute (Eds.), *Specific reading disability: A view of the spectrum* (pp. 75–120). Timonium, MD: York Press.

Scarborough, H. S. (2001). Connecting early language and literacy to later reading (dis)abilities: Evidence, theory, and practice. In S. Neuman & D. Dickinson (Eds.), *Handbook for research in early literacy* (pp. 97–110). New York, NY: Guilford Press.

Schmitt, N. (2008). Review article: Instructed second language vocabulary learning. *Language Teaching Research*, 12(3), 329–363. https://doi.org/10.1177/1362168808089921.

Schuele, M. C., & Boudreau, D. (2008). Phonological awareness intervention: Beyond the basics. *Language Speech and Hearing Services in Schools*, 39(1), 3–20. doi: 10.1044/0161-1461(2008/002).

Serravallo, J. (2015). *The reading strategies book*. Portsmouth, MA: Heinemann.

Shanahan, T. (2004). Critiques of the National Reading Panel report: Their implications for research, policy, and practice. In P. McCardle & V. Chhabra (Eds.), *The voice of evidence in reading research* (pp. 235–265). Baltimore, MD: Paul H Brookes Publishing.

Shanahan, T., & Shanahan, C. (2008). Teaching disciplinary literacy to adolescents: Rethinking content-area literacy. *Harvard Educational Review*, *78*(1), 40–59. doi: 10.17763/haer.78.1.v62444321p602101.

Shanahan, T., & Shanahan, C. (2012). What is disciplinary literacy and why does it matter? *Topics in Language Disorders*, *32*(1), 7–18. doi: 10.1097/TLD.0b013e318244557a.

Share, D. L. (1995). Phonological recoding and orthographic learning; A direct test of the self-teaching hypothesis. *Journal of Experimental Child Psychology*, *72*(4), 95–129.

Short, K. G., & Pierce, K. M. (1990). *Talking about books: Creating literature communities*. Portsmouth, NH: Heinemann.

Snow, C. E. (1991). The theoretical basis for relationships between language and literacy in development. *Journal of Research in Childhood Education*, *6*(1), 5–10. doi: 10.1080/02568549109594817.

Snow, C. E., Burns, M. S., & Griffin, P. (Eds.) (1998). *Preventing reading difficulties in young children*. Washington, D.C.: National Academy Press.

Snow, C. E., & Juel, C. (2005). Teaching children to read: What do we know about how to do it? In M. J. Snowling & C. Hulme (Eds.), *Blackwell handbooks of developmental psychology. The science of reading: A handbook* (pp. 501–520). Blackwell Publishing. https://doi.org/10.1002/9780470757642.ch26.

Soter, A., Wilkinson, I., Murphy, K., Rudge, L., Reninger, K., & Edwards, M. (2008). What the discourse tells us: Talk and indicators of high-level comprehension. *International Journal of Educational Research*, *47*, 372–391.

Souto-Manning, M., & Martell, J. (2016). *Reading, writing, and talk: Inclusive teaching strategies for diverse learners, K-2*. New York, NY: Teachers College Press.

Spiegal, D. L. (1998). Silver bullets, babies, and bath water: Literature response groups in a balanced literacy program. *The Reading Teacher*, *52*(2), 114–124.

Stahl, K. D. (2014). New insights about letter learning. *The Reading Teacher*, *68*(4), 261–265. doi: 10.1002/trtr.1320.

Stahl, S. A., Duffy-Hester, A. M., & Stahl, K. (1998). Everything you wanted to know about phonics (but were afraid to ask). *Reading Research Quarterly*, *33*(3), 338–355.

Stanovich, K. E. (1986). Matthew effects in reading: Some consequences of individual differences in the acquisition of literacy. *Reading Research Quarterly*, *21*, 360–405.

Strickland, D. S. (1996). In search of balance: Restructuring our literacy programs. *Reading Today*, *14*(2), 32.

Sweller, J. (1998). Cognitive load during problem solving: Effects on learning. *Cognitive Science*, *12*, 257–285.

Squires, J. R. (2004). Extensive reading. In G. Cawelti (Ed.), *Handbook of research on improving student achievement* (Vol. 3, pp. 125–138). Arlington, VA: Educational Research Service.

Tharp, R., & S. Entz. (2003). From high chair to high school: Research-based principles for teaching complex thinking. *Young Children*, *58*(5), 38–44.

Torgerson, C., Brooks, G., & Hall, J. (2006). *A systematic review of the research literature on the use of phonics in the teaching of reading and spelling*. The University of Sheffield. Research Report No 711. Sheffield, UK.

Toulmin, S. (1958). *The uses of argument*. Cambridge, UK: Cambridge University Press.

Troia, G. A. (2004). Building word recognition skills through empirically validated instructional practices: Collaborative efforts of speech-language pathologists and teachers. In E. R. Silliman & L. C. Wilkinson (Eds.), *Language and literacy learning in schools* (pp. 98–129). New York, NY: The Guilford Press.

Tunmer, W. E., & Chapman, J. W. (2012). Does set for variability mediate the influence of vocabulary knowledge on the development of word recognition skills? *Scientific Studies of Reading*, *16*(2), 122–140, doi: 10.1080/10888438.2010.542527.

van Bergen, E., Snowling, M. J., de Zeeuw, E. L., van Beijsterveldt, C. E., Dolan, C. V., & Boomsma, D. I. (2018), Why do children read more? The influence of reading ability on voluntary reading practices. *Journal of Child Psychology and Psychiatry, 59*, 1205–1214. doi:10.1111/jcpp.12910.

Vaughn, S., & Linan-Thompson, S. (2003). What is special about special education for students with learning disabilities? *The Journal of Special Education, 37*(3), 140–147.

Vygotsky, L. S. (1978). *Mind in society: The development of higher psychological processes.* Cambridge, MA: Harvard University Press.

Vygotsky, L. S. (1986). *Thought and language.* Cambridge, MA: MIT Press.

Wagner, R. K., Torgesen, J. K., & Rashotte, C. A. (1994). Development of reading-related phonological processing abilities: New evidence of bidirectional causality from a latent variable longitudinal study. *Developmental Psychology, 30*, 73–87. doi: 10.1037/0012-1649.30.1.73.

Walton, P. D., Walton, L. M., & Felton, K. (2001). Teaching rime analogy or letter recoding reading strategies to prereaders: Effects on prereading skills and word reading. *Journal of Educational Psychology, 93*, 160–180.

Wartenberg, T. (2009). *Big ideas for little kids: Teaching philosophy through children's literature.* Lanham, MD: Rowman & Littlefield.

Wasik, B. A., & Bond, M. A. (2001). Beyond the pages of a book: Interactive book reading and language development in preschool classrooms. *Journal of Educational Psychology, 93*(2), 243–250.

Wexler, N. (2019). *The knowledge gap. The hidden cause of America's broken education system—and how to fix it.* New York, NY: Avery.

Whitehurst, G. J., Falco, F. L., Lonigan, C. J., Fischel, J. E., DeBaryshe, B. D., Valdez-Menchaca, M. C., & Caulfield, M. (1988). Accelerating language development through picture book reading. *Developmental Psychology, 24*, 552–559.

Whittingham, J., Huffman, S., Christensen, R., & McAllister, T. (2013). Use of audiobooks in a school library and positive effects of struggling readers' participation in a library-sponsored audiobook club. *American Association of School Librarians, 16*, 1–18.

Willingham, T. (2006) Knowledge in the classroom. *American Educator,* Spring, 2006.Retrieved from https://www.aft.org/periodical/american-educator/spring-2006/knowledge-classroom

Willingham, D. T. & Lovette, G. (2014). Can reading comprehension strategies be taught? Teachers College Record. Retrieved from http://www.danielwillingham.com/uploads/5/0/0/7/5007325/willingham&lovette_2014_can_reading_comprehension_be_taught_.pdf

Wiliam, D., & Leahy, S. (2015). *Embedding formative assessment: practical techniques for K-12 classrooms.* West Palm Beach, FL: Learning Sciences International.

Wilson, J. (2019). Assessing writing. In S. Graham, C. A. MacArthur, & M. Hebert (Eds.), *Best practices in writing instruction* (3rd ed., pp. 3–28). New York, NY: Guilford Press.

Wolf, M., & Bowers, P. G. (1999). The double-deficit hypothesis for the developmental dyslexias. *Journal of Educational Psychology, 91*, 415–438. http://dx.doi.org/10.1037/0022-0663.91.3.415.

Wolf, M. K., Crosson, A. C., & Resnick, L. B. (2005). *Accountable talk in reading comprehension instruction (CSE Technical Report 670).* Los Angeles, CA: Center for the Study of Evaluation, National Center for Research on Evaluation, Standards, and Student Testing.

Wolf, M., & Katzir-Cohen, T. (2001). Reading fluency and its intervention. *Scientific Studies of Reading, 5*(3), 211–239.

Worthy, J., Moorman, M., & Turner, M. (1999). What Johnny likes to read is hard to find in school. *Reading Research Quarterly, 34*, 12–27. doi: 10.1598/RRQ.34.1.2.

Wright, T. S., & Cervetti, G. N. (2017). A systematic review of the research on vocabulary instruction that impacts text comprehension. *Reading Research Quarterly, 52*(2), 203–226. doi: 10.1002/rrq.163.

Yeh, S. S., & Connell, D. B. (2008). Effects of rhyming, vocabulary and phonemic awareness instruction on phoneme awareness. *Journal of Research in Reading, 31*, 243–256. doi: 10.1111/j.1467-9817.2007.00353.x.

Yopp, H. K. (1988). The validity and reliability of phonemic awareness tests. *Reading Research Quarterly, 23*, 159–177.

Made in the USA
Monee, IL
20 October 2022